JACQUELINE PASCARL has worked in radio and television, and as a documentary film-maker – her work including the award-winning documentary *Empty Arms – Broken Hearts*. In 1995 she moved into the area of child literacy and established 'Operation Book Power', a project operating in Kenya and South Africa. In 1998, she was appointed Special Ambassador for CARE International and worked as an emergency aid worker in the war zones of Bosnia, Kosovo and East Timor.

Recognised internationally as an expert on the Hague Convention and International Parental Child Abduction, Jacqueline has lectured at the US State Department and the Australian Department of Foreign Affairs and Trade, as well as the European Union and the Hong Kong Family Law Association. Awarded the United Nations Special Commendation for the International Year of the Family, and two recognition awards from the National Center for Missing and Exploited Children, USA, Jacqueline has been a high-profile international lobbyist on human rights and refugee issues. In recognition of her humanitarian work, Jacqueline was appointed to a new role as a patron of CARE International in January 2007.

Jacqueline is the author of the bestselling *Once I Was a Princess*. She has four children, and now resides in Melbourne, where she is concentrating on her writing.

SINCE I WAS A PRINCESS

The Fourteen-Year Fight to Find My Children

Jacqueline Pascarl

MAINSTREAM
PUBLISHING

EDINBURGH AND LONDON

First published in Great Britain in 2007 by
MAINSTREAM PUBLISHING COMPANY (EDINBURGH) LTD
7 Albany Street
Edinburgh EH1 3UG

ISBN 9781845962166

This book is a work of non-fiction based on the life, experiences and
recollections of Jacqueline Pascarl. In some cases, names of people and
places, dates, sequences or the detail of events have been changed to protect
the privacy of others. The author has stated to the publishers that, except in
such respects, not affecting the substantial accuracy of the work, the
contents of this book are true

A catalogue record for this book is available from the British Library

Typeset in Bembo

Printed in Great Britain by
Clays Ltd, St Ives plc

For my four amazing, uniquely individual and fascinating children. Know that wherever life's journey takes you, I hold you close and proudly in my heart. Never give up on what you know to be just and truthful, or those you love and respect.

Author's Note

Princess is a state of mind, not a state of royal grace. Every child living on the globe has a right to a childhood, and to have a place in someone's heart as their prince or princess. Parental protection, nurturing, innocence and self-esteem contribute greatly to a young person's expectations, self-image and sense of place in the world – without them we all have the potential to founder.

'Always live in hope . . .'

Prologue

May 1999

The wailing permeated my gut, and travelled to that plateau just above the breasts where pain and empathy reside so closely.

Even before I could pinpoint its location, I recognised the cry as the timeless sound of great loss and grief. I knew its origins well; I was familiar with its resonance and acquainted with its depth. In my past, I had, myself, been the originator of many such cries. It was a call to which there was no answer and no panacea – nor did it expect one. Its vibrations spread to my temples and the back of my skull, finally settling as a great, unyielding lump in the back of my throat. As I stumbled across the rock-strewn terrain of the refugee camp, I thought how strange, and yet somehow comforting, that the sounds of tragedy do not differ from one section of humanity to another.

High-pitched screams now punctuated the wails of grief, competing with the dull 'thump, thump' emitted by the rotors of a passing armoured helicopter. The chopper, probably carrying missiles, a reconnaissance team, or some other NATO cargo, was visible only as a blackened presence against the night sky. This tract of land over which it passed was wedged between the battle zone of Kosovo and the bright lights of the Macedonian capital, Skopje, 30 kilometres down the unlit road. Our small sanctuary, just 11 minutes within the Macedonian border, provided a meagre haven for 27,000 displaced souls — women, children and men who had fled the armed conflict of Kosovo and the relentless pursuit of the Serbian military forces.

Stenkovec II was one of the three major processing and refugee camps in Macedonia set up under the protection of the United Nations High Commission for Refugees (UNHCR), and run on a day-to-day basis by CARE International, the global humanitarian aid and development agency. The camp was bleak and unforgiving, occupying a series of high-walled rabbit-warren gullies, interconnected by excavated cuttings just wide enough for a tank to pass through. A small hill at its core provided a vantage point, up which children scrambled during the daylight hours, and where an effort had been made by the United Nations International Children's Emergency Fund (UNICEF) to cobble together the semblance of a school and kindergarten. Formerly a stone quarry that had served, until recently, as a heavy artillery and weapons range, the locale was devoid of trees, running water, electricity and sewerage.

The moon reflected off the battered face of my Swatch watch – 3.27 a.m. We had been processing and unloading these latest busloads of refugees (or 'Internally Displaced People', as the politically correct amongst us insisted on saying) since just after 1 a.m. The initial headcounts reckoned about 800 souls had been crammed aboard six buses, each normally intended to carry fifty-five passengers.

Closing in on the weeping, I picked my way around the rear of the huge khaki-coloured 'horse tents' – so named, I assumed, because the military arm who had donated them to the relief effort was a cavalry regiment. It was here that our new arrivals were to be sheltered. Each human being would be allotted a one-metre-wide space which would have to serve as sleeping quarters, living room and storage for whatever possessions they had managed to carry on their back, or shove into plastic shopping bags as they began their escape to safety. A requisite two metres separating the rows served as a central walkway between the two sides of a tent. These were the minimum allowances under World Health Organisation (WHO) and UNHCR guidelines during a time of emergency. This was the theory; but in practice, nearly one hundred weary people would that night sleep in a tent meant to accommodate thirty, cheek by jowl with complete strangers in utter darkness. This was just one of the frustrating realities we faced as aid workers: we witnessed humanity at its lowest ebb forced to masquerade as sardines.

I checked each canvas, trying to pinpoint the location of the grieving woman. The miner's lamp on my head bounced light off startled faces peering back at me from the darkness. There was quiet sobbing in every shelter I visited, whispering, groaning and sometimes the whimpering of babies and children, but the sound I sought was on a different level – it had a different intensity. Tangles of guy ropes and tent pegs running off our makeshift town hampered my path; I tripped and broke my fall by making a grab for the cyclone wire perimeter fence, and that is how I found her.

My torch illuminated her feet, shod in battered tan high-heeled shoes. Knees drawn tightly up to her chest, she sat on the ground oblivious to my approach. Her brown gabardine skirt was heavily stained, that much I could see, and she now emitted guttural howls as she repeatedly banged her forehead with the heel of her hand. To witness such grief, and then to be capable of identifying it from the outside looking in, is an unspeakable invasion of person. Even now as I write, my chest compresses hard against my lungs and my eyes are drawn out of their sockets by the insight it affords.

Her brown hair was short and streaked with blonde, her hands and nails grubby and torn. The blouse she wore had once been white – a teacher's or secretary's garb, I guessed – but marred now by a few missing buttons and what appeared to be dried blood. Thirty-plus, I estimated, around my own age – young enough, yet ancient, too, if life has imploded all normality.

Grasping her pounding fist, I dragged it downwards as she threw back her head. Her jaw slackened with a huge expulsion of air and wailing from the back of her throat. Another woman emerged from the shadows, a grandmother, judging from the little girl clutching at her long cardigan. She spoke to me in Albanian, a tumble of words I couldn't understand. I tried a few words in Bosnian and there was a flicker of comprehension. The grandmother called to a teenage boy who had hung back against the tent wall.

Selma was the distressed woman's name, according to the boy, translating the grandmother's words. Two days earlier, at a pre-border check by the Serbian paramilitary, she had been subjected to a body cavity search. The soldiers had found a roll of cash secreted on her person. Her punishment for attempting to smuggle cash out of Kosovo was the murder of her child.

Apparently, she was on her knees as she struggled to stop the thugs from tearing her seven-year-old son from her arms. One military type grabbed her by the hair while another wrenched the small child's arms above his head, put a pistol to the base of his skull and pulled the trigger.

'His eyes, his eyes,' was what I now understood Selma sobbed as I held her tightly in my arms, her head against my shoulder. The last image of her terrorised child had seared itself into her mind with the efficiency of a precision laser and marked her as a mother shattered by its final brutality.

It was then, for the first and only time ever, that I broke the cardinal rule of aid work – never cry in front of your charges. Fuck that; I was crying with her not for her, and some of my tears were for the awfulness of our fellow human beings and the deeds of which they were capable.

The incongruity of my journey to that point in time was not entirely lost on me. How had I come to be wading through such violence, poverty, desperation and shining hope? I've often thought it bizarre that an Australian mother of two had become the common denominator linking a refugee camp in the foothills of the Balkans, a child literacy project amid the Maasai of Kenya, hunky French paramedics, Parisian couture, heavy-duty army boots and an international furore over parental child abduction.

But the straight truth of the matter is that nothing surprises me much any more. A stiff vodka on ice sipped decorously in the private bar at the House of Lords and a

...p of coffee imbibed squatting beside the casings of ...d uranium armaments aren't that different in terms of ...d conversation or company; and, besides, I now just accept the vagaries of life as a natural progression towards some distant point in the future. Years ago I had to make a choice: to either shut down my faculties, my heartbeat, my potential for joy and wallow in unassuageable grief and torment, or decide I would survive and create a new life for myself by harnessing all my negative experiences into one positive and stubborn force and following the direction in which it led me. That was *the* single most important decision I have made since I *was* a princess.

Chapter 1
What's a Nice Girl Like You ...

I t was an ill-conceived compulsion – dangerous, and one I knew I'd regret even as my hand ferreted in the bottom of my duffle bag and shakily withdrew the small album of family photographs. The images contained within flung me onto a rollercoaster ride of emotion. They buoyed and mocked me with their simplicity and happiness and reminded me of a life that was no longer mine, of children whom were no longer embraceable and a time so long past. The small album I held in my hands was my private talisman of determination, my future and my past. Sleep would now be unattainable, but the reminder of what had once been allowed, of a sanity I once knew, was worth it.

I lay still and quiet in my bed, watching the occasional light from a helicopter gunship float past my window, as I waited for dawn to release me from my unwelcome thoughts. I contemplated how the years following a tragedy can pass in the blink of an eye or with the protracted and torturous ache of an unhealed and suppurating amputation.

It depends entirely on the mindset of the person counting the minutes. For me, that experience of time passed through both dimensions depending on my relationships, surroundings and activities. Losing both my children had devastated and galvanised me on the most unpredictable levels of pain and survival. For me, I came to understand that the human mind remembers moments or days, but the overriding psychological imprint is that of emotions and milestones – missed and shredded.

Decisions I had made as a seventeen year old, when I was swept off my feet by a seemingly mild-mannered foreign architecture student who had attended Prince Charles's alma mater, Geelong Grammar, left me and my children dealing with the consequences of my wilfulness decades later.

The quiet young man I had met and fallen in love with was the clichéd tall, dark and handsome gallant; he also turned out to be the grandson of the late Sultan of Terengganu and a royal Prince in his own right. I see now why Bahrin was attracted to me – he had been married (and divorced) once already to a fellow student of the same age who had left him for an Aussie gardener. In me, as a fairly damaged teenager from a dysfunctional home who just wanted a family to love, he had found a girl he could mould into the sort of Princess he wanted. Fresh enough in terms of genealogy, parentless in terms of interference, and always an outsider in Australia because of my mixed racial background (Australian born of French, Irish, English and Chinese decent) in a then xenophobic country, I longed to fit in and that is what he offered – complete acceptance under Islam and a firm place in his family.

We settled down to a strange married life within Bahrin's

family, a branch of the Malaysian royals in Terengganu – quite a wealthy state where the royals benefited from its gas, oil and mining reserves, as well as the logging of rainforest timbers. I was a breeder and he took a punt that my bloodlines would enhance his. Our ten-year age difference seemed inconsequential at the time of our union, but like many hopeful fairy tales, the gilt wore off the marriage fairly quickly when our cultural differences became apparent. I objected to his philandering and physical poundings and he disliked my objections. The other problem was that once I became a mother, even though I was a teenager, my malleability dissolved and I grew a brain – a very Westernised brain – which provoked my husband's blue blood to the point of boiling.

My erstwhile Prince became increasingly abusive towards me, but the straw that broke this camel's back was his polygamous marriage to a scantily clad nightclub singer a couple of weeks after the birth of our youngest child. Subsequently, the children and I returned to my home town of Melbourne.

Following a protracted legal battle in the Australian Family Court regarding the correct forum for a hearing (the Prince had wanted me deported from my own birthplace to stand before an Islamic Syriah Court in Malaysia), Bahrin voluntarily signed over full custody of our children to me, allowing me to forge a new life with my children in Australia.

Contrary to various media reports at the time, the Prince was not hard done by legally or emotionally and had liberal, although conditional, access to our little ones.

Iddin and Shahirah lived in Australia with me from the ages of two years and five months, respectively. We were happy and self-contained, a marked contrast to my turbulent life in a royal Islamic household. I worked in the early years following our divorce as a waitress, typist, ballet teacher and later a public relations consultant, always juggling childcare and income, with the priority being the children and our time together. Money was tight, but the children and I lived happily in a rambling old house I renovated with my own hands.

There was what I can only describe as a lightness in my children's existence then – they were shiny and joyous and giggling. I remember climbing the old apricot tree in the garden with them and dangling from its branches, and teddy bear picnics in the park. I suppose, at that time, we were growing up together, as I was a single mother at the age of twenty-two. There were raucous afternoons spent quite literally rolling in the mud and snorkelling in the bathtub and making cereal boxes into hats and spaceships. But most of all, we were together, and however modest my income, my children were never hungry and never dirty and there was always plenty of love and cuddles. I think that is what, even after all the years of separation from Iddin and Shah, I missed the most – the cuddles; the heart-wrenching and primal instinct to softly sniff your child's scent as they snuggle in, and the knowledge that the heartbeats you can faintly feel as they press against you first began in your own body.

Iddin and Shahirah were seven and five when I remarried in 1990 – five years after leaving their father. Iain Gillespie was light and laughter compared to my past, the quintessential Pied Piper/Peter Pan I had missed in my childhood. He came as a package deal with teenage children and worked as a documentary film-maker and journalist. Our children fell in love with each other and we lived a happy, busy suburban life in a leafy Melbourne suburb. Bike rides, weekends at Iain's family farm, loud dinner parties and a frenzy of domestic activity – what more could anyone expect with five children often residing in the house together and the occasional foster child or sleepover. Perhaps we were too bright and smug in our domesticity, for when the guillotine of abduction came hurtling down, the heart of our family was cut out with the removal of our two youngest members.

I can remember the great gaping maw of emptiness and shock, the point where emotional pain and physical stress collide and all your body can do is retch uncontrollably and shake with spasms of open-ended grief and longing. All this was played out for months in the full glare of the media and with all the drama of a television crime show, for the cachet of royalty and my role on television and radio as a reporter and broadcaster were like fresh blood to a school of sharks. It caused a feeding frenzy as I agitated every angle that could be found in the hope of first locating my children on Australian territory and later, causing enough of a political furore to make the government do something to retrieve Shah and Iddin from Malaysia. My children were dual nationals at the time of their abduction. Both children held Australian and Malaysian citizenship, having been born in Terengganu and registered by my husband and me with the Australian diplomatic mission as Australian citizens.

I oversaw petitions, pressed for parliamentary questions, lobbied opposition members, made midnight phone calls to union leaders and former prime ministers, who either behaved like arseholes when asked for assistance, or took my calls late into the night and offered wise counsel. And always the newspapers and other media, ever present and later perverse as they chased the new angle, then decided I was too boring and turned against me for a ratings point or two. Our family became fodder for the tabloids but I understood that much of it was necessary to fight the good fight.

I was urged to keep going, to present the most attractive face I could to the public to obtain the sympathy and support we needed to meet the political and international challenges I faced in my fight for the children. Some days I loathed myself as I looked in the mirror and reached for the camouflage make-up to conceal the dark circles under my eyes, and cleaned my teeth and brushed my hair as it fell in great clumps from my head (for I had developed rapid alopecia), before facing another media maelstrom. 'Sweetheart, pretty women get more sympathy than ugly ones,' Iain told me a few times. The viewing public didn't want to see a sleep-deprived, near-suicidal woman on their screens every night – I had to appeal to everyman and everywoman, and I hated myself for being so calculating when all I truly wanted to do was sit in my filthy bathrobe and weep for my lost babies. Desperation takes you down many paths and makes very strange acquaintances best friends. Fame, notoriety and celebrity harness together the strangest acolytes and yoke them to you until the direction you wanted to go in is only the vaguest of memories.

But grief and longing for your children, that's a different matter – you learn to cope outwardly, to ensure the comfort of others, to not break down and upset them with your pain. But the grief stays there, the pain ever present, even as I lay in my bed in faraway Macedonia. It was as if a giant apple corer had excised an enormous chunk of my soul, and in its place a tight, drum-like membrane had grown that reverberated with every whisper of a word that reminded me of my lost ones.

The mourning continued as well; I mourned for the 'what-ifs' and the lost moments – I mourned for all the first's I'd missed and the childhood secrets to which I could never be privy. I mourned the lost opportunity to nurture and guide, and I even missed the smelly teenage socks and the messy rooms I would never see. Death robs a parent of all future and quashes their dreams; abduction tortures a parent with the emptiness of the future, and all of the potential never witnessed in its fruition.

Life in the preceding years, before this point in which I found myself in the middle of an armed conflict in the former Yugoslavia, had proved to be unchartered territory for which I had no compass and no complete plan, but reflecting back, I realised how far the journey had brought me.

When questioned by strangers about my past, I would trot out the prickly and succinct family history, almost as a challenge.

'On the 9th of July 1992, my two children, Iddin and Shah, were kidnapped and I haven't seen or spoken to them since.'

Chapter 2
Life Limps On

Since the day they were kidnapped by my ex-husband, Bahrin, I'd been trying desperately to get my children back. But the Australian Labour government were negotiating a defence treaty with Malaysia, to extend the use of an air force base in Butterworth, on the island of Penang, and Iddin and Shahirah had been sacrificed on the altar of strategic diplomacy and defence training.

I'd been accused of using the media to further their cause, and for that I would make no apology. I chose to keep agitating in the media, and any other avenue I could identify, all the while holding onto a tiny bead of hope that perhaps news of my continued fight would permeate through to Iddin and Shahirah in their cloistered existence in Malaysia, so that they would know how much I loved them both and that I would never give up fighting for their return.

My media expertise, and that of my most immediate circle, lent itself to this avenue. Had I been a doctor, would I have been expected to stand idly by after an accident in which my own child was injured and give no first aid, waiting ineffectually for an ambulance to arrive? I used the only skills I had to help my kids.

The time would eventually come to give other children and parents a voice too – using those same media skills.

Running away from all the turmoil and the grief of Iddin and Shahirah's abduction was not an option for me. I could attempt to numb the pain for fleeting nano-seconds of respite, but the puncture in my existence was unpatchable. It permeated every element of my existence – it peered over the shoulder of any intimacy with my husband, Iain, and mocked me as I carried out the most routine chores. Loading the washing machine was like a slap in the face: the absence of the children's clothing screamed at me that life should stand still. But it wouldn't, no matter how hard I tried to push it away. Life – real everyday, mundane functioning – felt like a betrayal and a divorce from the pain and confusion my children, I knew, would be experiencing.

Were they bewildered and frightened? Were they trying to comfort each other? Were they crying themselves to sleep every night? When an inkling came through from the Australian government that the 'children are in Indonesia, travelling towards Malaysia', I moved heaven and earth, marshalling lawyers on a number of Indonesian islands in an attempt to legally block my ex-husband's journey through the archipelago, but my efforts proved futile and were particularly thwarted by the intractability of my own government when the powerbrokers refused to pinpoint the exact location of the children even though the intelligence services and the Foreign Ministry had it.

If I am very honest and delve downwards to the darker, most painful elements of self-analysis, I know I began to shrink back into an emotional life where an estrangement from the familiar phrases of living equated themselves to utter loneliness – even though surrounded by others. My shopping list was now devoid of reminders like 'must buy cornflakes' or 'pick up Vicks for Iddin's chest', and I pined for the mundanity. Too hard to maintain the normality of relationships from within the context of the family lost, I began to redraw boundaries, to re-contextualise the format of my intimacies. Parts of me hardened like grapes withering on a maternal vine. Other parts began to awaken to the pressure of the invisible band of copper wire entwining my torso and constricting my capacity to be who I had been in the *other* life, and so disallowing me the ability to move entirely outside of its deceptive malleability as a metal. It was a restrictor nonetheless that allowed me growth only in *its* chosen direction, and that direction compelled me to search out other parents who had a parity of grief and isolation to my own.

Knowledge, I felt, would arm and sustain me, and the repository of this knowledge, must, I had reasoned, be other parents of abducted children.

With a resigned wisdom very uncommon in my personality in those days, and after some urging from an insightful friend, Marie Mohr, I realised it was time for me to speak to an independent professional who could help me with the seemingly bottomless well of grief into which I had plunged. Instinctively I had begun to realise, too, that I needed help to 'age' my stolen children in my mind – to accept the passing of time and to better comprehend the manifestations of the traumas they would be going through. If I was to fulfil my role as their mother in the future, I would need to understand their developmental phases.

But, the bottom line was that I was teetering on the brink of my own emotional implosion, spreading myself so thin my nerve endings were transparent. Simultaneously, I was writing my first book, *Once I Was a Princess*, dealing with the sheer hard slog of arranging and researching a multi-country film shoot, and skeltering through life at a frenetic pace. I was doing anything I could put my hand to so I didn't have a spare moment to think and could fall into bed every night exhausted. It was also becoming harder to ignore the obvious fissures in my marriage – random and oddly placed, the cracks were beginning to resemble the plasterwork in an earthquake shattered building. Forces (some of which I had manufactured to cope after the abduction) were pushing me over a brink I felt I could never rescale if I didn't take definitive action.

Because of the sexual abuse I'd suffered as a child at the hands of my mother and stepfather, and their subsequent machinations, I was pretty skittish about baring my naked anguish more than necessary. However, once I had begun my twice-weekly discussions with Dr Julie Jones, a clarity of thought allowed me to look at the broader picture of my life, and to sketch out what sort of condition I wanted to be in once I reached my final destination and the day when I could hold my children again.

The freedom to express my emotions to Julie – unfettered by social constraints – was like water to a parched man in the desert. Liberated at last from the social niceties and sensitivities which had tainted all my conversations since the abduction of the children, it was a relief to be able to dissect the torments sleep presented for me and to rail against the platitudes people felt compelled to mouth in my direction. What could I say when faced with a sympathetic look on a stranger's face, a comforting hand touching my own and the never-to-be-forgotten line delivered in a quavering tone: 'I know how you feel, my cat just died.' (In a deeper part of myself, I realised that grief is relative – only the inner emotional experiences of the person empathising with me could weigh their commiserations – so I had learned to take a deep breath and utter comforting words in return.)

Fortunately, I could laugh and cry with Julie about what became known as the 'cat bereavement' episode, and so many others, unconstrained by the fear of causing offence or my deeply ingrained need to be polite. Julie was such a tremendously skilled and sensible psychotherapist, a clinical child psychiatrist specialising in grief counselling, that nothing seemed to throw this compassionate woman at all. Despite all my initial misgivings, she managed to arm me with self-knowledge and new foundations for coping. The next phase of life I was about to enter – travelling overseas to report on the very crime that had so upset my own life – would require all my new-found equilibrium, but with Julie's encouragement I straightened my shoulders and leapt across the breach.

Chapter 3
Two Candles

I'll be the first to admit that deciding to embark on a complicated four-and-a-half-week film shoot across twenty-three cities, eight nations and three continents with a budget as tight as an opera singer's corset was probably not one of my most rational decisions, but it did seem logical at the time.

I wanted to create a cohesive documentary on what child abduction is, and how it is dealt with around the world; to show the social, emotional and political ramifications, and to try to educate parents not to use their children like cudgels with which to beat each other around the head. I decided to profile a number of parental child abduction cases across the world – the children and the families left behind, from New York to Israel, France to Algeria, Belgium to Morocco, Sydney to South Africa via Monaco, and England to Egypt, rounding off with a look at the workings of the United Nations Committee on the Rights of the Child in Geneva.

The title came easily. It would be called *Empty Arms* –

Broken Hearts. This simple phrase was a succinct summation of my own thoughts and the exhausting futility of all my legal challenges to date, and the personal pleas I made to my former husband's representatives for just one single phone conversation with Shahirah and Iddin.

My inner battle would be to make my mind function and my intellect work during the filming, even as my soul screamed with every breath: 'I love you, I love you, come home safe, my babies.'

So my odyssey began. In order to make *Empty Arms – Broken Hearts* a well-rounded documentary that I hoped wouldn't be overly parochial, I'd devised a filming schedule which, had I known better, I would have taken an extra set of feet, three more weeks, energy supplements and a lock pick.

Fortunately, the three-member film crew consisted of personal friends and Iain (who was also co-producer alongside me), as the four of us would be living in close proximity for over a month with only two rest days. On our tight budget, we were travelling economy class on all flights – a big concession when you consider that two of the crew were over 6 feet tall – and sharing rooms. When we marshalled at the airport, even with the camera, lights and sound kit pared back to only the barest necessities, our luggage totalled eighteen individually tagged pieces. All the equipment had been registered with international import and export authorities, separately itemised, guaranteed, insured and held under international 'carnet' documents (a pre-paid bond arrangement to ensure that no nefarious on-selling activities were taking place).

By the time we finished filming we had travelled to

twenty-six locations and been strapped inside all manner of aircraft. We'd rented seven self-drive cars, hired one dilapidated limousine, escaped with our lives in a battered old Mercedes Benz, journeyed in umpteen taxis, sped along in a French bullet train and hadn't lost one item of luggage.

In many ways the documentary was a confrontation with my greatest fears and nightmares – one that was necessary, though, if I was to stay true to my children and what they might one day know of me. On my odyssey I would re-enter an Islamic state, with much trepidation, and walk the streets of London on a bright spring day with a young boy who had been abducted by his father four times in a campaign of terror and control. Most often, I would see my own face in those of the other parents – a mirror to which, in my lowest moments, I wished my eyes were blinded.

The huge amount of coverage my family's case had generated led to the public perception that I had some sort of extra power or sterling connections in the palm of my hand and led to other desperate parents contacting me, begging for my assistance or offering information for the documentary. Looking back now, I realise how bizarre it is to research anything without using the Internet. It seems incongruous that in 1994 I didn't even have email. Instead I burned up telephone lines at all hours of the day and night, following leads and fleshing out snippets of individual stories and family tragedy that often reflected my own.

Before we left Australia, I had made contact with scores of parents around the globe who'd lost their children to kidnap, and I had become privy to some of their darkest moments. Now I wanted the documentary to show that none of us was alone in our despair. I'd also discovered the correct terminology to identify myself: I was now officially a 'left-behind' parent.

Shockingly, I had found that far from parental child abduction being confined to a handful of rocky relationships, the international statistics were ominously robust and rapidly increasing.

In 1994, not many nations kept centralised databases on the numbers of children abducted overseas (today, in 2007, this is changing and laws have tightened); however, according to Reunite, an affiliate of the British Lord Chancellor's Department and the British charitable organisation responsible for assisting victims of child abduction, the United Kingdom was losing an estimated 1,400 children each year. That's the equivalent of forty kindergartens suddenly being removed from the face of Britain. In France, the estimates for 1994 put the number at 1,000 *dossiers*, a term used to identify the individual family names, masking the probability that multiple siblings from those thousand families had been kidnapped in that year. Australia kept no comprehensive records in the early 1990s, but official estimates stood at eighty to one hundred cases per year. From the United States, more than 800 children had been taken overseas in 1993 and categorised under the heading of 'Hague Convention Abductions' – those statistics were even higher if you added the hundreds of children abducted by family members to countries outside the jurisdiction of the Hague Convention.

Thirteen years on, the estimated numbers of kidnapped children involved in unresolved cases, and hailing from Western nations, still stands at the 1994 figure of 30,000. Many of these children are trapped in a legal void – scattered and hidden in different parts of the world, cut off from all they once knew and loved.

The *Hague Convention on the Civil Aspects of Child Abduction* is a multilateral international treaty, which came into being in the mid–1980s, to combat the escalating incidence of international parental child abduction.

Simply put, a child taken from a Hague Convention country to another Hague Convention signatory nation must be returned to his or her normal country of residence. Working along the lines of an extradition agreement, the Convention isn't meant to be used to determine custody rights or other matters. Its primary function is to ensure the safe return of a child to their habitual domicile and to entrust the appropriate courts in that country to hear all the issues pertaining to welfare and custody. Gradually, over the past fifteen years, the Hague Convention has been adopted and ratified by more and more nations. (In 2007, the number of signatory nations was seventy-six, compared to only forty-one in 1995.) Many Middle Eastern, African, Asian and South American nations are still non-signatories to the treaty, which means that children abducted to or from these places have no legal safety net to protect them and assist in their repatriation to their homelands. Iddin and Shahirah weren't covered by the Hague Convention as Malaysia is not a signatory – there was no safety net for my children.

In any case, even signatory countries sometimes evince confusion or plain pig-headedness when faced with a Hague Convention matter. A significant sector of European Union member states, although Convention signatories, do not readily return children. France and Germany are very difficult countries to deal with in this area of law as there appears to be great internal confusion about the rights of sovereignty versus the precedence of international treaties and self-determination. Tragically this often hampers the proper implementation of the Convention. A strange form of nationalism, sometimes tinged with racism or sexism, can also put a spoke in the wheels of a child's future. Quite a number of former European colonies and protectorates (such as Algeria and Morocco) are known to automatically refuse to return a child if the abducting parent is one of their own nationals – it is a strange form of what I term 'post-colonial backlash'.

Coming into New York City from the airport, we saw the enormous buildings of Manhattan and the myriad lights reflecting off the Hudson River in the twilight. Then, from our midtown hotel, we took a cab to Brooklyn.

In front of an uninspiring brownstone building there, Larry Leinoff was waiting for us – a father whose little girl, Audrey Bloom-Leinoff, had vanished, aged four, six years earlier in 1988. Quietly mannered, with a neat salt-and-pepper beard and hound-dog eyes, Larry took us into his spartan living room. He sat and spoke about Audrey as the cameras rolled and the hot television lights reflected off the blinds. As he talked, Larry's hands constantly wandered to the dog-eared photographs of his small daughter arrayed on the arm of his chair.

Marcia Bloom-Leinoff, Larry's former wife, had scrambled for valid reasons to disallow Audrey's grandparents and father from having contact with the child. Unsubstantiated claims were thrown into the legal arena, definitively investigated by the authorities and a battery of child abuse specialists – and proved to be unfounded. However, by bamboozling the legal system into months of mandatory but fruitless investigations, Marcia had enough time to spirit Audrey out of America and into Israel, where the mother and daughter simply disappeared and have not been heard of since. How bitter it was to reflect on the grave disservice women inflict on each other and society with such untrue allegations.

Larry now maintains a website in the hope that one day his daughter, Audrey, may contact him, even if only out of curiosity – if she knows he exists.

My first instance of face-to-face contact with another left-behind parent of longstanding provided me with a concrete example of the effect of a child's long absence. Before me – devoid of window dressing – the emotions and the heartache had been so nakedly revealed in Larry's eyes.

A frustrating misconception that only fathers abduct children has prevailed for a long time. But abduction is not a gender issue – it's so often about power and revenge.

Leaving Brooklyn that night, I turned my head to look out the window of the cab so the others wouldn't see the tears that welled in my eyes and trickled down my cheeks. As we headed back to Manhattan, steam rose wraith-like from the subway manholes that dotted the city's streets and whispered upwards against the chill of the early April night as if to echo my wavering hopes that my own children would return before I, too, had six years of yearning etched deeply on my face.

Rising early next morning after a fitful sleep, I headed out onto the New York streets, pulling my black overcoat tighter around me and my velvet cloche hat tightly down around my ears and melded with the commuters emerging from the subway stations. No filming was scheduled until later that day, so I had the luxury of time on my own and the privacy of my own thoughts. Turning uptown from 38th Street, I swung onto Fifth Avenue in search of a deli to answer my hankering for a smoked salmon bagel. Instead I came upon the towering Victorian Gothic facade of St Patrick's Cathedral. The enormous circular stained-glass window suspended above the main entrance caught the sunlight and refracted its colours onto the forecourt. Drawn up the front steps by some strange imperative, I noticed a side door standing open and found myself poised within the threshold.

I hadn't been inside a church for a long time. With the exception of Christmas and my beloved nanna's funeral, I'd purposefully stayed away from any building of Christian worship to guard against public conclusions that religion was a huge mainstay in my life. The Christianity versus Islam debate had become such an issue in the media after the kidnap of Iddin and Shah that I had perhaps over-analysed how my attendance at a church would be perceived publicly. Nor had I wanted to further inflame my former husband's religious sensibilities, or those of his supporters, who considered my children's abduction an act of jihad – Muslim holy war. Here though, in a city thousands of miles away from prying eyes, I was anonymous.

I *never* prayed; I simply wasn't what one would call religious. In fact, I certainly wasn't a Catholic by virtue of my own convictions on abortion and divorce; but instinctively I reached out my hand for two tapers. Touching the wicks of both slim candles to one of the small flames, I added mine to the long bank of votive candles flickering in the draughty vestibule of the cathedral. Sinking to my knees in the nearest pew, I murmured under my breath a plea to some higher power I could not even name or identify, but knew existed.

'Please bring them home to me, please keep them safe, please let them know I love them with all my heart and soul – always.'

And so began a pattern for me wherever I was in the world (except Australia). I would seek out the oldest church, regardless of denomination, and light two votive candles, always compelled to murmur the same hopeful words about my children. That simple and private action became as much an imperative of hope to me as it was an act of defiance. The flames flickering in their holders were primitive and ancient, spiritual and timeless, symbolising humankind's ingenuity and resourcefulness and my own burning desire to keep my kidnapped children safe from the coldness of the act perpetrated against them.

Choosing to make *Empty Arms – Broken Hearts* was not a very effective way to combat my yearning for Iddin and Shahirah. Everywhere we travelled my thoughts would turn to them and the knowledge that, for the moment, the closest we could all be was the presence of their photographs pinned inside my pocket every day as I dressed for the filming ahead – a kind of talisman of faith.

The documentary introduced me to friends who have stood by me and been on the same wavelength for many years. Most significantly, I met Patsy Heymans and chronicled her desperate seven-year search for her three children – Simon, Marina and Moriah – which ended with their joyous reunion in 1993.

Patsy is petite and blonde, a no-nonsense woman with a generous spirit and a wicked sense of humour. Violently opposed to make-up and the frivolity of fashion, her one concession to adornment is her diamond jewellery. Teamed with faded denim jeans and T-shirts, the stones glitter and wink incongruously from her fingers and neck. Patsy presides over her brood with love, logic and laughter in a rambling stone house, complete with menagerie of pets, in Ambly, a beautiful village in the French-speaking part of Belgium.

When I first met Patsy, she had painted the windows of the house with bunnies and Easter eggs and her home seemed to embrace all who entered with its warmth and welcome. Patsy and her second husband, Walter, had produced three more little ones during the period Simon, Marina and Moriah were missing – Olivier, Gautier and Noelie – all of whom adored their older siblings. I felt like I already knew Patsy well, as we had spent hours talking on the phone about child abduction before I even set foot in Ambly. Patsy is a pivotal force in the field of parental child abduction in Belgium and Europe, counselling and giving practical assistance to other parents whose children have vanished.

Patsy's older children had been abducted by her estranged first husband in 1987, and for the years they were missing Patsy had fought hard to maintain her reason. Her sheer nervous energy fuelled an exhaustive international search and public campaign for her three children, which she spearheaded with her amazingly tenacious father, Jacques, and the Belgian police inspector Jean Dooms.

In 1990 the children's father was arrested by the FBI in New York, extradited to Belgium and jailed for three years. During this time he refused to divulge the whereabouts of the children. He relished his revenge and enjoyed Patsy's suffering. Domestic violence became a link between Patsy's story and my own – that, and the newly found religious fundamentalism of the fathers involved.

Just when hope had worn thin, the FBI followed up a tip from the public and finally located Patsy's children in a Hassidic Jewish community in New York State. The children had been told their mother was dead, and the youngest, Moriah, could not remember Patsy at all. Haim, their father, had dumped them with the ultra-Orthodox group years earlier and never returned.

While we were in the US, I had wanted to speak to the normally cloistered Hassidic community in an attempt to understand why they'd aided and abetted a child abduction; and, in particular, whether or not the family with whom the three children had lived for over three years were aware of their complicity in an illegal action, or had been duped.

My excursion with the film crew to Bedford Hills in upstate New York turned into one of the most bizarre nights of my life. The only way we could make the three-hour journey, cost being a major consideration, was to hire a 'limousine' from the cousin of our hotel doorman. When the vehicle creaked up to the hotel entrance, we all clambered in, slamming the door behind us – an action which promptly caused the door to become unhinged and fall to the sidewalk. It did not augur well.

After hasty repairs, we set off at a reasonable hour from the city, but after many hours' travelling time and noting the fading light, I began to get a little apprehensive about our tight schedule. For 150 miles, Juan, our driver from the Bronx, had assured us he knew where he was going, until he suddenly pulled over and informed us he was lost. I found myself standing in wintry darkness, illuminated like a startled rabbit in the headlights of our vehicle, outside a white clapboard picture theatre in a small town of quintessential American apple-pie charm. The hope was that someone inside would provide directions to the community we were seeking. Luckily, the ticket seller had a vague idea, and after much discussion we set off again with a hand-drawn map scribbled on the back of a movie flyer, taking it in turns to cling to the loose door lest it detach itself from the vehicle once more.

Our excursion to upstate New York, however, turned out to be fruitless. We'd travelled at a snail's pace along fog-bound country laneways to reach the remote Bedford Hills compound – a walled former Victorian tuberculosis quarantine facility – only to be startled by a group of bearded and black-clad men who suddenly appeared from the mist surrounding the darkened outbuildings. Their menacing tones and belligerent gestures made it abundantly clear we weren't welcome. Explaining that we had an appointment proved futile. We had no alternative but to load ourselves back into the car and trundle back to Manhattan.

Chapter 4

Them's the Breaks

From the window of my hotel in Paris — a strange crooked building on the Rue de Rivoli with minuscule balconies and creaking, crooked floors — I saw the Eiffel Tower for the first time. That most romantic of images. The sky was the deep azure that only a European twilight can provide and all of Paris seemed to glow golden. For a few moments my breath was taken away by the sheer beauty and enchantment of that magical city. But then my chest grew tight, and the absence of my children became a palpable void in my body.

Instinctively, I reached inside my jacket pocket and touched Iddin and Shah's photograph. Their spiritual presence, if not their physical, made my resolve strengthen even though I had begun to feel daunted and drained by the confrontations with officialdom and the mutual tears with parents who'd also been deprived of the joy of watching their children grow and mature.

I made my way to Notre Dame Cathedral for a modicum

of respite, pulled again by some illogical reasoning that urged me to seek out the votive tapers in the nave and light two for Iddin and Shahirah. As always, I uttered my mantra of love and protection and stumbled out into the evening, squaring my shoulders for the tasks ahead.

My marriage to Iain had fallen apart a third of the way through the filming – at the end of our shoot in the United States. We were airborne on a United Airlines flight above the Atlantic Ocean, between Washington and Paris, when just in time for the late-night meal service Iain opened his eyes from what had appeared to be a very deep sleep and spewed forth the words 'I divorce you, I divorce you, I divorce you', looking straight into my eyes with unblinking clarity. Oddly, he chose the Islamic method to pronounce this. I sat speechless, trying to find words to counter his startling statement. Continuing, he said that he had decided that he didn't 'want to be married to a famous woman', that he was 'the senior journalist and should have written the first book'. There had been no arguments, no sniping to precipitate these statements. In part, I understood how he felt – I wouldn't have wanted to be married to me at that stage of my existence either.

I tried whispered pleadings and reasoning, but amidst a planeload of strangers it was difficult to come up with the words to save our crushed marriage. Shattered, I retreated to the airline toilets to weep, and remained there until turbulence forced me out to a vacant seat in another part of the plane at the flight attendant's insistence.

Although Iain later asserted he hadn't meant what he said, to me, in my deepest emotional core, I knew that he had been brutally and horrifyingly frank. It spelled the death knell of trust, eroding what had remained of my feelings of security and the certainty of stability I had placed in our marriage. In my mind it was a blow from which our relationship would never recover and a betrayal. The edge of the cliff had simply crumbled beneath my feet and ironically, I hadn't even realised I was standing at the precipice.

Iain and I would continue to work together for some time after his pronouncement. Our intimacy had dissolved even though we ostensibly resided at the same address. On a barely conscious level, because of what had transpired on the flight, I realise that I began to go into self-preservation mode, which was barely perceptible to outsiders because I had so much experience as a survivor of child abuse in putting up a facade. I withdrew into survival mode, locked off parts of myself and sought a new existence, purpose and identity away from our disintegrated marriage.

Interviewing children was by far the most difficult aspect of filming. Prior to leaving Australia, I had spent many hours with a psychiatrist specialising in children's trauma to learn how best to interview kidnapped children while trying to avoid further compounding their distress. Although these children had now been returned to their original homes, I was extremely mindful that it was inappropriate to ask them which parent they preferred, and that it was vital that the final decision on whether or not an interview would proceed was made by the children themselves. A number of the children, by this time aged between nine and nineteen, had experienced parental violence and abuse while with the abducting parent, and some had believed for many years that their left-behind parent was dead. The trust these vulnerable children and adults were placing in me was an enormous responsibility. I could only imagine what it had been like for Shahirah and Iddin when two very callous Australian reporters had interviewed them after their abduction with no thought of the emotional consequences. My own experiences with the media had taught me that a chunk of the interviewee's life is carried away by the interviewer: the subject is at the writer's mercy as to how they are portrayed.

Following the abduction of my children, Bahrin had returned to Malaysia and pulled strings to have a retrospective Islamic court order issued. It was retrospective indeed, in light of the dates: the kidnapping took place in 1992; the court order he obtained that year was backdated to 1984 and in essence awarded Bahrin full custody of both the children even though we were still married on that date and I was pregnant with Shahirah! A retrospective custody order over my womb did strike me as convoluted, even knowing the vagaries of the Islamic Court and the clout of the royal family. By design, though, it meant that in Malaysia I was deemed a kidnapper of my own children, and would be arrested if I entered the country. Frustratingly, the Australian Labour government made it very clear that if I attempted to enter Malaysia either to retrieve my children, or just to try to see them, my inevitable arrest would leave the Australian authorities unable and unwilling to assist in my release from a foreign prison. Coupled with this was the knowledge that as the children were an eight-hour drive from the capital, I would not even come close to seeing them if I were arrested; it would be an exercise in futile grandstanding.

It was daunting, then, for me to enter Morocco, a Muslim country, but another bizarre judicial decision was behind this leg of the filming. In order to silence the annoying diplomatic and political demands of the Belgian government for the return of two kidnapped boys, Karim and Mehdi, aged nine and seven respectively, the courts in a provincial town in Morocco had ruled that as the father, Chikhaoui, had refused to produce the children in court, he must have killed them. Death certificates were issued in the boys' names and the father convicted of murder, only to be released from jail after serving just six months, whereupon, as reports would have it, he returned to his home town, opened a petrol station and reverted to living openly with his two sons.

Valerie, the children's mother and a Belgian national, had warned us that her husband, Chikhaoui, had powerful government connections who had threatened her. Perhaps that was why Moroccan airport officials impounded our camera and equipment as soon as we landed from Paris, even though we had the necessary permits for their importation, and for filming. My heart had skipped a beat when the customs inspectors began to scrutinise our documents and question us closely in French and English.

It took several days of negotiations, and two long car trips, to speak with officials in the ancient city of Rabat and to obtain further clearances for our equipment and its release. In the meantime we used a professional video camera to film around the marketplaces and walled portions of Casablanca.

I was feeling very claustrophobic and more than a little irrationally jumpy at finding myself back in an Islamic society. The strict conditioning of the Malaysian royal family continually tainted my enjoyment of this colourful and exotic tourist destination. I felt inhibited and unable to stride out confidently like the myriad tourists milling about on the streets. My instincts were to don a veil and blend into the crowd as a docile daughter of Islam, attracting as little attention as possible.

I could see that Morocco was exciting and beautiful, rich with the smell of spice and the riotous clamour of markets set against a background of ochre-painted buildings with shady archways and cool white colonial structures. Sunrise against Casablanca's shoreline of breaking waves held the promise of romance and exotic adventure à la Bogart and Bergman. But the others had absolutely no notion that many of the men we encountered on the street and in marketplaces were cursing and insulting us in Arabic, all the while maintaining a smile. Shahirah was constantly on my mind as I caught myself taking second glances at many of the young girls wearing full Islamic dress and veil alongside more fashionably dressed friends. I wondered what my own daughter was wearing, now she was getting older.

At last, after many days' delay, we set out for the inland town of Oujda, an hour north-east of Casablanca by small plane. Here, I had arranged to hook up with a local university student, an activist in the fledgling feminist movement, who would act as our interpreter. We had resolved now to be as circumspect as possible and had stored the majority of our baggage and equipment, cultivating the outward appearance of tourists. We had reached Chikhaoui's home territory where his family ran many of the larger business concerns.

Oujda, when we finally came to it, was very different from Casablanca and Rabat. Small grey donkeys were a fixture on the roads, hauling enormous loads stacked upon rickety carts assembled from scrounged materials; and bored-looking boys perched precariously atop their cargo dressed in kaftans and shabby sandals. The landscape was sparsely dotted with trees and the earth dry and dusty. Our circumspection seemed wise in this remote place. The rocky Beni-Snassen Mountains spread out in the distance, beyond which lay the Algerian border. The call to prayer echoed through the town and marked the passing of the day.

Women were fully veiled in black; only their eyes were visible. They scurried from place to place without the gaiety of their urban sisters back at the coast. Here, the sight of a lone woman travelling with three males raised many eyebrows and it was not sensible for us to leave the establishment we were staying in more often than necessary. The bathrooms there were filth-encrusted and stank so badly I held out for ten hours before using the toilet – a long-drop arrangement. Our beds had a liberal application of previous occupiers' body hair, and the sheets and blankets were rank and stiff. All of us slept fully clothed on top of the covers but, even so, the next morning we were covered in bed-bug bites and itching all over.

Berkane, very close to the wild Algerian border, was the town where it was believed Karim and Mehdi lived with their father. I decided on a straightforward approach as the best way to discover whether the boys were alive. The five of us bundled into a dilapidated Mercedes for the bumpy ride. Our interpreter, Amina, was very concerned that we make this a brief visit and not cause too much of a disturbance, as Chikhaoui's reputation for violence had filtered back to her via discreet enquiries on our behalf.

Finding the petrol station owned by Chikhaoui was

simple, as was locating the man himself. You couldn't really miss him. He stood at over 6 feet 4 – a mountain of a man with large hands, broad shoulders and swarthy skin. He seemed extremely irritated to see us alighting outside his business. As we had driven into the station, I had spotted a young boy being hustled inside a doorway. It appeared to be the nine year old, Karim, and we were lucky enough to catch him on a few frames of film before the door was shut tight. Seeing the camera, Chikhaoui initially agreed to be filmed, ushered us inside the building, and even produced recent photographs of his sons as we talked. When, after a few anodyne questions, I asked him why he hadn't allowed the mother of his children any contact with the boys since June 1991, he replied that she didn't deserve it and that all his troubles were Valerie's fault.

'If she believes they are dead, that's her problem, not mine.' He gave a dismissive flick of his hand.

Looking at his face closely, I asked him through the interpreter, and again in French, if the boy we had seen earlier was his son. Startled, he dismissed my question and angrily brought the interview to a close, leaping to his feet and towering over me. Fingering the photographs of the boys and using a quiet voice, I asked him if we could at least film the images for Valerie back in Belgium so she could see that the boys were indeed alive. He refused vehemently and began to eject us from the building. Following us to the car, he made a lunge for the car keys, which had been left in the ignition, and refused to return them, screaming abuse at us and doing some serious jabbing of chests with fingers.

Then Chikhaoui began to demand that we hand over the videotape we had shot of him, and all our film. I was aware that Amina was cowering behind me, trying to drag me into the vehicle, and was whispering frantically into my ear that Chikhaoui was instructing someone to summon the police.

It was probably not the time to remember that this man had broken his former wife's thighbone with a swift kick.

Within minutes of this scene erupting, the local constabulary arrived in a cloud of dust and skid of tyres, immediately cutting us out of the conversational loop and taking Chikhaoui aside. I had to move swiftly to protect our footage. Gesturing to the cameraman, I had him give me the two small videotapes, about $3^1/_2$ inches by 3 inches, which we had partly filled. I thrust them down my baggy trousers, into the crotch of my underwear, followed by the tape from the camera itself. Surreptitiously I ripped open the packaging of a new blank tape while the others blocked my actions from view; this tape also joined the other three. Settling my jacket in place and straightening my posture, I tried to look as nonchalant as possible – just as the police officers strode over and demanded the films from the camera and the bags.

When we refused, we were all arrested and taken to the local cells, where we found the chief of police and the mayor waiting for us.

All our travel documents and passports were confiscated, along with my international media pass and the Moroccan Film Board accreditation naming me as head of the project. After searching the car and our bags, the police chief demanded the surrender of our tapes – which was obviously out of the question. The mayor and Chikhaoui were incensed by this refusal and, after searching the crew and driver, the police ejected them all from the building and detained me. Amina was also released and told to think about the consequences of her involvement with us.

It was at this point that I became quite apprehensive, as the manner of the Moroccans still inside the police station was intensely belligerent. I suddenly wasn't feeling that defiant any more – the prospect of a police check being done and the Malaysian warrant coming to light started to play on my mind. But there was simply no way I was going to meekly hand over the tapes.

The mayor and the police chief put me in a brightly lit, if somewhat smelly, room with an earth floor. For seven hours, at regular ninety-minute intervals, my jailers opened the door and demanded I tell them where the footage was hidden. Finally, shortly before sunset, by pressing my ear to the door, I picked up a few Arabic words I recognised. They were discussing strip-searching me.

Trying not to panic, I began to scream out at the top of my voice a muddle of words in Arabic, roughly translating to, 'I am unclean, I have my period! You cannot touch me, I am unclean.' I don't know who was more shocked at that moment, them or me. Until that time, all the stilted conversation between us had taken place in broken English and my terrible French. I had been cautious not to let them know that I had knowledge of Islam or Arabic, in case it made them too curious. In any case, my protestations in their own tongue did the trick. I was brought from my holding cell and into the main chamber of the police station, where negotiations commenced over a plate of peaches that the police chief sliced delicately with a long-bladed knife, and proffered in my direction as a conciliatory gesture.

Back and forth we went, with Chikhaoui adding his opinions and accusations for good measure, until an agreement was reached. I acquiesced to handing over the videotape Chikhaoui and everyone else kept referring to, and in return, my party and I would be free to leave town. Rising to my feet with as much dignity as I could muster, I turned my back for the sake of decorum and fished out the blank videotape from its hiding place inside my trousers. I handed it over to the police chief, who gingerly took possession of it between forefinger and thumb, holding it as if it were a contaminated object then passing it to Chikhaoui with great distaste. Rising triumphantly from his place beside the police chief's desk, the great oaf of a man ceremoniously tore the fragile tape from its casing, and for good measure laid it on the chief's desk and smashed it with a large paperweight.

Emerging from the police station, I found our driver and the film crew sitting beside the vehicle. When I looked over at Amina, she was ashen-faced, and I noticed her hands were shaking slightly. In a quavering voice she suggested we leave Berkane as quickly as possible.

When our vehicle finally trundled through the outskirts of Oujda, my breathing eased a little. The main concern by this stage was getting Amina safely to her front door. She had put her family and herself at risk by volunteering to interpret for us, of this I was sure. I hoped that she would not encounter repercussions from Chikhaoui or his cohorts. After exchanging our postal addresses I bade her goodbye with a warm hug and a cash bonus.

Back at the hotel that night, all four of us shared one room, barely dozing and very much on edge. I listened with one ear, half-expecting the police to burst through the door at any moment and cart me away. I counted the minutes until shortly before dawn, when we could get to the airport and take the first flight back to Casablanca and then our connection to London.

As the jet touched down, I've never been so pleased to land at Heathrow in my life. I finally understood the Pope's compulsion to kiss the tarmac, but I doubt if he ever had to deal with the delicate placement of three videotapes on his person when he did so.

We were like a caravan of movie-making gypsies, barely one step ahead of collapse. A lightning-fast visit to the United Nations in Geneva to film a session of the Committee on the Rights of the Child and hold an interview with the official Rapporteur of the Committee, Marta Santos Pais, proved frustrating – the committee obviously lacked real international power and were stagnating in a pool of their own complacency. Arrive, film, depart; we were hopping back and forth across the English Channel between Europe and the United Kingdom, still filming, tracing lost children and speaking to others who had been able to find their way home. The pace was exhausting but I manically drove the crew and myself on. We were approaching the documentary's finishing line.

Sleep by now was a futile exercise in tossing and turning, my thoughts filled with montages of my children and the smashed normality of the life we once had as a family. Every roll of film we shot symbolised moving an inch closer to Iddin and Shah and the possibility of one day being able to hug them and tell them I love them with all my heart and soul.

Despite my resolve, it was becoming increasingly difficult for me to work with Iain. I was no longer able to agree with what he wanted me to say in the film, or how he wanted me to behave on camera. I developed an iron-hard and secretive resentment against my husband. The love, though, took a lot longer to die, much longer than the liking, which had begun to evaporate in the days and weeks after the aircraft incident. Eventually I understood that Iain didn't even realise he was hurting me; the pressures – emotional, professional and financial – of the abduction had utterly changed the dynamic of our relationship. Iain had predicted this on the first night following the children's kidnap.

In London again in the final week of the shoot, I could no longer ignore that my right breast was terribly swollen, and seemed to be on fire. During filming in Monaco, I had been attacked by a woman I was interviewing about the role she played as a paid accomplice in an abduction. She had long, sharp talons and had inflicted painful wounds on my chest. Though it meant the loss of a day's shooting, I finally had no choice but to take myself off to the Princess Grace Hospital in search of a physician. It seemed like a fittingly named facility, considering the country in which I'd received the wound.

I was in a fever and fast becoming a sweating, shaking mess. It seemed that the wound to my breast had become an abscess; there was no choice but to submit to an overnight stay in hospital, the draining of the abscess and massive doses of intravenous antibiotics.

Three days later, with a stiff arm and a heavily bandaged chest, I boarded a flight for Australia. The filming was all but complete.

Empty Arms – Broken Hearts went on to screen

internationally and was awarded a special commendation for outstanding contribution to the United Nations Year of the Family. Around the world, the documentary has been used as a teaching film for judges and practitioners working in the areas of parental child abduction and family law.

My hope is that the documentary changed the attitudes of people towards this crime of revenge and power. As one thirteen-year-old child, a victim of abduction interviewed for the film, said, 'I hope that any parent who watches this film and is thinking of kidnapping their own children will stop and think about how much it will hurt the children. Don't do it.'

Simple, sage advice from the mouth of a babe.

Chapter 5

The Empty Arms Network

It was a decided anticlimax to have finished the film and to leave the editing and post-production to others; all that was left for me to do was record the final voice-over track. My other skills, nurturing and mothering, I had little use for now.

I became more and more despondent on the day of Shahirah's ninth birthday and the second anniversary of the children's kidnap. A heavy bout of depression had settled on my shoulders after completing the documentary filming and I felt unable to shake it off. In hindsight, one of the main contributors was the film itself and the gradual realisation that it might be years before I saw my own children once more. The deep reflection that writing my first book required had also brought all the demons of my childhood abuse to the surface: issues I'd never dealt with had seemed to engulf me and I no longer had my identity as a mother of young children, with which I had defined my self-worthiness.

For all intents and purposes, Iddin and Shah had been, I

believe, in Bahrin's eyes, surgically excised from my life with commendable efficiency. Their absence confronted me daily at all levels of my life and I felt my inactivity as a nurturer keenly. Conforming to Bahrin's dictates that I only communicate with my children via the cold and impersonal offices of his lawyers in Melbourne, I set about choosing a birthday present for Shahirah and also a small gift for Iddin. Two years is a lot of growing time and I felt as if I were inflicting my own disembowelment as I attempted to write a loving birthday card and upbeat notes to my children whose tastes were now unknown to me. Especially as I knew I could probably expect no response or acknowledgement of my tokens or love. It was a horrible pattern of attempted contact which I would continue for over a decade.

I was mentally and physically exhausted, having for months pushed myself to the limit. Sleep continued to elude me, or was filled with nightmarish images and unrequited longings for the children. Tears flowed unbidden at the most inconvenient moments and wouldn't stop; sometimes they were prompted by recognisable issues or triggers, in other instances not. Gradually, the vaguely enticing option of a chemically induced repose began to take on an attraction. Until that time, I had always been adamantly opposed to sedating away the pain. Prescription drugs offered to me by medicos, or from the secret stashes of well-meaning friends, were crutches I had steadfastly rejected, and recreational drugs offered no solution to my insomnia.

'Three hours of relaxed sleep and then the natural body clock will take over. It's a way of resetting your sleep patterns,' was how my doctor described the effect of the mild sleeping tablets I obtained in my capitulation. Tinged somewhat with a fatalistic attitude, and fuelled by a desperation simply to 'switch off' and escape, I downed ten pills in one swallow and snuggled into my duvet and comfortably arranged pillows. The promise of a deep sleep was sensually attractive after two years of broken rest. There was also a feeling of playing Russian roulette with the possibility of not waking up, of simply sleeping for as long as my body decided it needed to. Exhaustion led me into a delusion of hope, of being able to find Iddin and Shahirah in my undisturbed sleep, of being able to touch their faces and smell the uniqueness of them once more. In some convoluted way I reasoned that by giving up control to a chemical, I was conversely taking control of my ability to find a dream where I might encounter Iddin and Shah without the terrors of separation and overwhelming grief that coloured everyday life as I now knew it.

It's easy to understand why sleep deprivation is such a favoured tool with interrogators and torturers: reality is suspended for the victim, and rational thought is bent and worn down.

Even though I was obviously in a quite deep despair, I was still a control freak: I took the precaution of leaving a note explaining what I had ingested and why, along with a few instructions, such as not to call an ambulance and to just let me rest. Not terribly sensible and, in hindsight, overly dramatic, I admit, but at the time, it seemed organised and responsible. However, when I was discovered sleeping so heavily about three hours into a blissfully dreamless and deep sleep, panic ensued and an ambulance was summoned.

I came to a rude awakening on a hospital trolley surrounded by strangers. A very young and earnest-looking doctor was bent over me, demanding to know why I had attempted suicide and threatening a commitment – not of the romantic kind – should I offer the incorrect answer. Evaluating my situation as hurriedly as my still foggy brain allowed, I ascertained that I was a new arrival in the hospital and hadn't had my stomach pumped, but was in serious jeopardy of ending up in either a straightjacket or, worse, in an open-backed hospital gown. Even more horrendous was the thought of ending up on the front page of the morning newspapers in lurid bold type: KIDNAP MUM'S TRAGIC SUICIDE BID, PICTURES INSIDE! or PRINCESS POPS PILLS! Scrambling for the right words to prove my sanity and liberate myself, I attempted to explain the situation with as much clarity as possible but only managed a pretty good imitation of a fish – my mouth opening and closing accompanied by a groaning 'orruummm'. My tongue seemed to be incredibly attracted to the roof of my mouth and rather too large for its normal space.

So much for the first try. The situation was now serious and my befuddlement was starting to clear, accelerated by the patronising look on the young doctor's face, which was rather blurred as my spectacles, no doubt, were still sitting atop my nightstand. Concentrating on the doctor's next question, I realised that he was speaking with a broad Scottish accent. The foreign brogue explained the absence of a spark of recognition in his eyes which was all too present in the attending nurses' faces I could see hovering behind his shoulder.

'If you commit me overnight, I will sue you,' seemed to have the desired effect of at least holding his attention. I followed up with a slurred, 'I am fully in control of my faculties and do not need to be committed, thank you very much.'

'Tell me why you are so depressed, Jacqueline,' the doctor questioned.

I was rather tempted to point out that as we had not been formally introduced, I'd prefer him to refrain from using my Christian name, but thought holding my tongue on that point the wiser option. Instead I answered with the obvious.

'Because my children were kidnapped by their father and—'

'I think you're confused, Jacqueline,' he interjected with saccharine tones and careful enunciation, even adding a vague pat to my hand. 'Your husband hasn't ... he's ... er ...' The doctor was cut off by an urgent tugging on his sleeve and a hurried whisper in his ear from one of the nurses. Comprehension and curiosity suddenly lit up his face. I was going to have to choose – would I sing for my supper or take the 'high dungeon' road? I chose 'high dungeon'.

'If you would kindly telephone my doctor,' I said, rattling off the name and number, '... she'll be able to confirm that I'm not a candidate for a straightjacket and you can discharge me.' In hindsight, I suppose most unhinged people say things like that when push comes to shove. Nevertheless, warming to my theme, I marshalled a very pompous voice, adding, 'I'm fully aware of my depression and its causes and, with all due respect, I will discuss it with my therapist, and only her. Please phone her now. And what the nurse has been whispering to you is correct, I am *that* woman, the one who is a fixture on the television and in magazines, and I'll take it as a breach of doctor–patient confidentiality if the media becomes aware of this highly personal incident.'

Ten minutes later I was discharged.

Did I really try to commit suicide that night? In truth I'm

not sure. At the point when I took those pills, did I want to die? Let's just say that as I was floating away I didn't want to wake up; I was just too tired. (In any case, the dose I took probably wouldn't have proved lethal.)

Thank goodness my stupid actions remained off the front page and I was able to salvage some shreds of rational thought and determination. I would have to make a choice – either become an eternal victim, in which case I might as well have crawled into a corner and died, or attempt to turn a negative into a positive and try to hang on until I saw Shah and Iddin again.

I knew that I had to keep busy to fill the void left by my absent children; to make some sense of the empty existence I was close to leading.

I decided to harness all the knowledge I'd gathered during the making of the documentary, and establish an organisation – called the Empty Arms Network – to offer support to victims of parental child abduction, both on a domestic and an international level.

I was still receiving so many phone calls from parents in similar circumstances to my own. All these parents, male and female, from Australia and overseas, asked me for guidance or assistance with their cases. I felt strongly that no one should have to go through this nightmare alone. Setting up the Empty Arms Network seemed the logical thing to do. After all, I couldn't jump up and down in the media, pointing out the failure of legal and diplomatic responses to a human rights issue as emotionally fraught as child abduction and then take a wholly selfish view.

An organisation similar to Reunite in the UK, and the Missing Children's Network in Belgium, was clearly needed in

Australia. In the 1990s, Australian government bodies were not equipped to offer emotional support to the increasing number of left-behind parents, nor could they stray outside their bureaucratic parameters. If, for example, a case was a non-Hague Convention matter like my own, even obtaining information from a government agency was exceptionally difficult, and almost impossible when seeking assistance in a foreign jurisdiction. For any left-behind parent the whole process of fact gathering was like trying to abseil down the face of Mount Rushmore on a line of embroidery thread, juggling a set of steak knives and singing 'What I Did for Love'.

So, I decided to formalise what I was already doing. And to ensure autonomy, I'd fund the network myself using the royalties from my first book and any other income I could garner. I was determined that the Empty Arms Network would be a 'not for profit' organisation able to call on the expertise of a broad cross-section of skilled solicitors, psychologists and like-minded support organisations around the world with whom I had already established viable contacts while filming. By putting in place reciprocal arrangements with my international counterparts for my skill set, much of the ruinous costs for left-behind parents would be circumvented or reduced. There would be no full-time staff except me, as wages were out of the question. It all seemed to make perfect sense. Although my decision to not recoup expenses (such as international phone calls) from the parents I helped was quite a financial drain, I wanted no fingers pointed for profiteering.

And so Empty Arms began. One of the first international cases concerned a young English boy, Anthony, who'd been kidnapped by his mother. The left-behind parent, Andrew, telephoned me from Sittingbourne, Kent, after being referred by Reunite in London.

The seven-year-old boy had been abducted by his non-custodial mother during a rare contact visit and had been missing for several months. Anthony had been in his father's sole care for many years and had had little interaction with his mother. Now she had taken the child to Australia, where she had relatives.

Andrew had recently been retrenched and couldn't afford a place to stay in Australia while searching for his son. So for the first, but not the last, time over a number of years a parent would come temporarily to occupy my guestroom.

Andrew had scraped around to borrow the money for his fare to Melbourne and, hopefully, for Anthony's return to England under the Hague Convention. It felt rather odd collecting a stranger from the airport at midnight. We'd spoken on the telephone five times. Now I met a tall, slim man with blond colouring and a ready smile – even after the exhausting flight. As we sallied forth from the terminal Andrew mentioned he couldn't understand why everyone had been looking at us – I promised to explain all in the morning and bundled him into the car, fearing that too much information would be too bewildering at such an hour. In my phone conversations with Andrew, I'd not mentioned my job as a television host, nor my kidnapped children. I had made it a policy that the Empty Arms Network was not an opportunity for me to push my own personal barrow about my children. Discussing my family situation was something I would not do with my 'clients', unless, as in Andrew's case, it was unavoidable. Approaching the work professionally was all important if it was to make any difference to the cause. The network was not designed for distressed people to discuss problems and grief with me or other parents; this was no mutual 'slash your wrists and bleed' society, this was a fighting force.

For most of September and October, Andrew lived in my home, retreating to the spare bedroom as his 'cave' when the fight for his child became overwhelming. At first he was totally overwhelmed by the entire situation, but gradually he relaxed and came to overlook my television job and royal past. I helped in his dealings with the Attorneys General, making sense of legal jargon and Hague procedures, coordinating court dates and requests for evidence and documents – and attending court hearings with Andrew when Anthony was finally located.

The engine of the Hague Convention went into motion. This was terribly nerve-racking for Andrew and his elderly parents back in Kent, as the outcome of any proceeding under the Hague Convention is never a foregone conclusion. To enable Andrew to see his son regularly after the boy was located by the police, it was necessary for me to give legal undertakings to mediate the contact between father and mother and supervise visits. One thing was absolutely certain – this man loved his son fiercely and was investing all his energies in what he believed were Anthony's best interests. Never once, even in his most despairing moments, did Andrew express a desire to inflict revenge on his former wife, and he was adamant that Anthony would always be allowed to see his mother, should the court case go in his favour.

After a few private conversations I had with Anthony's mother, she decided not to complicate the court procedures too much with ambit protestations. In the meantime, the Family Court of Australia ordered that seven-year-old Anthony and his father reside with me for a few days while final court orders were hammered out. Eventually, indeed, a favourable Hague Convention ruling was made. Andrew and his son could return to live in their tiny council house in Kent with his parents!

Watching Anthony fly into his father's arms on the day they were reunited was an amazing moment to be privy to. A miniature version of Andrew launched himself with great velocity across the crowded foyer of the court building, joy emblazoned on his small face. The marble flagstones provided no traction and the child found himself sliding delightedly on his knees towards us, coming to a stop at his father's feet. Andrew, tears running freely down his cheeks, clutched Anthony to his chest and smiled at me above the little blond head. For a split second I felt the ghost of Iddin and Shah's arms about my neck and my throat closed. A little selfishly I wondered if it would always be so. Would I have to vicariously experience the joy of reunion, and if so, for how long?

'Ma'am, my wife she done stole my chillun and she done sold my cows!'

I held the phone close to my ear in the 3 a.m. dark and thought I'd never heard a better opening line. It cut right to the crux of the matter. Recommended to me by Meredith Morrison, a case worker at the USA's National Center for Missing and Exploited Children, it would be another eighteen months before my Midwestern American caller saw his sons again, but this father never failed to use the same opening line to introduce himself to those helping with his case. His case will always stick in my mind for its quirkiness and hilarity, even in the most strained of circumstances.

Sometimes, though, it was the abducting parent, who'd fled to Australia, who would contact me. Bizarre as it seems, they'd call from their hiding places, seeking my assistance. What they needed was a negotiator – for their voluntary return to the child's home country, and to avoid the criminal charges in Hague Convention nations. I would contact welfare groups and hostels for them, too, and find solicitors back in their originating country.

From the years 1994 to 2006, I was involved in the safe repatriation of sixty-four abducted children from country to country all around the world. Hong Kong to Columbia, Australia to Lebanon, the United Kingdom to Malaysia, the United States to Australia, France to New Zealand via Australia, Germany to the United States, Argentina to Jordan, Sweden to Australia, Finland to Belgium, Ireland to Indonesia, Singapore to Canada, New Zealand to Libya, Australia to Greece, USA to Thailand, Great Britain to Haiti, Palestine to Paris. The list goes on.

On the level playing field of the Hague Convention, many of the cases I was involved with were resolved with speed and efficiency. Oddly, though, cases involving the USA often became complicated. The USA has no federal family law jurisdiction, and many states lack judges familiar with and proficient in family law matters. A judge in Tennessee can be hearing a parking ticket violation one day and be presiding over an international abduction case the next. It can be a long and financially ruinous exercise for the adults involved, but the biggest cost is to the children, who must remain in limbo, belonging nowhere and unable to put down roots.

France is another hotbed of contention when it comes to the Hague Convention, as French judges often fall back on one of the provisions in the Convention (sections 13A and 13B) to disallow the repatriation of a kidnapped child. Broadly speaking, these provisions were included to deal with the physical and emotional welfare of the kidnapped child in the event of mistreatment in their country of origin – either sexual, physical or psychological. It is a safety mechanism to ensure that the child is not returned to a situation of potential harm. However, the French often define such 'welfare' to include intellectual stimulation and access to cultural heritage.

'Why,' one French judge asked, 'would I send a half-French child back to a country utterly devoid of cultural sophistication [Australia], a land of kangaroos, beaches and sheep farmers? France is the cradle of intellectual life, the home of Voltaire and the Arts.'

Simply replace 'Australia' with America or Canada, Great Britain or Germany and you begin to get the picture of how frustratingly difficult the implementation of the Hague Convention can be in a nation where middle-class judges can apply their misunderstandings and prejudices to what constitutes the best welfare of a child.

Following the success of *Empty Arms – Broken Hearts* and the headway I was making with my work at the abduction coalface, it seemed I'd finally earned my battle stripes, or at least that was the unwritten text of an invitation I received to give a speech on parental child abduction at an international family law conference. Ironically, I had crossed into the ranks of experts and was no longer on the victim side of the river. My gratitude to the then Chief Justice of the Family Court of Australia, Alastair Nicholson, will always be something I feel deeply. Justice Nicholson took a risk in pushing for my inclusion on the programme of speakers, and his trust in me is something I can never repay, for it was to set me on a path that would reshape my life and give me purpose.

With some trepidation I embarked on my first public speaking engagement, so nauseous from nerves that I had refrained from eating for twenty-four hours. Opening my lecture with an audio-visual montage of comments made by children who had been abducted, projected behind me on a screen, was a choice I made to instil maximum impact. Using their words to segue into an overall picture of jurisdictional attitudes proved to be a device that captured their attention. Standing behind the lectern, and quaking in my carefully chosen red suit and black suede shoes, I delivered my paper on the sociological effects of child abduction, not realising that it would be the first of many such seminars and conferences I would find myself attending in far-flung places from Brussels to San Francisco, Hong Kong, Buenos Aires and Johannesburg.

As the third year after the abduction of my children loomed, Bryan Walter Wickham, one of Bahrin's paid accomplices (the other two being Singapore nationals), was apprehended by officers of the US Marshals Service in Florida, USA. My first reaction was 'good old American know-how'. This news came to me in a late-night telephone call from Tim Pallesen, a staff writer with the *Palm Beach Post* newspaper.

Interpol, and ironically the media, had searched for Wickham all over the world, from the Philippines (where it was suspected he had nefarious links) to Scotland, where he had lived until he emigrated to Australia. When this utter stranger had assisted in the abduction of my children, he had left his own kids and his wife, Sheila, behind in Australia. (Hypocritically, at a later time he was to repeatedly espouse the sanctity of family ties and children!) Neither Wickham nor his wife had met Iddin or Shah prior to the abduction, but in every interview Sheila Wickham gave following her husband's arrest, she condoned their illegal removal from the only secure home and family they had ever known. I suppose it was the gleam of all the cash and gold bullion paid to her husband for his part in the crime that eased her moral qualms – although one wonders whether Bryan Wickham has ever possessed any morals.

Wickham had been working in West Palm Beach, Florida, on various building sites since December 1992. From what I could gather, the FBI and US law enforcement agents had successfully pieced together his trail from fingerprints and a random vehicle registration check which some sharp-eyed officer had picked up as being connected to Wickham. Apparently, he had arrived in West Palm Beach five months after the kidnap and settled comfortably into an apartment provided by Mr Orville Rodberg, a local businessman, and his son, whose connection to Wickham was never explained. Complete with swimming pool and salubrious surrounds, Wickham had slipped into a sunny Florida lifestyle with great ease and little apparent complication.

Assistant US Attorney, Thomas O'Malley, ensured that the American proceedings went smoothly, so with minimal delay following his arrest, Wickham was successfully extradited from the United States and arrived in Australia for trial, pleading guilty to the abduction of Iddin and Shahirah.

Wickham is a convicted criminal with alleged links to prostitution, tax evasion and money laundering – so it makes my flesh creep to know that he was anywhere near my children. In court, he told an extraordinary tale of deceit, double-crossing and his own eventual abandonment by Bahrin. He implicated the government of Indonesia and its military in the kidnap, and maintained that he had assisted Bahrin because of his love of children.

He was sentenced on 5 May 1995 to eighteen months' imprisonment, a reduced sentence because he had pleaded guilty. Subsequently he served only nine months of his sentence, as he was given a probation period of nine months. The usual maximum penalty for the crime of kidnapping is three years per offence. However, Wickham was not through with us yet.

From prison he sent a message, offering to sell me the full details of the kidnap of my children – what they purportedly said, what was done to them, how they behaved and reacted, and so on. Apparently, he felt very clever at having pleaded guilty, and so avoiding cross-examination in court: he had preserved the juicy bits of his story intact so he could cash in on the abduction. It was, the messenger told me, his insurance policy.

Of course, part of me felt compelled to know even the minutest detail of my babies' ordeal. But this was a disgusting ploy to extract money from me. He had already ripped the essence of my life away; I was damned if he'd get one more thing from me.

Another Christmas loomed, taunting me with the children's absence. I placed the children's photograph under the tree and took another snapshot to mark the passing of time. Unbelievably, it had now become years since I last saw or spoke to Iddin and Shahirah. I'd missed their birthdays, Shah's teeth falling out and, most of all, their wonderful personalities and laughter. The pain didn't ease but I learned to cope with it for the most part. I've heard that amputees often retain a memory of a lost limb, feel its presence and sensations – maybe that's what I was experiencing.

I had written my first book, about the kidnap and my earlier life, as a way of allowing Shahirah and Iddin some insight into my personality, and to communicate my reactions, motivations and the choices I had made in my life. I wanted them to have tangible proof of my love for them. It seemed important to put it all down on paper – given how unpredictable life can be. I felt that *Once I Was a Princess* was my insurance policy against an uncertain timeline and left a part of me for them, to delve into one day in the future. Though it was a double-edged blade I had drawn from the scabbard, making me even more exposed to strangers by the nakedness of thought I'd included in the book.

The emotional minefield of the children's absence deployed itself in my daily path, and the grieving continued in a vicious circle of ebbing and flowing tides that washed over me. I wasn't coping as well on certain levels as I did in the first year or two; I just lived in hope.

Chapter 6

Warrior Professors and the Power of Tears

Our convoy of Land Cruisers rattled its way through the Rift Valley, across open savannah country and a dry lake bed stretching 20 kilometres in either direction – one chalky shimmering mass of compacted earth corrugated by thousands of years of tide and wind. Above, vultures circled in search of weakened prey and the odd flock of migrating birds cast geometric shadows on the parched plain that was dotted by trees and low spiky shrubs. Across the border in Tanzania, Mount Kilimanjaro, the highest peak in Africa, loomed starkly in the distance, pure white snow caps atop rugged dark contours, revealed only when the low-lying clouds dissipated as if by magic. The sky, a somewhat overcast grey-blue, undisturbed by commercial jets, stretched endlessly to meet the horizon.

We were driving across the cradle of humanity, the hollow of creation, through the middle of the Amboseli Game Reserve, home to the largest population of elephants in East Africa, where animals roam free and humans are as dependent on Mother Nature as the beasts and flora. It was the kind of journey that shakes bones loose and covers everything in a fine red dust which clings to the skin and colours every strand of hair a warm terracotta.

Wildebeest, horned, bearded and broad-backed, pelts a musty grey, slowed the progress of our vehicles as we lessened our pace to allow these strange-looking animals right of way. Scores of gazelle ran beside us, leaping and darting, hooves barely touching the ground. Two hundred kilometres at a snail's pace on rocky roads and dusty tracks, most of which were little more than vague lines etched across clay river beds – and not one complaint entered my head. I wanted to inhale the horizon and stretch my arms open to the sun. My nostrils were full of Africa, rich and spicy, clean and uncontaminated; time seemed organic, hanging in the air. Whenever we paused in our journey I opened the windows of the truck and sniffed deeply to try to imprint the moment in my mind.

Not even the heat could quell my joy in the surroundings. It was all exhilarating. The zebras grazing in enormous herds, and the giraffes loping nonchalantly in graceful rhythm, made me wonder why I'd wasted so much precious time before getting to Africa!

In January 1995, my friend Bill Searle, executive producer for *Neighbours*, had been developing an innovative storyline for the show with a charitable theme linked to the humanitarian organisation World Vision. The soap would be filmed in Africa. I had flippantly put my hand up when I heard about the shoot, but hadn't really expected to end up travelling with the actors and becoming part of the film crew, it just sort of fell into place. I was aware of the popularity of *Neighbours* around the world, and its long run on British television, but as far as I was concerned it was a half-hour of television I never watched.

I'd pre-recorded enough stories for *House Hunt*, the Australian lifestyle show I was presenting on Melbourne television, been vaccinated for nine different tropical and potentially deadly diseases, and studied rudimentary Swahili!

Occasionally now a cloud of dust in the distance would begin to take shape, gradually revealing a tall slim figure clad in bright red and cobalt blue *shukas* – one length of fabric worn as a sarong and the other over the shoulder like a Scottish plaid. Without exception these men held long 6-foot staffs or spears and would nod or wave a greeting as we passed. They were Maasai warriors out for an evenly paced trek across the vast plain. Amboseli was not only host to a plethora of animals, it was also a part of Maasailand, the traditional home of the Maasai tribespeople, some of whom would be taking part in the shoot.

Towards the end of the day we reached vivid green swamplands fed by underground streams from the melting snows of Kilimanjaro. Birds in abundance swooped and dallied around the water's edge, while ripples and several sets of ears and eyes peeking up from the centre of one pool indicated hippos swimming and romancing in the water. All of us found it hard to contain our whoops of delight when we caught sight of our first herd of elephants. A cow and her baby played in the shallows, swimming in circles with trunks raised like periscopes; the rest of the family bathed and snorted water into the air as little white birds hopped casually back and forth on the elephants' backs, feeding off tiny parasites. Ever since my first trip to the zoo as a small child, I'd been fascinated by elephants. To at last see them wild and unrestrained only metres away brought a lump to my throat, and enormous happiness. Cameras were hastily pulled out, and everyone scrambled to photograph these majestic creatures enjoying one of the game reserve's rare watering holes.

I wished my children could've been beside me to revel in this cornucopia of wildlife and nature. I could almost hear Iddin's exclamations of excitement as he drew my attention to a baby elephant swimming awkwardly, or Shahirah's voice, along with a tugging on my sleeve, as a giraffe strolled into view. As always, Iddin and Shah's laminated photograph was in the depths of my pocket. I remembered a quote from some wise soul: 'Being a mother means that your heart is no longer yours; it wanders wherever your children do.'

Tortillis was one of the new breed of small, luxury eco-tourism developments designed to have the least impact on the surrounding environment. I'd envisaged roughing it in tents, not the amazing set-up I found in this slice of paradise.

The dining room, reception and lounge bar were on a hilltop overlooking a steep valley, with an unsurpassed view of Mount Kilimanjaro. These buildings were open-air pavilions, roofed in thatch with dark polished wooden floors and exposed ceiling beams. A flagstoned terrace on a lower level served as an additional living area, with divans of carved wood and rattan smothered by comfortable cushions in riotous colours to relax on. Most evenings, after filming had finished for the day and all the grime of the open plains had been washed off, I would sit on this terrace nursing a cold vodka, watching groups of elephant, zebra or gazelle make their way to the watering hole, a mere 40 metres away, to drink their fill.

This was the production's base camp – home for the next two weeks. Among the *Neighbours* group, actors Jackie Woodburne (who still plays Susan Kennedy) and Brett Blewitt (who played Brett Stark) were tremendous fun to be with on location.

Jackie, an intelligent woman with little time for diva antics, is originally from Ireland, has a quick sense of humour and often kept us in stitches. Brett, only a teenager at the time, was incredibly absent-minded, leaving his passport and wallet in airport terminals and wandering off vaguely at the most inopportune moments, such as boarding time for flights. He gained rather a reputation for being accident-prone and we all wondered how he made it through to the end of the shoot with all limbs still attached.

Our accommodation was a ten-minute walk down the hill from the main pavillions; we followed a twisting flagstone path, which in the evening was lit at regular intervals by kerosene lamps. At dusk, an old man, dressed incongruously in an ancient grey trench coat and Maasai shuka, would make his way from lamp to lamp, lighting each one as he slowly climbed the hill – never anxious, never hurried, simply careful and methodical.

Each of us stayed in large 20-foot-high thatch-roofed tents, fronted by a verandah and open-sided living room complete with easy chairs, coffee tables and a comfortable divan. Inside, the tent was floored in polished wood and had big zip-open windows with built-in mosquito netting. A large double bed was centred in the middle of the structure directly opposite the entrance. And to my great surprise, I had the luxury of an en suite bathroom with a solar-heated, gravity-fed shower. Electric light powered by solar batteries would run for a couple of hours every evening; after that it was hand-held torches. I'd never heard of camping in such comfort and style! (I half-wondered when Grace Kelly would turn up and order tea with a wave of her hand.) The only trick was remembering to zip up securely at night to ensure no curious four-legged visitors wandered in to sample the new selection of imported flesh – we were only separated from the other inhabitants of the game reserve by the slim single wire of an electric fence!

Mornings would see all of us out of our tents and marshalling for breakfast before dawn, after which we'd set off to that day's location, sometimes a two-hour drive across rocky terrain. I would snatch a few moments to stand at the top of the hill to catch the sunrise and then hustle myself along to join the rest of the film crew in the trucks.

The heat and often long treks to location made filming exhausting. By the end of the day we'd return to Tortillis and dive into refreshing showers before a drink in the bar and dinner. Afterwards, some would linger in the lounge, talking and drinking; a number would withdraw to the terrace to watch the animals; and the rest would retreat to their tents and fall into bed as early as possible to gear up for the next day. I tried all of those approaches on the first four evenings to ensure a full night's sleep, but to no avail. It was not such a problem falling asleep as it was staying so.

Like clockwork I'd find myself awakening at 3 a.m., my ears fully alert and listening to the amazing silence of the bush. It's very stillness like a heavy velvet curtain, Indian ink blue and full of timeless secrets. The odd animal call or rustling in the darkness seemed only to enhance the silence rather than break it. Opening my tent flap I could discern the vague outline of Mount Kilimanjaro, snow peaks glistening in the moonlight, and sometimes I could pick up the faintest scent of a passing animal. No glow of light came from the other tents, no shadows moved against canvas; I alone was awake in the Kenyan night. 'It', the thing that made me wake, had no reason or form, no logic or debatable points.

I could almost hear my own heart beating and feel its slow measured rhythm: no pounding or thumping, no adrenalin rush of fear – just an uncomplicated and dependently steady pulsing. Yet for all my lack of anxiety, for all the calm and stillness surrounding me, it was as if my entire emotional being was a large transparent bowl of marbles. Every marble a different size, weight or colour, and each seemed to encapsulate a facet of my inner, unidentifiable essence. I would watch as the bowl hurled its contents into the air in front of me, and it was as if I were watching my own emotions descend with no sense or order in slow motion to the ground and arrange themselves in patterns on the bare earth, each one different from the last.

With this emotional 'awakeness' came tears. Not anguished or despairing, not angry or bereft. I simply cried big warm dollops of salt water. Each time I wiped them away more would form and spill from my eyes; each time I attempted to curb them, to halt their flow, my body would vehemently object and erupt in spine-shaking sobs. So I let the tears come. Until just before dawn, the rivulets of my inner essence coursed down my cheeks as I 'watched' the African silence outside my tent.

On the fifth night I slept through until Kilimanjaro's snow cap was tinged pink by the dawn. I slept and dreamed endless images of my children with no nightmares or terrors, just happy open memories. 'It' came no more.

Perhaps because I had listened to Africa's silence, or perhaps it was because I'd finally listened to my own, I felt ready for more of life.

Until that time, guilt and longing for Iddin and Shahirah had curtailed even my most fleeting moments of elation and happiness. Each time I wandered off the path of grief, a trip switch was thrown in the very centre of me and I would plunge into self-castigation at my disloyalty to my children. But this place changed things: Africa gave me permission to be happy, yet still grieve. Without for a moment forgetting the loss of my children and the love I felt for them, I simply discovered the capacity to enjoy the present moment without a feeling of betrayal.

This new experience of happiness was with me the day I first entered the village of Engkonganarok.

We were welcomed into the *boma*, or corralled Maasai village, by a massing of all 160 members of the tribe, dressed in their best shukas and chanting a traditional welcome in melodious voices.

The village was built in a circle, with huts on the outer rim, and a circular promenade on the inner edge protecting the main focus of the boma – an enormous cattle corral shaped from prickly thorn bushes. Here the main source of Maasai wealth, their livestock, was penned overnight.

Formerly nomadic tribespeople, the inhabitants of

Engkonganarok had opted, with the shrinking of their traditional lands and hunting grounds, to put down permanent roots. Here also they had access to fresh water, thanks to a new well dug with humanitarian aid monies.

The *engkagi*, or houses, of the village were constructed by the Maasai tribeswomen from mud, cow dung and sticks, all patted into a tall, round structure, which dried to a yellowish clay that was roofed with thatch. The entrance to each home contained an ingenious safeguard: it was built with a narrow S-bend to give the occupants some warning should a predatory animal like a hyena attempt to snatch a baby in the middle of the night. Entering an engkagi requires a feat of flexibility – you have to bend over double to negotiate the S-shaped foyer. Even inside, it's impossible to stand upright, and near-darkness prevails; the only light comes down a 15-centimetre chimney hole, which carries the smoke from the cow dung fire to the outside. The engkagi must accommodate an extended family of up to seven or eight people in this one tiny space. Maasai sleeping arrangements usually mean that all family members sleep curled into one another, cheek by jowl, although, at adolescence, the boys will relocate to a nearby boma constructed for the sole use of the *morans* (warriors) in training and the marriageable men of the tribe.

Standing in the middle of scores of Maasai people that day, learning all these things and awash in the vibrancy of their red and cobalt-blue robes and layers of beaded jewellery and painted faces, I felt elated and welcomed. Rich chocolate-brown skin shimmered in the sun, artfully highlighted by touches of red ochre painted in geometric patterns over faces and arms. Many of the young male warriors had also decorated their bare legs and hair with this natural pigment dug from the earth. Serenely beautiful women stood upright, often with babies suspended in slings from their backs; small children peered shyly and curiously at the invading *mzungu* (white people) from the safe folds of their parent's shuka. Almost all the tribespeople wore their hair shaved or very short.

In the Maasai culture it is considered de rigueur to reply to a greeting in Maasai in the same language. We had been taught this by members of the tribal management committee who had earlier been sent to meet us to examine the intentions of the film crew and our attitudes and worthiness. Each person in the film crew was to reply individually to all 160 inhabitants who had sung their welcome to us. The villagers, who had formed an enormous human circle around us, then filed past us and our replies were to be delivered in gender-specific language while using the equivalent of a Maasai secret handshake – involving the intertwining of fingers, interlacing of thumbs and squeezing of palms and wrists. Having achieved this, some of us were granted the first social dance of greeting.

To the chanting of a hundred voices and the excited calls of all assembled, we moved to the centre of the cattle corral, and amidst years of accumulated cow dung and buzzing flies, we began to dance. A kind of jump, jump, step, a rubbing of shoulders and intertwining of forearms held at right angles from the body, followed by a rhythmic shaking of the shoulders – the steps were instigated by one of the elder women of the tribe, and we did our best to imitate. Apparently my dance skills (I blessed the years of childhood dance classes!) weren't too bad for a mzungu. At the time many of the warriors fell about laughing, but a couple of days later I was offered four cows as a bride price for my hand in marriage. One warrior was impressed by my musicality and willing to overlook my lack of social refinement! He and the others had also discovered that I could milk a cow. A life skill for which I have to thank my beloved godparents, Auntie Connie and Uncle Kevin, dairy farmers in the lush green pastures of Victoria's South Gippsland, with whom I spent all of my childhood school holidays and who had raised me for months on end when things at home got tricky.

At the age of three, I remember sitting in their milking shed on a small three-legged stool reserved for my use. A crackly transistor radio was blaring out in the background as my auntie taught me to first peg the tail of my pet cow, a docile and gentle Jersey called Buttercup, tie up her near hind leg with a slip loop, and then rinse down her udder and teats with warm soapy water. Auntie Connie then showed me how to firmly squeeze Buttercup's teats and shoot a warm and frothy stream of her milk into a bucket. Amazing how an obscure skill learned as a preschooler can come in handy thirty years later in Africa! It was quite an ice-breaker and very practical too.

And smiling brought me a healing and wonderful gift here too – Naipanti. I met her on my second day in the village. From a distance a young girl began to call to me in broken English. Bedecked in fine necklaces of multicoloured beads, she sported the full ochre paint normally reserved for eligible teenage girls. Naipanti was eleven years old and more than a little cheeky, yet I felt inexplicably drawn to the child as we began to communicate in broken Swahili, English and sign language. She was vibrant and possessed a smile bright as a thousand-watt bulb. Her eyes had a spark of inquisitiveness that reminded me of Shahirah.

Naipanti had been withdrawn from school, it seemed – her father's herd of cattle had been wiped out by drought and a raid by a pride of lions. The only way to rebuild the family resources had been to put Naipanti on the marriage market with a bride price of several cows and a goat.

Over a few days I learned what sort of money was needed to get Naipanti back into school and off the prospective bride list. Her father, Murongo Ole, described her as a handful and quick-witted, and professed regret that Naipanti had been withdrawn from school as it was the only thing that kept her intelligent mind occupied.

We sat, Naipanti's mother and I, against the outside wall of their boma, singing and laughing and looking into each other's eyes; two mothers talking of one child's future and that of her family – for if Naipanti were to continue her education to high school or beyond, the economic future for her family could change dramatically. Naipanti would learn to read and write, and this would enable her to find work when she was older. It would mean that the whole family would have a regular and steady supply of food and medical assistance.

Finally, we agreed, via delicate negotiations, that I would sponsor Naipanti's schooling and supplement the family income. For the price of one good bottle of red wine per month, I could assist her family with day-to-day living and ensure that Naipanti could explore her potential scholastically. As a bonus, I was able to obtain an undertaking from Murongo Ole that Naipanti would not be subjected to the traditional female genital mutilation ceremony, as it would be superfluous if she was to eventually extend her education. Not undergoing the ceremony would make her less marriageable within her tribe, but not in the more sophisticated environs of Nairobi, where Naipanti's future schooling would inevitably take her. The girl would keep her clitoris and genitalia intact, and if she studied hard would achieve an autonomy and respect within her tribe that many African women don't even dream of.

Naipanti's immediate future settled, I found myself in the role of foster mother as well as a new official member of the Maasai community of Engkonganarok. From that moment on, for the remainder of shooting, Naipanti followed me everywhere, her small strong hand tucked into mine, and her chattering filling the silences.

To foster a child in Maasailand is to be welcomed and accepted into the clan as a full member, regardless of race, religion or nationality. I was given handmade Maasai jewellery, a *kamishina,* to wear that identified me as a member of Engkonganarok village. This was a great honour. The Maasai believe that they are the chosen people, but acknowledge that someone coming to them in peace and becoming involved in the village community by contributing a skill is also a Maasai. To them, the colour of someone's skin only affects their ability to cope with the hot African sun – nothing else.

One lunchtime, Mongo, a tall and majestic warrior who was fluent in English, Maasai, Swahili and Italian (he'd had a scholarship education in Rome), asked me to accompany him to the local school. We walked about 100 metres outside the main village to a clearing facing Mount Kilimanjaro – elephants to the left of me, and wildebeest and zebra to the right. There, beneath the umbrella-like shade of a thorny tortillis tree, were thirty perfectly aligned white rocks. This, said Mongo proudly, was his school.

After finishing university in Rome, Mongo had decided to return to his people to give the children of the village an education. He reasoned that his people would be better equipped to deal with all manner of problems if they had the power of the written word. So Mongo had gamely set up this venture with one dog-eared dictionary, a few lead pencils and one exercise book. There were no textbooks or coloured pencils for the children, no brightly illustrated storybooks or encyclopaedias, just this one determined and dedicated man balancing before me on one leg in the Maasai way.

Covered in red ochre, heavily beautified with beads and tribal scarring on his cheeks, carrying a hunting spear and a fly switch made from a wild boar's tail, and wearing a shuka flung casually over one shoulder, Mongo was a teacher with more tenacity than I had ever before encountered. Mongo's pupils might learn to write the alphabet in the dirt and to read and spell by rote, but they were taught by an amazing and dedicated person who was willing to work with all his heart and soul to give them an education. It didn't take long to realise that what Mongo lacked in equipment was more than made up for by his determination and utter commitment to his people.

Remembering that I had four children's books packed in my bag for emergency gifts (a practice I had begun when still living with the royal family), I delivered them to Mongo at the first opportunity. Seven days later, when filming in the village came to an end and it was time to bid farewell to my new family, Mongo invited me back to his school. This time, thirty small children, with Naipanti in their ranks, stood and gleefully recited the entire contents of one of the books I had given Mongo. To say I was astonished would be an understatement; in awe is a more appropriate description. This man, this teacher, who, in Western terms, possessed nothing of material value or wealth, had given thirty children the great gift of imagination, in under a week!

Chapter 7

Operation Book Power

From the day I left Africa, my life evolved with more meaning and focus than I had ever believed possible after losing Iddin and Shah. I threw myself into work: I was still presenting *House Hunt*, which I detested doing for its advertorial content, and fronting a lot of corporate films as host, although it had become merely a means to an end – a way to earn money to help realise my dream. For what came out of Maasailand with me was the spark of an idea – if four books could stimulate children in the middle of the bush and help them to read, what would a full library do for them? The youngsters I'd met sat on the ground and used the bare earth as both blackboard and notebook, writing lessons in the dirt, yet these conditions did nothing to hamper their voracious desire to learn. When Naipanti and her schoolmates had held those small books I'd given them, I saw a delight and wonder on their faces that would put to shame the affluent educational institutions of the first world.

So, when I first returned from Kenya, I contacted my

Australian publisher and convinced them to give me a selection of children's books valued at A$25,000 to donate to some of the schools and the orphanage I had visited. Organising the shipment of the books to Kenya, and their distribution, took a little bit of wrangling, but it didn't prove too difficult once the customs and export details were sorted through. The royalties from *Once I Was a Princess* helped pay the shipping costs.

Following this small success, I reflected on what reading and writing had meant to me over the years, and also on how much importance Mongo had placed on his people learning to read and write. Literacy had given me a personal bolt hole all my life: books had educated me, proven to be faithful friends, and given me the confidence to have opinions. Surely if children in Africa were given the opportunity to read and write, their futures could only be improved.

This fledgling project was another small connection with my own children. I had read them their favourite Mem Fox books, along with many others, when they were little. Later, I'd seen delight in their faces as we explored the *Chronicles of Narnia* together. I hoped that Shahirah and Iddin recalled our bedtime stories and the secret worlds only accessible through reading; I wanted them to hold onto that treasure tenaciously no matter what they were encountering as they grew.

Nourishment comes in so many forms that sometimes it is easy to neglect intellectual needs in favour of purely physical sustenance. Many humanitarian organisations do a magnificent job in setting up feeding stations and health programmes, but I wanted to feed children's intellects as well.

If you give people the ability to read, you give them the ability to be self-determining and independent. A woman can read a contraceptive packet, or a government notice about immunisation for her children. Factual and life-saving knowledge of HIV-AIDS becomes accessible. A farmer can gather information on rotational crops and irrigation. A villager can apply for funding for a well to be dug, thereby securing a safe water supply for an entire community, and individuals can make informed decisions about political reform and democracy.

Widespread literacy is a way of ensuring that a nation is not forever dependent on international aid. This is what Mongo saw for the Maasai and understood to be the practical impact of words and comprehension.

To make these goals a reality, an understanding that reading and books can be both fun and educational has to be instilled in children – so it's vitally important that the tools of education and discovery are made available to them. I believe the best way to do this is through exposure to vividly illustrated and well-written children's books, and through storytelling. Reading seemed to me a natural progression for people, such as the Maasai, who already have a strong tradition of oral history. Hilarious joketelling sessions run by the elderly women of the tribe could segue neatly into vibrant book and literacy programmes. I longed to make Mongo's hopes a reality.

Exactly how to do this on a large scale was what stumped me. It was frustrating to be so enthusiastic, but to lack the key that would make it all happen.

Snatching a few moments of down time one afternoon, I flicked on the television and sat down to watch Oprah

Winfrey's talk show. This was my illicit pleasure, during which I would wolf down my lunch of chocolate (I have a terrible addiction to the stuff, and practically existed on roasted almond milk chocolate and orange juice for more than twenty months after the children were taken), and try to switch off from the demands of my own television programme. A segment ran that day with Oprah exhorting children to read, encouraging her audience to explore books and ask questions outside their safety zone. A couple of days later, Oprah profiled some women who had come up with various forms of self-employment, and had run full tilt at new lives with great success. Another darker and more sorrowful story came up the next week: it was a tale of great tragedy and emotional redemption, I remember that much, and I also remember Oprah saying something about life being a great journey and that we all take different paths to find our potential and reach our destination.

I felt a switch flick on inside me; her comments echoed those of my very dear and trusted friend, John Udorovic, who had repeatedly told me that God was giving me tasks to tackle and skills to use that were solely meant for me. John was adamant that what I was going through would eventually make sense, and that the pain of my children's abduction was an opportunity to help other people, to offer insight or empathy others probably didn't have. I'd pooh-poohed that notion, but now harnessing my experience made sense. The *Oprah* stories all ran during the time I was grappling with my idea for a child literacy project in Africa; all my friends were either telling me it couldn't be done, or looked at me blankly when I tried to explain what I wanted to achieve.

I decided that I would stop procrastinating and take a leap

of faith, using my instinct that the notion of taking thousands of books to Africa to build libraries and reading centres would work. I decided to follow my own motto – 'We live in hope'.

After all, hope is truly what allows the human race to continue existing. Hope shines in all children if someone helps to light and tend the flame. So I picked up the phone and began to talk to the powers that be, people in publishing and in the airlines who could help me realise my mission. I did not ask for money, as being responsible for funds and financial transactions was well beyond my capabilities and would make the project just another charity. I was after goods and services, not cash.

In this way Operation Book Power was born in 1996 – a non-profit programme to facilitate child literacy in third-world countries. There were no salaries to pay, mostly because there was no staff – there was just me, and whatever help I could pick up along the way. Justine Gregov, who worked as our secretary and general office trouble-shooter on *House Hunt*, helped out in her own time whenever she could – she was wonderfully supportive as I think her imagination was captured by what I wanted to achieve.

After dipping a toe in the water following my first trip to Kenya, I decided to take the full immersion approach in 1996. It was simple really to approach Australia's top publishing houses; for once I felt it was appropriate to trade on my public profile, and it did open the doors of some tremendous firms. I know that I was almost over the top in my enthusiasm, but I understood that to harness people's imagination and take them on a journey, I had to make them understand the important part they had to play in making

Operation Book Power a success. I was overwhelmed by the positive response from well-known publishing names such as Penguin, Pan Macmillan, Rigby Heinemann, Random House, Reader's Digest and Macmillan Education. They had no hesitation in donating a huge and diverse range of books – from children's fiction and illustrated books through to encyclopaedias and textbooks. In total, 28 tonnes of books were earmarked for shipment, with a retail value topping A$750,000.

What delighted me so much was that the people at the publishing houses instinctively understood what Operation Book Power was all about and threw themselves behind it with a passion. Having had one book of my own published, I had learned a little about what goes on in the warehouses of the industry. Prior to the days of full computerisation and the use of scanning codes to monitor stock levels and reprinting, many books were printed in too great a number. The excess were classified as remainders and either sold at a huge discount in less than glamorous retail outlets, or to paper recyclers for pulping. My plan was to offer the publishing houses tax deductibility for the remaindered books donated to the project by partnering with other aid agencies who could offer full tax deductions to donors who participated in Operation Book Power. The firms would garner a greater financial offset than they would have received for the publications as pulp, and the books would also find their way to a future marketplace.

I bombarded potential donors and supporters with my verbal pictures and enthusiasm and the clincher was pledging that I would personally be at each and every one of the deliveries and would see the whole project through from start to finish. In other words, I would be getting my hands dirty in the field and guarantee that none of the donations would be wasted or diverted.

As a thank you, I organised magazine coverage and television and radio stories that mentioned all the companies supporting Book Power – which we termed a 'Christmas Present for the Children of Africa'.

So many people had been sceptical about my idea, warning that it wouldn't work or that I wouldn't be able to arrange things on my own without years of preparation and a lot of money, so it was enormously satisfying to see Book Power coming to fruition. To avoid problems with the various African nations' customs departments, I approached the Ambassadors and High Commissioners from those countries at their respective embassies and opened a frank and cheeky dialogue with all of them. Each of the diplomats proved to be an enthusiastic supporter of the project and bent over backwards to smooth the way with the various bureaucracies. Having the support of the embassies also short-circuited the prospect of being coerced into paying bribes by lower-ranking officials on the ground in Africa.

Next step was the mammoth task of airlifting the 28 tonnes of cargo to South Africa, Kenya, Tanzania and Ethiopia. After I met with Brian Garside, the sales manager for South African Airways in Sydney, the airline generously agreed to transport the books and me halfway around the world. In exchange, I would write an article for their in-flight magazine and mention their assistance. The key was thinking laterally when faced with the problem of having no money to pay for things.

By travelling with the shipment I could assure the donors that the books were really reaching the children who needed them, as well as sort out any problems that might crop up. Distributing such a large number of books by ourselves was problematic, so I began to tap into the already established infrastructure of education projects and humanitarian aid organisations in Africa.

Book Power could distribute thousands of books in Kenya under the auspices of World Vision International's educational programmes and also through CARE International affiliates. Similarly, READ Education Trust, President Nelson Mandela's brainchild, would help with distribution in South Africa. After consultation with these agencies, I was able to work out which areas and schools were most in need. Each school would then receive a consignment of approximately 2,000 publications – a cross-section of all the books donated – as well as teachers' packs and some stationery. If Book Power was going into an area without an established school, then the community had to have a secure, weatherproof structure in which to house the books. This meant that a whole community could benefit, in terms of accessing the materials, as an undertaking had to be given that an evening reading programme would be set up to assist semi-literate adults as well.

Though most of the aid agencies I dealt with were terrific organisations, there was a downside to my contact with one particular Christian international development agency, and that was the discovery that development aid and children's education were directly linked to religious proselytising. As I saw more of the agency's programmes and interacted with their national staff members I realised how deeply ingrained this policy was, yet how assiduously the organisation downplayed this mission quest in its literature and during interviews. There were even blatant attempts to limit my conversations with various communities.

In one instance, I caught a representative of the aid agency bullying a villager to whom I had just spoken, insisting that the villager hand over my business card and not attempt to contact me. In another, a tribal elder admitted in a snatched private moment that singing hymns prior to class and reciting Christian prayers were prerequisites for the village children being granted an education in the school partly funded by the aid agency. Because of their limited finances, the village – and the government – apparently saw no other choice but to turn a blind eye to this practice.

I find the idea of humanitarian aid being tied to religious conversion very troubling. In my opinion, it's a form of cultural genocide and is especially invidious when tied to fresh water or education – both vital to a people's developing autonomy. It is my strong belief that humanitarian relief and development assistance must be secular: non-religious, non-political and with no expectation of anything in return except for the satisfaction of having helped to make a difference. Eventually, Book Power withdrew from partnerships with this particular aid agency.

In Johannesburg, Book Power caused quite a stir as, according to the READ Education Trust, 95 per cent of black children in the poorest areas of the city, Soweto and Orange Farm, did not have books in their schools. The old apartheid regime had followed a passive policy of illiteracy for the black population – often building schools, but not stocking the libraries or supplying textbooks. The spectre of an educated black majority was obviously one the architects of apartheid had greatly feared.

Driving through the urban slums of Johannesburg was rather daunting at first, as poverty, violence and crime were the norm rather than the exception, and diplomats, government representatives and my South African friends had stressed the need for tight personal security. I was not unhappy that a police patrol car had been assigned to follow our van into the more volatile districts of Soweto. Few trees softened the grey urban landscape there; instead, an expanse of rigidly symmetrical streets were lined with dwellings that were often little more than converted metal shipping containers. Each residence boasted a freestanding lavatory cupboard in its front yard. This had been a government initiative, introduced after the dismantling of apartheid, a way of ensuring better hygiene and running water for the people of the ghettos. Wide bitumen roads with soft dirt shoulders fronted these homes, promising mobility but not departure. No flower gardens bloomed here. Much of the surrounding area consisted of the remnants of open-cut mining, with slagheaps piled high in a desolate wasteland that seemed to serve as a no-man's-land for the city of Johannesburg. Unlike other cities, there was no genteel descent from the most affluent suburbs to a middle-class suburbia, working-class earnestness and eventually squalid slums: these slums were a self-contained satellite of the city, metaphorically and physically distant from the world of commerce and private education. There was a dishonesty about this element of South African life which I found depressing – an out-of-sight, out-of-mind attitude.

It was a little embarrassing and very humbling to see the

enthusiasm on the faces of the children in the schools of Soweto. Often, driving into a school car park, I'd see handmade posters and banners proclaiming how grateful the students were for the arrival of Book Power. And always there'd be a choir of hundreds of children gathered to sing welcoming songs in the traditional way. To realise that in a school of 600 children there might only be thirty-five books made me doubly disgusted with past South African governments. How could any nation with a moderately affluent society and a large middle-class debase the right to read into a question of black and white?

After Johannesburg, the prospect of returning to Kenya filled me with elation. Not only would I be visiting unfamiliar parts of the country, I would also make a repeat trip into Maasailand.

It was a three-hour plane journey north to Kenya. I'd passed through Nairobi a year earlier. A place of contradictions, parts of the city were lush with tropical vegetation and manicured lawns, tourist-oriented and sophisticated in the extreme. Others were squalid and dusty, haunted by child beggars and purse-snatchers. A confusion of traffic crowded the roads, and hubbub from a thousand voices filled my ears whenever I took to the streets. And a feeling of false charm and commercialism permeated most social interactions with the inhabitants of the city and reminded me that the fate of entire extended families often rested on the shoulders of one person.

Tourism and international humanitarian aid were vital economic factors in the city. Many large aid organisations –

from various agencies of the United Nations to charitable foundations – were based in Kenya because of its relative political and social stability. Nairobi is frequently used as a staging post for aid convoys and medical teams responding to humanitarian emergencies in East Africa. I had met many veteran aid workers there, who had done everything from driving convoys of essential food into Ethiopia during famine, to wading bravely into the middle of the genocide in Rwanda to assist orphaned children and handle evacuations, and nursing the wounded victims of bloody guerilla warfare. The gentility of Hollywood's Africa, shown in films like *Out of Africa*, bore no resemblance to the realities of economic survival in a city dependent on humanitarian aid and tourism. But this was also the city where I'd fostered Rasoa. I'd been sending financial support for a few years, and on my first trip to Kenya, I'd managed to fit in a side-trip to finally meet her.

Before I could head east to Maasailand, I had a delivery to make to her orphanage in the slums of Kibera. Rasoa was now four years old, an impish child with large brown eyes, a lopsided grin and a fascination with my long hair. From the Kikuyu tribe, she spoke Swahili and a few words of English.

On this day, when she saw me again Rasoa sprinted towards me on sturdy little legs and suddenly stopped short, waiting to see if I beckoned her closer. When I did, she became shy, walking slowly to my side and slipping her hand into mine. Seeing her again after nearly a year was wonderful, and I relished the cuddles.

The Mukuru Centre, where Rasoa lives, functions not only as an orphanage but also as a school and halfway house for the wider community. In the area surrounding Mukuru, people live in some of the worst poverty I've seen anywhere in the world: there's no running water, sewerage or electricity, and the dwellings are barely hovels. Goats vie with children for the scraps from the rubbish heaps and raw effluent runs past doorways. Without access to medicine, children regularly die from malaria, bronchitis and measles.

When I arrived at the centre, the food storage shed was almost empty and further funding was not expected for almost a fortnight. The centre's director, Mary, told me that most days only 120 children, out of the nearly 200 kids, were lucky enough to be fed the one meal of porridge provided by the centre. How Mary chose which child would eat each day I couldn't imagine.

Setting up a library in the Mukuru Centre would make a huge difference to the children's education. But they had to have food too, and from my savings I bought plenty of sacks of maize and dried beans for the storehouse. I shuddered at the thought of Iddin and Shahirah going hungry, and at the awful prospect of having to choose which of them to feed.

I had two days with Rasoa and the other children – singing, playing games, doing animal impressions, telling stories, and, of course, reading books. On the bonnet of a four-wheel drive I sat, and the children crowded around, *aahh*ing and *oohh*ing while I turned the pages of a book and let loose with ridiculous character voices and silly animal sounds to match the illustrations. Some of the children remembered my kookaburra call from the earlier visit, and this time I'd brought hand-puppets of Australian native animals and birds, and photographs of the Australian outback and beaches.

Rattling along the familiar route to Engkonganarok, I could hardly contain my excitement. Kilimanjaro came into sight, then a herd of elephants in the distance. We were close.

The people of Engkonganarok knew I was coming back, but not exactly when. If there'd been any doubt in my mind that I'd be remembered, though, it was dispelled the moment I jumped down from the vehicle. I was surrounded by laughing and hugging as people surged around and pulled me into the cattle corral for a ceremonial welcome.

We danced and sang until the sun began to sink onto Kilimanjaro's shoulder. I inspected babies born in my absence and played with those children I'd known from my previous trip. As darkness fell, we settled in front of a camp fire, Naipanti's head cradled in my arm, and my back against her mother's as we listened to raucous and bawdy knock-knock jokes from one of the matriarchs of the tribe. Something about monkeys, cold testicles and attempts to pilfer food! The moon shone luminously and the clean air was perfumed by the smell of roasting goat and burning charcoal.

Next day, community business was taken care of over a beverage of still-warm cow's blood and milk. This delicacy, I knew, was reserved for honoured guests or the very sick, and it was a point of etiquette that I not hesitate as I drank deeply. The Maasai 'elixir of life' tasted tepidly metallic, with reminders of my childhood milking efforts as an underflavour, and I tried hard not to think of the tuberculosis it could be harbouring. Strangely, I was the only woman at this gathering and I wondered why.

Then Mongo and his friend Kapito, along with Daniel, the head of the village, asked me to follow them back into the middle of the corral. Here, all was revealed. Before all the members of the village, I was pronounced an honorary man by the warriors and presented with a hand-beaded belt that, by tradition, only men may wear. With a grin, Mongo explained Daniel's edict: although I was only short and smiled like a woman, I walked tall like a man. It is one of the best compliments I've ever received.

And one of the greatest privileges of my life is to have been present when groups of children saw their very first books. Kids would congregate, chattering and craning over each other's shoulders to glimpse a book, eyes ablaze with curiosity. After about 15 minutes each child would withdraw from the huddle, in possession of a book. With a single finger extended, a painstaking reading would begin to take place as each child sank to the ground, turning its pages. It was as if all the years of learning by rote had suddenly flicked on a light of comprehension and reading an actual book was now more than a fantasy.

There were so many exasperating, funny and poignant moments in which adopting a roll-with-the-punches attitude proved best. 'T.I.A.' – This is Africa – I had quickly learned to quip, with a shrug of the shoulders for good measure.

There was an emergency landing one day, on a remote airstrip 200 kilometres from Johannesburg, in a tiny Piper Cherokee, piloted by my good friend South African cinematographer Harmon Cusack, during a ferocious storm. And I remember the hysterical response of Joy, my assistant and travelling companion, when she was confronted by large toads in the shower recess of our simple accommodation in Namelok, Kenya. Then there was Joy's infestation of head lice, after she failed to tie her hair back when delivering books to one of the orphanages. Railing against bad luck when things go wrong simply doesn't cut it in Africa; you have to work with the tools available, and save the hissy fits for true catastrophes in which blood, theft or violence are involved.

Operation Book Power proved to me that a single person can make a difference – all you need is conviction and a bit of stubbornness. Everyone who came on board with the project made a difference; it was like tossing a pebble into a pond and watching the ripples grow into a tidal wave of goodwill.

By 1999, Mongo's school at Engkonganarok had mushroomed from thirty pupils to over 130, many of whom walk up to two hours across the savannah to attend. Three government teachers have been appointed to help Mongo, and government funding has built a small library and two classrooms. In the evenings, the village runs adult reading classes. All this came from a germ of an idea, four small books, and a dedicated and wonderful teacher, Mongo, who never gave up on his people.

Operation Book Power ran until 2000. It had extended to Bosnia in 1997, assisting in the re-establishment of schools throughout the Tuzla and Sarajevo regions, in a bid to restore some normality to the lives of children affected by the long war. Later, we distributed books to Swaziland, Malawi and Zimbabwe, as well as keeping up our work in South Africa and Kenya.

Seeing the children in the Book Power programmes was a balm for my longing for my own two dear ones. I was meeting thousands of children each year, reading stories to them in the middle of a war zone, or sitting in a field with giraffes and zebras – but I didn't know if I could still identify Shahirah's giggle or Iddin's voice. Beyond my need, though, I was confident in the belief that literacy is every child's right. Just like clean water, medical care and enough food to eat, literacy is a genuine core need – it is the tool that delivers independence and self-sufficiency.

I'd once travelled to and from Africa with the Australian author Bryce Courtenay. Originally from South Africa, Bryce had emigrated to Australia as a young man and become hugely successful in advertising. In his semi-retirement, Bryce had begun to explore the love of his life – writing. His first book, *The Power of One*, was an enormous runaway bestseller that eventually became a Hollywood film. In his 60s, his writing had become a second, even more successful, career. A father of adult children, Bryce had known deep personal loss. His son had tragically passed away from medically acquired AIDS in his early 20s. It was refreshing that he mouthed none of the standard platitudes to me about Iddin and Shahirah – he understood.

Bryce and I had first met in the airport lounge in Sydney. There we'd slipped into a surprisingly relaxed chat. We'd talked about South Africa and Kenya, and excitement lit in Bryce's eyes when I told him about the child literacy project. Bryce's personality is full of expansive gestures and an enthusiasm that is boundless. We passed a pleasant few hours in the airport lounge, as our flight had been delayed, then exchanged telephone numbers and parted, boarding different parts of the aircraft – he to first class and me to economy.

Weeks later, when I entered the Johannesburg airport lounge for my trip home, there was his beaming face again, and his hearty wave.

'Jackson,' as he had apparently decided to call me, 'over here, you're just the woman I was hoping to see.' A rush of words: Bryce had remembered I was to fly home on the same day as him and had arranged an upgrade for me, to the pointy end of the aircraft. There was little I could do to protest; when Bryce makes up his mind, he can be rather like a force of nature.

So we talked all the way to Australia: about the children I had met, about the schools and the strange assortment of vehicles we had used, but primarily we discussed our mutual love of Africa, and writing.

'Follow your heart, Jackson, keep writing, you must,' he exhorted, 'and keep on doing what you are doing – all this work with the kids, the kidnapped and the others ... and your own. Stay true to your heart and don't let any bastard distract you.

'I got you this in Zimbabwe,' he continued, reaching into his pocket and withdrawing a pale blue, folded piece of paper. 'This is to remind you to stay true to your heart. I don't want you to wear it until you feel deep love again, just hang on to it – you'll know when it's time.' So saying, he unfolded the paper and revealed a three-carat purple amethyst heart, finely faceted but unset.

Tipping the beautiful stone into my hand he grinned from ear to ear like a schoolboy. 'This is my thank you on behalf of the children of Africa,' he pronounced and sat back in his chair.

What could I say, presented with this amazing gift coupled

with such touching words – some of which had a deeper resonance emotionally than anyone had dared voice to me as I limped along behind the facade of my crumbled relationship. He knew that I was facing a complex situation when I got home to Melbourne and that I needed to maintain my privacy about my failed marriage and the almost separate existences Iain and I now led under the same roof in order to have the best chance of having contact with Iddin and Shahirah.

Bryce seemed able to read my deep loneliness and unhappiness, and had been brave enough to speak to me about it, though we barely knew one another. Bryce's face was wonderfully guileless – there was no hidden agenda there at all – and I relaxed back in my seat and squeezed his hand in thanks for his beautiful gift.

On my flight to Melbourne after Bryce and I had parted company, I held the amethyst tightly and contemplated where I would go from here. I was a mother with no children, and a woman growing a carapace of cynicism to ward off love.

Chapter 8
The Cavernous Shell

It was late afternoon when the cab drew up to my house, but this was not the home I wanted it to be. I was afraid to go inside and confront my grief. I almost turned around and flung myself on a plane back to Kenya, to the people who accepted me as I was and knew little about my past, my children. But I was due to begin my three-monthly ritual of making formal requests for access to Iddin and Shahirah, and that could only be done if I remained in Melbourne for a time. So I stiffened my shoulders and headed up the front steps.

We had moved to this large, two-storey residence just months after the kidnap, when our original rented home was put up for sale. Daisy, my rocking horse, stood sentinel in the upstairs window here – a beacon to Iddin and Shahirah that this was their home. Solid and safe, on a big block of land with a private garden, the house was in the same suburb from which the children had been taken, and therefore easier for them to come home to in the future.

In these high, large rooms, I bunkered down now, barely going out except to work or shop for groceries, or occasionally to a movie or the theatre.

Most people didn't seem to know what to make of me. My reactions weren't victim-like; I didn't want to put on a show of grief for public consumption. Some members of the media seemed to resent my infrequent outings. I accepted some invitations extended by the television network to opening nights, but still those journalists were viciously judgemental – apparently they would have been happier had I slashed my wrists and been done with it, or maintained an air of black-clad perpetual mourning. It was far more comfortable for them if I sat in the victim box they had chosen for me. I was resented for making a living and I was resented for not being quiet about the abduction of my children. A woman who shows strength following a personal tragedy is often vilified by the media, whereas a man is allowed to move on, and even acquires kudos for his fortitude and the new life he builds for himself.

So I developed ploys to minimise my contact with the outside world. For example, I often pretended to be my own secretary so that I could choose whether or not to continue a conversation. And I shifted the production office for the television show to the house, so that I didn't need to have unnecessary contact with outsiders. I won't deny that I liked the idea of hosting *House Hunt* and very much enjoyed researching and putting together my own stories on architecture and interior design or environmental issues. But stories aside, presenting houses on television in an advertorial capacity was tedious. How many times can one wax lyrical about a granite-topped bench? But I kept reminding myself that financially keeping the programme going was the imperative. I would have happily joined another lifestyle or travel show if the opportunity had arisen, but Iain and I were often seen by the industry as a professional duo, which was a difficult impression to dispel.

It must have been strange for the production staff to work in a family home. With the help of a dear friend, Deb Gribble, I had transformed the new house into a welcoming place, a home that could at any moment be bursting at the seams with children ... except that the only child living here was my teenage stepdaughter, Skye; the two small kids for whom I pined were still missing. But Iddin and Shahirah's rooms were set up, their treasures carefully stored and the playhouse in the garden stocked with their bicycles and sundry summer amusements. Their early paintings I had framed and hung in pride of place in the family room next to the kitchen, and I displayed their sculptural achievements and swimming certificates on the sideboard. Photographs were everywhere, a huge family pinboard echoed life long past, and reminders of Iddin and Shah's existence adorned every room in the house. I kept Iddin's handwritten recipe for spaghetti on the door of the fridge until it faded and disintegrated, and I cried when it could no longer be salvaged with stickytape.

This private world was insular and narrow; as long as I held onto the possibility of the children returning I would still be their mother and could kid myself I was in charge somehow.

However, there were some things that I couldn't bear to look at or think about, and the sewing machine was one. Craft and creativity had been such a big part of my life with the children that the machine was now too painful to touch – and besides, I had no creativity of that nature left in me. After the children were kidnapped, I used my sewing machine only twice: once when a girlfriend was getting married and asked me to make a special outfit for her infant son, and again when Skye asked me to make a dress for her school dance. On the dining table I cut out the red crêpe material she had chosen for the formal gown and pinned it together for the first fitting; Skye was ecstatic as only a teenager can be. But I was gutted. At the first opportunity, I locked myself in the bathroom upstairs, to feign taking a shower, so I could sob out my frustration and an enormous dose of grief. I wanted to be sewing for my stepdaughter *and* my biological children. I had made things for Iddin and Shah since before they'd been born; it was a big part of who I was. I'd loved making dress-up clothes, tailoring summer frocks and boardshorts, and fabricating dolls' clothing from scraps and remnants.

In truth, I had turned the house into a prison as much as a refuge. And I was too frightened to leave permanently.

To leave would be to acknowledge that our family of two small children and three big ones, with two parents in love with each other, all living in a house where kids and visitors happily came and went, was over. It would also have thrown up a whole other set of problems under Islamic law – another complication in trying to obtain contact with the children.

If it were known I was single, Bahrin would ensure I was branded an immoral woman, with no rights to her children.

Iddin and Shah and I had a far better chance of reuniting if I was ostensibly a married woman. It was not the best of situations, but the needs of my children took priority, and any glimmer of hope that one day I might be allowed a phone call or a letter was what kept me sane, and ruthless about keeping up appearances.

No one except my closest girlfriends knew that my heart and soul were in tatters behind my relatively composed facade. They were my loyal and understanding sounding boards. They kept my secret thoughts safe and were tolerant of my foibles and my hare-brained schemes. They were the truest friends imaginable. Deb Gribble, especially, allowed me to express myself with no judgements on her side, just unwavering support. Mandy Fudge (now Holdensen) lived next door to me for some years and I was lucky to have her as a friend and amazing stalwart – I could laugh with both of these incredible women and just be me, no matter what. Sue MacArthur was a gentle and comforting soul and one of my oldest friends: she and Rob, her husband, were godparents to Shahirah and Iddin and loved them and me fiercely. My partner in crime, Sally Nicholes, often joined my adventures and loved me in my most privately outrageous moments; she and I would later be travelling companions, cutting loose in San Francisco and Washington. Heather Brown was always there in the background; she allowed me to dip in and out of her life and to gauge Iddin's probable growth against that of her son – Iddin's best friend, Jack. But most of all, I could be sad with these five women; they would always allow me that luxury. And when I doubted myself, I would pick up the phone and speak to beloved Patsy in Belgium; she was always determined and always soothed my fears and tiredness.

The peace I had found in Africa sustained me too, though it truly felt as if I had started to live three, almost separate, lives: an intellectual one, in which I could feel the pull of aid work and the need to help, and couldn't stop my mind planning humanitarian projects; the second, where I went through the daily motions of cooking, working and engaging with others; and the third, in which I lived in the past but hoped and prayed for a future with my children. I had no idea how to integrate my three lives and the effort to do so left me perplexed and exhausted.

The fight to see Iddin and Shahirah went on. I never gave up, although as years went past, it was necessary to scale back my demands and just hope to be allowed a phone call, if not face-to-face contact. I was now allowed to write letters to a formula prescribed by Bahrin. But they shredded my insides. I could include no words of love and was not allowed to tell the children I wanted them to come home. I was required to send the letters via Bahrin's solicitors in Melbourne, who would inspect every item before deciding whether or not to send them on to my own children! This whole grand concession, which was made around 1995, had been a public relations exercise for Bahrin and his lawyers. And I was very sceptical that the children would ever receive anything I sent them, either through sanctioned means or via normal post services. But write to his formula I did, even when sending birthday presents, though I tried to circumvent the censorship in various ways. One year I secretly inserted a videotaped message to Shah and Iddin into a *Star Trek* film, hoping that the children might see the film on their own.

Desperation drove me to reach out in whatever way I could devise. I mailed postcards from wherever I travelled in the world, always careful of the words I used and aware of the double-edged sword I was handing my former husband. The postcards' meaning could so easily be twisted – 'There is your mother, having a wonderful time flitting all over the globe.'

But the three-monthly attempts at contact were terribly draining. I'd be paralysed with apprehension for hours beforehand, procrastinating and finding distractions to keep me away from the task. Finally, I would place a businesslike phone call to Bahrin's legal representatives in Melbourne requesting telephone access to my own children; next, I'd try all the telephone numbers I had for the various residences of the royal family, then I'd move on to their business contact numbers. Finally, I would sit in my bedroom cradling the Malaysian phonebook that a friend had obtained for me on a business sojourn in Malaysia, and try listings for anyone who might remotely be able to help. Begging strangers for assistance became second nature to me – asking them to help me slip a message to my children, or give me some insight into Shahirah's and Iddin's appearance and activities. I had no shame in making my requests. The humiliation mattered not a jot; the foul language directed at me rolled off my back like drops of oil, though the nasty laughter as I burst into tears incensed me with the probability of what Shahirah and Iddin were going through. I felt beaten down and distressed for my children – they were being raised by these seemingly heartless people, surrounded by human beings prejudiced by a religion and deaf to their humanity. Only one of them in all those years spoke to me kindly, and he was later to ridicule me on the Internet for political gain. How could I help my babies when they were so far away and deliberately alienated from me?

For another six-and-a-half years I would continue this ritual of abasement, this challenge to get through to my children or to garner news of them.

But beating my head against a brick wall might have been more effective in the long run – I could have killed a few brain cells and felt a lot less pain. (In 2006 the children told me that none of my letters or gifts had reached them.)

A journalist from a Sunday newspaper phoned me one Saturday afternoon, just before her publication went to print, to let me know she had interviewed my former husband in Malaysia.

'Your children hate you, the prince told me,' she crowed. 'They are far better off in Malaysia – that's obvious.'

This woman had travelled to Malaysia and been entertained royally for her exclusive story, but had not clapped eyes on the children, let alone spoken to them. Nor had she ever met me. When I asked her for my children's telephone number she admitted having it but refused to give it to me, citing journalistic ethics. It seemed a convenient chestnut that could so abrogate parental rights.

By the end of the conversation I was enraged. Tracking down her editor on a Saturday was no mean feat. But if the journalist had my children's contact numbers – the direct telephone numbers for the house in which they were living – then surely I had a right to have them? After all, under Australian law, I was the legal custodial guardian and parent of the two children.

But the hour-long telephone conversation with the editor proved to be another demoralising exercise in futility: I could 'attempt to obtain a court order for the number', but the editor assured me the newspaper would not otherwise release the children's contact details. Iddin and Shah might still be minors and I might still be the legal custodial parent in Australia, but the editor had to protect her sources. I simply couldn't afford what it would cost me to try to garner a telephone number via court order. It would have taken a least a week in court in any case, and by that time the article would have gone to print and Bahrin would have again changed his telephone number.

So I was a mother stripped of all role in my children's existence, and a journalist had more access to them than I did.

I hung up the phone. My chest tightened to suffocation point – then coughing and retching took over, for the first time in two years. I had to get out, I had to go somewhere away from this phone where I knew I would be compelled to dial and redial the editor in my manic state of grief. I didn't want to beg strangers for help any more; I was repelled to think that my family and I would be the hot topic of conversation for that journalist and her editor that night, over casual drinks or a quiet dinner in a restaurant.

The children's absence from the house was too tangible. Night was falling. I threw myself into the car and drove to the last park the children had played in before they were taken. It sprawled next to the river, and a hill overlooked the playing fields below. I chose an old oak tree at the top of the hill; I could see the lights of the city in the distance as I slid down the trunk of the tree to sit on the grass beneath, the fabric of my dress catching on the jagged bark, my knees drawn closely to my chest. I teetered on the brink of simply taking myself out of life's equation, removing the temptation for self-serving members of the media to try to make a name for themselves by climbing on the shoulders of Iddin and Shahirah. If I ceased to exist, the story was over; the children would be left alone, at least.

I sat there most of the night as the rain fell, turning a pack of razor blades over and over in my hands. For a short while I did make horizontal cuts into my skin and watched with detached pain as the blood slowly oozed out. I suddenly understood why self-mutilation in abused girls is so prevalent; for those delicious minutes I could channel all the hurt and grief and all the pain and yearning to one tangible and visible place on my body. It was a release, a glorious and seductive release, to be able to pinpoint my pain and shift it from my soul to somewhere else.

Did I have the guts to slash my wrists more effectively? Apparently not. At 4 a.m. I got back into my car and drove to a friend's house and knocked on the door. When Andrew opened it he hardly blinked at my drenched and bedraggled state; instead, he led me unquestioningly to his guest room as I muttered about newspapers and the children, tears all the while running down my face. Grabbing a towel and a T-shirt from a drying rack, he tossed them to me and left me to get changed, returning with a cup of hot tea. He told me to get into bed and covered me with the duvet, watched me drink the tea, then switched off the light. I slept for five hours, then sheepishly surfaced.

I found Andrew in his kitchen making coffee, a newspaper spread on the counter.

'Thanks for last night, umm, this morning,' I volunteered.

'No sweat, mate,' he answered with a gentle grin. 'You've done the same for me in the past when I was going through a rough patch.'

We said no more; he was a mate in the old Aussie way and he didn't expect any explanations. Instead we sat in silence at the table, and he began to flick through the pages of the dreaded Sunday paper.

Something had to give: I couldn't go on like this.

Chapter 9
Finding Oxygen

'Nicolas van Waard,' he offered by way of introduction, inclining his head slightly. I blinked a little; for a split second I wasn't sure if he had also clicked his heels – he was so much of a European caricature that I stifled a titter.

Around us, the 'A-list' were making the rounds of a sumptuous buffet: lobster, prawns, smoked salmon and ice sculptures covered the tables. It was 7 a.m. on Melbourne Cup day, the first Tuesday in November, when the whole of Australia comes to a standstill for a horse race. Attending one of the pre-race early morning breakfasts was de rigueur for socialites and visiting and local celebrities. I had no intentions of going to the racecourse, I was merely fulfilling my commitment to the television network by rousing myself at the crack of dawn and dressing to the nines in an apple green tailored suit, matching high-crowned hat, trimmed with silk roses in a shade of dusky pink my grandmother always described as 'ashes of roses', cream high-heeled shoes and bag. This would be my one appearance of the day. I planned to leave at 10 a.m. and head to my neighbour Mandy's barbecue where a comfortable pair of jeans and a sun hat would be my attire of choice once I wriggled out of the suit and heels.

Some of us were here for work, but still champagne flowed freely in the ballroom of the Grand Hyatt Hotel. Gentlemen were dressed in morning or lounge suits, feathers and flowers abounded upon the ladies' hats and press photographers circled their willing prey feverishly. Jewellery twinkled in the early morning light, cutting through the ceiling-height windows at an angle, as a pianist fingered the ivories in the midst of all the chatter.

Turning from scooping up some oysters, my fork slid sideways, clattering to the marble floor, and I met with a solid wall of grey striped morning coat. Glancing up, I had to lean backwards to see the face atop the shoulders – I stand 5 feet 3 inches and the owner of the broad-shouldered jacket was at least 6 feet 6. The face that grinned down at me was hovering at nose-bleed height, but we somehow managed to knock heads as each of us bobbed down to retrieve my lost fork.

With a flourish, Nicholas van Waard retrieved my oyster fork from the marble floor and held it for just a fraction too long.

His accent had a cultured Euro-traveller edge to it – his English impeccable and precise as we continued with some small talk. I had to stop myself from staring: Nicolas was tall and stomach-flippingly attractive, with greyish-green eyes, tightly cropped blond hair and a measured assurance, all wrapped up in immaculate tailoring and an elegant ease. Not handsome in a symmetrical or chiselled way, but handsome nonetheless. His eyes crinkled when he smiled, and he smiled almost constantly as we spoke.

At first I thought him to be German, and then realised probably Dutch or Swiss. Wrong on all counts, Nicolas pointed out, as he revealed he was in fact Belgian – Flemish, to be precise. Belgian, thank God, I muttered under my breath. Finally, here was something about which I could converse instead of gawping at him like an awkward schoolgirl. Mentally I blessed Patsy and my visits to the small French and Flemish (Dutch) speaking nation of Belgium – at least I knew my way around there and could namedrop the places I loved and had visited. Nicolas was genuinely surprised that I was so familiar with his country, and even the university he had attended, as I had a friend who was a professor there.

I was shocked at myself; this visceral lust was something I'd never before encountered. Grappling to get my brain into gear, I listened with, I suspect, a slightly glazed look in my eye: Nicolas was saying that he travelled regularly to Australia from Belgium. He handed me his business card with one of those mesmerising smiles I wondered how he could keep producing and I discovered he was *the* chocolate industry! Not just chocolate of a pedestrian nature, not dabbling in sales of the cruder forms of the sweet: he was a Director of the most wonderful chocolate company in the world! (I knew this unequivocally, for I am of course a chocolate aficionado; chocolate was the first true love of my life and my constant companion since I had been old enough to save my pocket money and spend it on the stuff.) I felt like a stumbling knight finally catching sight of the Holy Grail.

Now Nicolas was asking me very politely for my number! I swear I could see a halo around his head.

What a heady combination: chocolate, Belgium, a good wit and sex appeal to boot. Cue violins and cupids shooting arrows around us, fireworks, and rivers of chocolate praline. We parted then, melting back into the crowd of revellers, but I caught sight of Nicolas again fleetingly, and he inclined his head and smiled goodbye across the room as he was ushered by his hosts towards a waiting limousine.

Four days later, 10 kilograms of the finest Belgian chocolate, presented in beautiful tins, arrived at my front door by courier, accompanied by a note from Nicolas. It read simply: 'May I contact you? Respectfully, Nicolas.'

Devouring the first 2 kilos of pralines in twenty-four hours, I pondered my answer, and chatted with my trusted friends. Point by point we mulled over my position. I had no desire to carry out a romance in the full glare of the media, nor did I want to be anything less than discreet out of respect to Iain, especially if this was only a transient affair by letter. Nicolas was far away, safely removed from everything and everyone in Australia. He probably knew nothing of my story. Why not indulge in a flirtation? Anyway, perhaps it was time for a hobby.

So Nicolas and I began to correspond, and long-distance phone calls were soon arriving from all around the world.

An envelope posted from Tokyo might contain a page torn from an in-flight magazine – the image a set of fluffy clouds with an original poem scrawled in Nicolas's small script across the paper. A phone call from Buenos Aires as Nicolas stood at the window of his hotel might describe his view of an elderly couple dancing the tango in a cobblestoned laneway near the waterfront. A Parisian menu might turn up with 'Thoughts of you and what can be' penned on it.

This was fast turning into a dalliance of thoughts and words flitting in both directions – the articulation stimulating the cerebral nature of romance and seducing me with my own weakness. I was being wooed with charm and sophistication, and I relished every minute of this non-physical, but highly sensual affair.

Nicolas gave very, very, *very* good letter.

Around this time I was asked to participate in a television pilot being made by one of Rupert Murdoch's family's companies and overseen by Matt Hanbury, Mr Murdoch's nephew, and Jackie Frank, the editor of the Australian imprint of *Marie Claire* magazine. The idea was to translate the reportage element of *Marie Claire* into the television medium. Ordinary people thrust into extraordinary situations – this was the angle *Marie Claire* wanted for their first TV programme. The pilot *Marie Claire TV* would be shown at the Cannes television 'love fest' called MIPCOM. This, it was hoped, would launch another global idea in 'lifestyle/magazine' television. I would be the subject of the lead feature story for the pilot. My agreement to participate was mostly driven by the fact that this was another opportunity to highlight the international problem of parental child abduction and the impact on the children and families involved.

Jennifer, the producer for part one of the pilot, arrived at my home one February day in 1997 to film an in-depth profile, highlighting my work in the field of child abduction.

She and her crew gave off a vague air of disappointment that I picked up on during the two days of filming. In Jennifer's preconceived film treatment, she had pictured me to be 'Spartan' and pared back in my decorating style and had thought she'd capture me against a very minimalist atmosphere – all moody angles and modern furnishings. Confessing all to me in a fit of amused chuckles, she had been quite taken aback to find that I lived amidst a plethora of family photographs on every surface and with paintings and bright artwork adorning the walls. Candles covered every possible surface and were juxtaposed with my not inconsiderable collection of African stone sculptures and personal treasures.

Eventually, we worked out a compromise; I was filmed against a moody lighting arrangement on the tall staircase of my house, clad in a sombre but slinky long, grey dress, my disembodied voice running over the images. Part two of the film package was sprung on me quite suddenly. Could I fly to London and meet with Pamela Green, a left-behind parent I had been involved with, whose three children had finally been returned to her with some assistance from me and my contacts in Washington. It would, I was assured, be a whirlwind trip of just two days. Mr Murdoch's finances would make sure I did it in comfort and with haste. I was glad to hear that, as the journey from Melbourne to London would take twenty-nine hours or more – quite an exhausting slog in a couple of days.

Having been advised in the past by the Australian government that it was unwise for me to travel to Europe over Malaysian airspace (as I faced arrest and a quagmire of political and diplomatic complications), I had become used to taking the long way round – flying over Russia to arrive in Western Europe. So, after an uneventful transit of a few hours at Hong Kong airport, the flight took off just after 10.45 p.m.

But shortly into our ascent, a horrendously loud grinding was heard throughout the cabin. Nervous but silent looks were exchanged, and a great deal of shifting in seats went on. One of the flight attendants answered the intercom phone, then pulled her seatbelt a little tighter.

Presently, the captain's voice came across the cabin speakers. It seemed the landing gear would not retract properly, and we would have to return to Hong Kong. First, though, we would need to circle the ocean to dump our excess fuel.

'That'd be right!' was my first thought. 'I decide not to top myself so I can see my kids one day, and I end up going down in a fiery plane crash – just my bloody luck!' I automatically reached into my pocket and touched Iddin and Shahirah's photographs for reassurance.

A sudden yelp interrupted these self–pitying musings – the man across the aisle appeared to have a personal grooming aid tangled in his nose hairs; its duty-free packaging lay on the seat beside him. He had no option but to yank the gadget free! I stifled a nervous giggle with my hand. Where were the drinks in first class when you really needed one?

It took two hours to dump the excess fuel over the South China Sea. On the screen at the front of the cabin, a tiny image of our aircraft flew in seemingly aimless circles around an artificial ocean.

Finally, below us, we could see fire engines lined up at the edge of the tarmac, and Hong Kong airport and landing strip lit up like Christmas trees. The screeching from our engines was deafening, made louder by the pounding of my heart as I clasped my hands around my knees and had a meaningful conversation with my kneecaps and toes.

And then we painfully and awkwardly ground to a lopsided halt on the runway. A collective exhalation was audible to all; the passengers cheered and clapped as the cabin crew rose swiftly to pop the hatches.

In the end we all got to launch ourselves down the slippery, yellow rubber emergency slide!

I was relieved to have had a safe landing, but strangely hadn't experienced any real terror, just nervousness, during the ordeal. I didn't want to die, but I had become fatalistic about my life. If I couldn't be with Iddin and Shah, I didn't really care much what happened to me.

After finally clearing customs and immigration at Heathrow airport, I made my way wearily to the hotel. Arriving there in the early evening, I found an invitation in my room from the 'part two' *Marie Claire* producer, Judith Curran, welcoming me, and suggesting that we meet at 8 p.m. in the bar downstairs for a nightcap, and to introduce ourselves and go over the next day's shooting schedule.

I had already been told that Judith was in the middle of making *The Lacemaker,* a documentary special on Collette Dinnigan, the Australian designer who had begun to take the French and international fashion world by storm. I was well aware Judith had just finished filming a coterie of supermodels, including Helena Christiansen, and was taking a day out of her hectic schedule to slot in my shoot.

Judith admits she already had a vague impression of me formed by news reports; 'severely traumatised is how I remembered you' she has since told me. 'I had a hazy notion I would be meeting a beautiful and glamorous woman and, sure enough, you swung into that bar all black leather pants and long hair down to your bum. That was my first image.' (I plan to pay Judith handsomely for that description.)

'You sat down on that stool next to me, Jack, and smiled as you rejected a glass of wine in favour of a pot of chamomile tea. I, of course, opted for the wine, staying true to my Kiwi [New Zealand] blood. I thought you couldn't drink because of that Chinese gene – obviously I was later to discover how wrong I was.'

In point of fact, I was too jet-lagged to sit and sip wine; my head was already hazy enough. Besides, I wanted to take stock of my new companion. Judith was gorgeously blonde with blue eyes and a broad smile emanating from red-coated lips. Wearing a midnight-blue shirt in silk chiffon, I noted how fit and toned her arms were – there seemed to be muscle where most women had flaps. Her black tailored pants showed off her super-fit derriere and legs. She was full bosomed (which made me glance down sadly at my own 32B chest), utterly self-possessed and intelligent. I was mind-numbingly exhausted and barely able to string a coherent sentence together; I hoped I made a modicum of sense as I stared at Judith's face in a haze of travel-induced exhaustion as she ran through the shooting schedule for the next day.

We eventually parted to chase our pillows after an hour or more and I remember wondering, as I glanced over at Judith while we waited for the elevator, if this woman might possibly end up becoming a friend.

Next morning I drove with the crew down to Surrey for our scheduled meeting with Pamela Green, grateful that Judith's cameraman, Peter de Vries, and sound recordist, Paul Blackwell, seemed to be quietly good natured and not too gung-ho.

When she greeted us at her front door, Pamela was bursting with pride and excitement. She was delighted to be able to introduce me to her complete family at long last, and we filled the half-hour before filming with rapid exchanges of news, and private insights into the difficulties her family faced as they tried to reintegrate their disparate experiences and trauma.

The interview, which at *Marie Claire*'s request focused on the path I had played in this family's reunion, went off without a hitch. But it hammered home to me the terrible contrast now between my reality and hers. Pamela had her children back.

Pamela's finances were modest, almost parlous, and her family large. The abduction and the years her children had been missing had clearly taken a huge toll psychologically on all of them. As we left I wondered how Pamela would deal with the teenage rebellion just discernible beneath the surface of her children's now impeccable demeanour. I had no idea how I would handle my lost children when eventually they returned – but I would more than welcome the opportunity to deal with the challenge. I just needed the chance to have them home.

As we travelled back to London in the car, Judith and I talked about her work and her schedule for the next day, when she would resume work on *The Lacemaker*. An interview with Paula Yates, a British rock chick icon, was next on Judith's agenda. As my return flight to Australia wasn't until the next evening, I asked Judith if I could tag along. We seemed to have struck up a friendship.

'Jacqueline, good evening,' he called across the lobby as I came in, pronouncing my name in the French manner. 'I was in the neighbourhood, and thought I would say hello.'

In a beige trench coat, light-blue shirt and well-pressed jeans, Nicolas van Waard was beaming across the marble expanse like a naughty schoolboy.

Quite taken aback I shook my head to clear it. 'Since when is London your neighbourhood?' I'd had a big day, following a long and hair-raising flight – I'd almost forgotten emailing him about my trip!

'Well, Belgium's only next door if you take a plane.' He was as full of smiles and laughter as when I'd met him. 'Shall we go for a walk, perhaps have a drink? Come,' – he took my arm – 'let us walk,' and he turned me back into the revolving doors.

I tried to fall into step beside him, but our difference in height made me feel like a trotting Shetland beside a thoroughbred. I asked him to slow down. His hand encompassed mine in the crook of his arm, and I grappled for casual conversation.

I was still bemused by his sudden appearance. Missives and phone calls were one thing; a living, breathing 6 foot 6 male was entirely another kettle of fish. At that moment, I hadn't the foggiest if I wanted that fish fried or stuffed back in the cool room.

We chatted over snifters of brandy in the bar of Claridge's

Hotel. The spark between us was there again, undeniable and intense. But I felt awkward. If only his eyes would stop twinkling at me in that way, I thought, I might be able to drag my mind into better focus. His body language was relaxed and he spoke of inconsequential things, with a hint of self-consciousness that made him even more charming.

Eventually, we went out into the cool English night and began to walk back to my hotel. Nicolas was gazing at me intently and it was both compelling and disquieting.

We were strolling through a colonnade not far from the British Museum when some delicate bronze sculptures caught my eye in the window of a gallery. Turning back from the glass I felt Nicolas's arms go around me and draw me into an embrace, one large, strong hand in the small of my back and another very gently cradling my head, fingers tangling slightly in my hair as his lips came down to mine. Only the first brush of his mouth was tentative; in me, a dam burst and I found myself standing on my toes to better reach him and pull his mouth firmly to my own as I wrapped my arms around his neck and kissed him back. We drew away from each other and, breathless and electrified from our first kiss, I pushed every other thought from my mind and reached out one finger to trace his lips. Nicolas raised one eyebrow – part query, part statement – and then quickly turned and hailed a passing cab. He stroked my face and repeatedly kissed my hand and the inside of my wrist. In five quiet minutes the taxi brought us to my hotel.

We made love and talked in between times for most of the night. I felt freed for the first time in so long I couldn't recall what this liberation was; my mind was happy and guilt-free.

Nicolas was a passionate and imaginative man, I

discovered, not just in his correspondence to me, but also during the most intimate of moments, and for this I was grateful and relieved. I didn't want to have taken the risk of being so exposed, only to find myself counting down the minutes until I could extract myself from an awkward mistake. Up until then, I had felt leaden and quite dead within, and now I was waking up to my more womanly and secret side.

In the early dawn light, I watched Nicolas slide into his clothes after a quick shower, and attempted to frame my thoughts. I asked him if he could understand that I wanted our relationship to remain private from my world – Australia and everything else that made up the complications of my life. That was a place I needed to keep separate from what I had discovered the night before with him.

'Can we just be whatever this is?' I asked him, proud to be trying to keep control where I had failed abysmally in past relationships.

'Only if we can be together again soon,' he replied, not willing to hear my meaning. 'After all, we both travel. I'm decorating my new apartment in Antwerp, maybe you'd have some ideas on that.'

Then, more gently, he told me he'd read my book. 'If you'd been through only half the things you describe, I would still be honoured by your trust.' He bent and kissed my forehead.

I was quite taken aback. I had been researched by my lover! Somehow, I felt doubly exposed.

'Nicolas, I can't offer you a domestic situation if that's what you want, but if you can accept my life and all its erratic commitments, then – let's just be ourselves, warts and all.' I vaguely registered that my language became strangely formal.

Nicolas bent to kiss me deeply. Then he gathered up his trench coat and touched the tips of his fingers to his lips as he reached for the door handle.

'I will see you soon. Either I will come to you, or you to me.' He stated it as a matter of fact, and then he was gone.

Lying back against the pillows, imagining him soon on a plane, I ruminated on what Nicolas and I could be to each other. I wasn't heart-thumpingly in love with him, but this disarming Flemish man was deeply attractive and compelling. Though he spoke French, English, Flemish, Spanish and German, Nicolas was charmingly self-deprecating and was, I suspected, endowed with a very big brain and a formidable will. Profoundly colour blind, he'd said with a chuckle and a shrug that he couldn't even tell what hue my lingerie was the night before!

Rising from the bed and entering the shower, I turned the taps to as hot as I could bear and immersed myself under the water jets, still thinking of Nicolas. He'd said he was an avid sportsman. Handball was his passion; just a few years earlier, he had won a gold medal in the sport. Catholic, but lapsed, his family was influential in right-wing politics. It seemed Nicolas's father had played a significant role in Belgian life, and his siblings were all highly educated intellectuals.

With our different backgrounds, would Nicolas be willing to work out a relationship on terms agreeable to us both? And at long distance, as well? I didn't want to venture into the realms of proprietorial behaviour again; I was not willing to be someone's trophy any more, nor to give up my newly found determination and independence.

I knew that men always seemed to cling to an image of

me that was only a facet of my self, and bore no true resemblance to the many parts of me incorporated as a whole woman. I'd been defined by others as an *objet d'art*, a breeder, a beddable filly. Now I was heading into uncharted territory. I felt that I could do more, be more and achieve more to make my children proud, and I had no desire to be compartmentalised all over again. That was a price too high for passion, comfort and intimacy. Besides, when one is placed on a pedestal, it's an awfully long way to fall.

I would always conform to societal attitudes and expectations in terms of manners and the ebb and flow of social intercourse, but I knew I would now refuse to be limited by my gender or the projections of short-sighted males interested in jumping my bones, or simply shielding me from the big bad ways of the world.

I had paid an inordinately heavy price to arrive at this point in my life and though there weren't many jobs around for fallen princesses who had been to hell and back, I was not going to step backwards into a stifling cocoon. Whatever I became and whatever I did in the future would be as honest and as real as I hoped my children would be in their futures, royal or not.

Chapter 10

Westwood, Women and Wine

Beginning a new day in an utterly happy frame of mind was a forgotten art for me. It was only as I applied lipstick in the mirror and saw that I was smiling that the felicity of my mood registered. Grabbing my oversized handbag, I swung out of the hotel room and hurried to rendezvous with Judith and the crew downstairs. I felt relaxed and pleased to be just tagging along on someone else's shoot, and more than a little curious about the subject of the morning's filming.

Judith and I chatted in the car as four of us wended our way through the backstreets of Chelsea. Until we pulled up in front of a terrace house in a quiet street.

The front door was opened by a young woman. We were ushered into the front parlour and asked to wait. It was a quirky room, rather small and dimly lit: the bow window overlooking the street was taken up by an enormous empty birdcage resembling the Taj Mahal, wreathed in fairy lights and silk flowers. The room seemed crowded. The fireplace and mantelpiece were filled with flowers, small oil paintings and Russian religious icons; a couch was laden with plump cushions and leopard-skin throws; the bare wooden boards of the floor were strewn with baby toys. And the surfaces of the coffee tables and sideboards were groaning with children's artwork and packets of photographs. Vases of lilies threw out their heady scent.

Judith had the crew set up lighting and position the camera so that cables snaked their way across the floor, and an air of expectation now permeated the room.

Paula Yates tottered in casually. Slim-hipped and buxom, her blonde cropped hair ruffled and funky, ankle-strap shoes encasing her feet and a latte-coloured lace dress clinging to every curve of her body. On anyone else that dress would have looked dowdy, but on Paula Yates it was pure rock chick meets lady-who-lunches.

Paula Yates, it seemed, would give a testimonial to Dinnigan's designs. Following introductions all round, Judith and Paula settled down to the interview.

Paula chatted readily to Judith and seemed both relaxed and eloquent. The interview was over quickly: Paula's former career as a television host and interviewer meant she hit her mark swiftly and controlled the flow of conversation with Judith.

Afterwards, as Pieter and Mark packed up the camera gear, Paula turned her attention to me as Judith explained my presence, and why I was in London for such a brief visit. Paula's eyes sparked up at Judith's precised explanation. 'I've heard about you from a friend,' she said. 'I'd like to get a hold of your book.' She intimated that her divorce from Bob Geldof was becoming quite rocky and sought to find parallels between us, which made me feel a tad uncomfortable.

'Michael [Hutchence, of INXS fame] and Bob swapped houses to make sure the girls were happy,' she said, when I told her how much I liked her funky home. Going on, Paula explained that her ex-husband, Bob, had agreed to move into her partner Michael's house not far away and that she and Michael took up residence in Bob's house with the three girls and their own child, Tigerlily. This logical and generous decision seemed at odds with the other things she was saying about Bob, so I did my best to steer away from the topic all together.

We talked about our children, comparing notes on breastfeeding (of which we were both strong advocates) and the amazing perspective motherhood created in our lives. Casually discussing Michael and talking about her four daughters animated Paula more than anything else we touched upon. Her distress at the effect the tabloid media had on her day-to-day activities with her children was deep and bitter. Paparazzi, she told me, had once pushed one of her young daughters over as Paula and the children walked down the street. The result had been a photograph of Paula hauling her child to her feet with an enraged expression on her face, captioned 'Furious Paula belts teary daughter', or something to that effect. Clearly, Paula was a woman in love with and much loved by her girls. In the background, the baby, Tigerlily, could be heard beginning to demand a feed. Paula hastily snatched a piece of paper and a pen from a teetering stack on a shelf and scribbled down her telephone number and address, urging me to ring her and keep in touch.

'Give me yours too. Quick!' she demanded, as she thrust

the pen and a corner of the paper in my direction. 'Genuinely, ring me,' she emphasised, 'I want to talk some more; we'll go out and have dinner or something.' She hugged and kissed me goodbye.

Judith laughed as we emerged onto the footpath. 'Gawd, you two! What a lovely woman. Pity Michael wasn't there too,' Judith said with a twinkle in her eye.

'Yes, on both counts,' I agreed, 'but there's an undercurrent of fragility under all that front.'

Glancing quickly at my watch, I ventured a thought. 'Judith, do you want to go shopping?' I asked with a little grin and knowing that she had no more filming that day. 'We can fit in a bite of lunch, too, before I have to head for the airport.'

'Sure,' she replied casually.

To this day, Judith maintains that her head still spins when she remembers the first time we went shopping together. Reasonably confident that she was an efficient shopper, she says that she felt as if she only had a learner's permit as we attacked the first shop at the west end of the King's Road in Chelsea.

I pride myself on being a fast shopper, but we had less than an hour and a half to peruse and purchase, if we were to have lunch together. Nothing like a tight deadline to cut the crap from the couture, I always say. A quick glance inside one of the first shops showed me my first purchase of the day, a black velvet Vivienne Westwood vintage bustier. In quick succession, we hit Russell & Bromley for shoes, Jigsaw for T-shirts, a lingerie boutique that saw the lace flying, and sundry other establishments – never drawing breath in between. The further incentive of red-lettered 'Sale' signs hanging in every shopfront window boosted my normal speed to high octane. I do like a challenge. I can evaluate the merchandise of most boutiques from the threshold.

According to Judith, within what seemed like minutes we were carrying so many shopping bags that we were struggling. Soon she was happily purchasing pony hide leather jackets, several new handbags and lord knows how many pairs of shoes.

Then, our shopping lust sated at last, we retired to a café where we could gloat over our bargains and feed our growling stomachs. A glass or two of wine soon loosened our tongues, and we talked about all manner of things as I let down my guard. Gently probed by Judith, I felt an enormous weight lift from my shoulders as I let my shell slide to the floor. I took a risk at being myself, and Judith reciprocated.

In that tiny crowded café, Judith sat with tears streaming down her face as she listened to me unburden myself. I knew then that Judith was someone I could trust implicitly.

Even though time was tight, I asked our hotel-bound cab to detour via Trafalgar Square. There was something I simply had to do before leaving London.

St Martin-in-the-Fields is my favourite church, the place where I felt closer to the children than anywhere else. Its tower and blue-faced clock beckoned me inside whenever I was in the city. Reciting my mantra and lighting candles for the children there gave me a sense of peace I never felt anywhere else.

Judith did not bat an eyelid as I went through this most private of rituals. It was truly the start of an amazing friendship.

That evening, we both boarded flights home to different cities in Australia, but within a week had talked on the telephone, establishing a pattern of raucous laughter and unadulterated truth that still prevails, even though we are usually separated by oceans.

Chapter 11

We Are What We Make of Ourselves

I n early 1997, the various threads of my life began to intertwine to form some sort of self-determining tapestry. The week I arrived home from London, an invitation plopped into the letterbox asking me to speak at the World Congress on Family Law and the Rights of Children and Youth, in June. The congress was to take place in San Francisco, and would be chaired by Chief Justice Alastair Nicholson, the honorary chairperson being the then First Lady, Hillary Rodham Clinton. The topic of my presentation, the governing committee wrote, would be 'The Impact of Parental Child Abduction: From the Inside Looking Out – A Practical Guide to Casework'. Only a matter of days after that, I received another invitation, this time to brief the US State Department, specifically the division which handles international parental abduction. The State Department would be happy for me to set the date to coincide with the congress.

A foreign government had asked me to speak, but not my own. The irony was not lost on me.

Up until a few months earlier, the then incumbent Labour government had seemed to view me as a canker on the butt of ministerial dignity. My constant lobbying to try to force them to do something humane and supportive towards my two small children, who were Australian citizens, was met with animosity. Gareth Evans, the incumbent Foreign Affairs Minister of that period, seemed to have little interest in the welfare of Australians in need of consular assistance; his eye was very firmly fixed on a glittering international post and his departure from Australian politics. The fact that he detested me and resented my criticism had also contributed to his intractability.

But when a federal election rolled around in March 1997, there was a dramatic political change for Australia with the election of a Liberal (conservative) government under John Howard as Prime Minister. Just twenty-four hours later, I received a telephone call from Alexander Downer, the new Foreign Affairs Minister. He caught me in my car, returning from a speaking engagement in rural Victoria, so I pulled over to the side of the road.

How did I think his department, he asked, and he personally, could be of assistance with my abducted children?

To say I was gobsmacked would be an understatement! Until then, Senator Gareth Evans had refused any direct contact with me, and his stance over the preceding years since the kidnapping had been obstinate and resentful, which had only served to raise my ire and degenerate into a sniping match between us in the media. I felt Evans had pretentious intellectual delusions and grandiose delusions above us mere mortals. So, to get a call from the new Minister left me feeling as if I were having an out-of-body experience. Not only that, Downer then moved the conversation to the procedures and attitudes of his department in terms of international abduction and consular response, and simple, plain compassion and lateral thinking. The conversation went on for more than two hours and left me feeling bewildered and just a little more hopeful for the other parents who were experiencing, or would experience, the emotional, financial and legal quagmire of international parental kidnapping.

Alexander Downer had probably been advised that it was better to woo me with honey than vinegar, so I would prove to be less vitriolic towards the new political incumbents when discussing the plight of Iddin and Shahirah. I wasn't naive, but I was hopeful. And the change in attitude within the all-powerful Department of Foreign Affairs and Trade was noticeable within weeks. For this I was truthfully and humbly grateful.

Small changes, admittedly, but the wheels of change turn very slowly, I knew.

At this time, I was working on a tragic abduction case, through the Empty Arms Network, that brought me into close contact with Robert Hamilton, the head of the Consular Division of Australia's Department of Foreign Affairs and Trade, and later Ambassador to Mexico. The case involved a woman and three of her children who had been spirited to a Middle Eastern nation by her former husband. Her oldest child, a daughter, had been left behind in Australia. I was trying to find a conduit for her to establish contact with the three boys who had been taken; it was an exercise that was proving very difficult. But just before

Mother's Day, we received word that the eldest boy, aged sixteen, had fled the village where he had been held, making his way across perilous terrain to the capital city and managing to scrape together enough money to place a phone call home to Melbourne. The boy's mother now faced a terrible choice: she could move heaven and earth to get her boy home immediately, or she could counsel him to return to the village to watch over his much younger brothers.

If she chose the former option, then any hopes of being reunited with the younger boys would be dashed, and if she chose the latter, then hopes of seeing any of her sons were slim, as she had been diagnosed with aggressive uterine cancer.

This mother chose to bring her eldest son home, and I began the groundwork on her behalf.

When I telephoned Robert Hamilton to advise him, his response was magnificent. He felt that, under the new government, he had the leeway to make certain discretionary decisions, which is exactly what he did. Swinging into action in the small hours of the morning, he arranged for the boy to be collected by staff from the Embassy and taken to a safe house. (The police there were probably looking to apprehend the boy under his father's instructions.) Via a fax from my office to Robert proving the teenager's identity and citizenship, Mr Hamilton then arranged a temporary travel document and an airline ticket. Had he been a less resourceful diplomat, less humane, the paperwork probably would have taken another week to finalise.

Consular officials took the boy to the airport and waited until he safely boarded the plane home to Australia. As dawn broke on Mother's Day the boy arrived back in Melbourne;

half an hour after landing he was in his mother's arms. She died 48 hours later.

I will always be profoundly grateful for Robert Hamilton's compassion and efficiency. Had he been a less resourceful diplomat, the paperwork probably would have taken another week of checking and double-checking to finalise; Robert's lateral approach was courageous and humane.

Shortly before the new Prime Minister's first official state visit abroad – to Malaysia – his chief of staff called to say that the Prime Minister was willing to intercede on my behalf, on a personal and private basis, with the then Prime Minister of Malaysia, Mahathir Mohamad. Did I have any objections? Objections! What was there to object to? I'd had my fingers, toes, eyes and all other bodily parts crossed for years, wishing for such a profound change in political attitude!

If I wished, said the chief of staff, I could put together some personal possessions and mementos, which Mr Howard would deliver to the Malaysian Prime Minister with the request they be passed on to Iddin and Shah.

I wept as I hung up the phone. At last, my own government was willing to show some compassion towards my children. It had taken five long years and a change in the political landscape to effect this turnaround.

I decided to send Iddin and Shah a multi-image photo frame – pictures of myself, my nanna and other family members and friends, all labelled with our pet names in case the children's memories were a little hazy. I was sure that neither of the children would have seen a photo of me since the kidnapping. It had been too long since I had held them and they had seen me smile.

Allowing myself a little hope, I worked feverishly on the collage, obsessively rearranging it until I felt it to be just right.

The Prime Minister, I was told, wanted no political gain from his actions, nor did he expect any positive publicity from me waxing lyrical about what he was doing in the press. This was the kindness of one parent to another.

I went to ground for the duration of Mr Howard's state visit. No journalist would be able to elicit a comment from me on the Prime Minister's trip; too much was at stake. In private, I bit my nails and paced the floor – all I could think of was that my children might finally be receiving tangible proof that I was still fighting for them, that I loved them with every fibre of my being.

Confirmation of the safe delivery of the package came through twenty-four hours after the Prime Minister's return to Australia. His aide assured me that Mr Howard had politely but firmly put my case to the Malaysian Prime Minister for compassionate contact with Iddin and Shahirah, and that the Malaysian leader told him he would make a personal request to the Terengganu royal family that the children be allowed to receive my gift on humanitarian grounds. I was tentatively hopeful.

In January the following year, a parcel was delivered to me – it contained the large picture frame.

The back had been defaced with slogans in Malay, and my gift had then been deposited on the reception desk of Australia's High Commission in Kuala Lumpur by one of my former husband's minions. It was obvious it had never reached my children. From there, the gift was returned by diplomatic pouch to Australia, and back to me.

At least I'd had ten months imagining that I had been watching over my children with a loving smile.

Nicolas had managed to make two business trips to Australia in as many months, but now he was urging me to come to Belgium. The thought appealed, and I had work to do in several parts of the world. As well, Antwerp might be a good base for the aid activities I'd been increasingly involved in, and which were becoming focused on the Balkans; *and* I could visit my friend Patsy in Ambly. As well, it made it simple to meet up with Paula Yates and Michael Hutchence to examine a proposal Paula had come up with during what had become a flood of phone calls from her to me. At all hours of the day and night, Paula had taken to ringing me; sometimes she insisted doggedly that I expand on specific incidents that she had read about in my first book. For her, the telling of my story in black and white did not sate her, she wanted the smaller details, the exact nature of what I felt when I met my father for the first time at the age of thirteen and he was dying from cancer.

Often her train of thought went off on tangents mid-conversation. 'How do you keep going when everyone is out to get you?' she cryptically asked me one night during a tearful phone call that had interrupted a dinner party I was hosting. 'Don't they get it, I just love my children and that should be what counts,' she sobbed, as she audibly dragged in a breath of air. 'I'm fighting for my girls everyday, harder and harder, just like you are for your two.'

I found it hard to decipher if the battle Paula was referring to was against the insatiable media, or against a legal system over custody issues. More and more I got the impression that Paula swung from wanting to defend herself, her love life and her children in the media, to not giving a fig if she was the subject of tabloid gossip and moral outrage in Britain.

Australia, though, was a different kettle of fish. Seemingly, Paula had become anxious to change the perception people in Michael's country had of her; she was determined to dispel the innuendo and mistrust that swirled around her in Australia as well as Britain, garnered mostly from very negative press coverage. Michael also had chipped in during a couple of telephone calls.

'I'm f★★★ing sick of people heaping shit on Paula. She's an amazing woman and an incredible mum,' he told me heatedly. 'They just don't get it, or us, and it's hurting the kids.' Michael conveyed his frustrations about Paula's divorce proceedings and the scandal which had come to light about their apparent drug use. He came across as a man determined to protect his woman, and was clearly deeply hurt and bewildered by the vitriol spurting forth in the scandal sheets about her. For a man at home strutting the international rock stage, his vulnerability and bewilderment were obviously a new phenomena to him, and probably exacerbated by the emotional upheaval of becoming a father.

INXS, Michael's band, were working in the UK on the release of a new album. 'Come on over to us and we can work out a way for you to write,' she said. Michael and Paula would speak to me about their personal lives and the baby they shared, Tigerlily. 'We'll give you an exclusive to write about us for a magazine; Michael says the *Women's Weekly* is the one to go for in Australia,' Paula pushed. 'I trust you, I like how you wrote your book and we could handle you being around the family as a friend. How about it, will you ask the magazine if they're interested?'

We agreed that I would spend a couple of weeks hanging about with Paula and her family, and that anything that happened during that time would remain off the record unless Paula and Michael gave the green light. Then, the formal interview would take place – if Michael judged me to be OK. The *Women's Weekly* editor jumped at the offer of the exclusive, even with such bizarre conditions attached.

I was perplexed. I had only written a few magazine pieces at that point. This was a story that was much sought after. And I still didn't know Paula very well – snatched phone calls don't really constitute a proper friendship. But she did seem to relate to me as if we were both going through the same sort of experience. I racked my brain, trying to see what parallels she saw between us and what I could do to help steady her unvoiced anxiety. Still, I wanted to have an excuse to be in Europe for a while, and the money would also help.

I decided to stay away from Australia for a few months.

First to Los Angeles, to meet with my agents regarding the optioning of film rights to my first book. Then, next morning, a plane to Belgium and a few days of solitude. Nicolas would be in Hong Kong on business when I arrived.

A close friend of Nicholas's kindly collected me from the airport and drove me into Antwerp. She gave me the key to the newly renovated flat and left me at the vestibule, to explore my new abode and the picturesque old city.

As soon as I entered the spacious art deco apartment, I noticed that every aspect of the decor was in a derivation of beige. Perhaps, I thought ruefully, I should have had a look at the interior designer's sketches when Nicolas had asked me to. (A year later, during a conversation at a literary dinner with the writer and respected American neurologist Oliver Sacks, author of *The Man who Mistook his Wife for a Hat* and *Awakenings,* I came to understand the implications of Nicolas's profound colour blindness, and his perceptions of the world around him. My fair skin, which Nicolas kept urging me to suntan, apparently appeared grey to him, similar to the rotting flesh of a corpse! Flattering stuff indeed.)

'Beige, Jacqueline,' Nicolas himself would explain, 'is the only colour I know I can identify.' Well, the decorator had taken him at his word – unrelentingly. The apartment was like being trapped inside a giant puddle of milky coffee, with no cookie or cake on the side to expand the tastebuds.

Outside, though, a gracious city was waiting. I fell in love with the home of the great artist Rubens and the amazing architecture of the town. Five days on my own gave me time to walk the side streets and wander into the Gros Platz (Town Square) with its aged cobblestones and medieval rooflines. In the ancient cathedral I lit votive candles for my children; this religious focal point of Antwerp had stood solidly for centuries, and I felt my mantra of hope and protection echoing among thousands of whispered supplications already uttered in this holy place.

Having come across the flower and produce market, I staggered back to the apartment laden with long-stemmed roses, pungent cheeses and punnets of fresh, sweet raspberries. It was blissful to have no television in the house and to be able to concentrate on my writing and my forays of exploration. It had been a long time since I'd had the luxury of aloneness. (I'd spent so much time in recent years either working in television, in the abduction arena or doing media for my book. All this activity involved speaking to people. On top of that, I was simply never able to go outside in Australia without being recognised and approached by strangers. I relished the thought of being alone and silent.)

Then I contacted Paula and arranged to dash over to London for dinner with her and Michael. I hopped on the Eurostar and then cabbed it to the house in Chelsea. The older girls were out for the evening, so Paula, Michael and I sat and talked for a while before dinner. The attraction they had for each other was palpable and evident in the way all the little intimacies gelled together. I envied their easy body language as they sat draped over one another, Michael's leg across her lap as he half-reclined on the compact couch in front of the window.

It was a bizarre evening that left me feeling like Alice through the looking glass. A whirl of paparazzi jostling us as we made our way into the restaurant, meeting vaguely named people, all of whom seemed to want a piece of the high-profile couple whenever they stepped outside their front door. A day later I was safely back in Antwerp wondering what the next instalment of that scenario would be. Phoning Anthony Williams, my mentor and literary agent in Sydney, I told him about it.

'Play it through, my dear,' he drawled, 'just play it through.'

Chapter 12

A Continental Inspection

If there is one thing I loathe, it's being evaluated for my suitability – for anything. All my old insecurities come to the fore, and I immediately feel on the defensive – as if I'm a horse having its withers and teeth checked.

Over dinner with Nicolas's friends, though, this sensation of being inspected quickly dispelled. I was amidst new bosom buddies! They were a diverse but accepting crowd: one an artist, another a newspaper editor; one woman was a partner in a multinational accounting firm and her husband an architect.

'Watch out for this man,' one teased, 'we're sick of him sabotaging a good thing every time we get used to someone.'

Nicolas looked more uncomfortable than pleased.

'Shush,' chided his wife under her breath. Then, in French: 'She'll run and we'll have to do this all over again with another new one. Besides, this one has a brain and deportment, thank God.'

I maintained a fixed smile and pretended not to

understand what she had just said; discretion was an automatic part of my disease to please!

But a few nights later, in a restaurant near Antwerp's waterfront, my feeling of unease was further compounded when Nicolas began to make derogatory comments to his friends about a couple sitting at a nearby table.

'Homophile,' Nicolas muttered to one of his friends with a disapproving grimace, 'let's move.' Regrettably, I chose not to question this quiet comment as we were in a group. Luckily we stayed put at our original table. But the remark didn't bode well for the future if this was an example of his prejudices or homophobic fears. I had a number of homosexual friends and I wasn't about to have them insulted by anyone with whom I was associated, romantically or otherwise.

For the next couple of weeks I was in a holding pattern with the Paula and Michael story. I met up with them again a couple of times, and Paula phoned strangely often. Her anger at her former husband seemed to be building as Michael and she melded their lives even more closely than before, but also had to contend with the legalities of the British family law system. I still had difficulty understanding why Paula's diatribes about Geldof grew, and had to bite my tongue a couple of times as she kept wanting to make Geldof and my former husband interchangeable. Finally I told Paula that I worried she was not making sense about her worries that Bob would gain the children full time via court order. Perhaps I was naive, but I wanted to add some perspective to her view.

'Paula, if you and Michael aren't shooting up or beating the kids, no one, not the British High Court or anyone, is going to take your kids away. And I don't think that Bob would have gone to all the trouble of making sure his girls were secure in a familiar environment at the house if he just wants to screw you over. No one is going to kidnap your girls.' I finished with ill-concealed exasperation that I immediately regretted.

There was a stunned silence and I waited for her to tell me to go to hell. But she didn't and when she did speak I was surprised that she sounded chastened for a couple of minutes and then exasperated yet again when she ended our call with: 'But you don't know him. The stuff in court and everything else – he's the devil incarnate.'

'Paula,' I growled, 'things get bad when a marriage crumbles and everyone gets angry, but this isn't helping the kids.'

'Hmm . . . OK,' she replied, then said goodbye.

I went to sleep that night pondering the improbability of 'Saint Bob' of Live Aid renown crossing the ring of fire and becoming Hades' new recruit.

Nicolas had commitments during the day, taking business trips to Spain, Germany and France, and occasionally staying away overnight, which allowed me the freedom of doing exactly what I wanted. My beloved friend Patsy drove up to see me a couple of times from her home in the south of Belgium, which was wonderful. We walked to the park opposite the apartment to accommodate her need to be outdoors and talked until our voices were hoarse. But when they met, Nicolas and Patsy took an instant dislike to each other – so vehement was Patsy's hostility that I was left speechless. What passed quickly between them in French and Flemish was a bit of a mystery to me. Patsy refused to speak Flemish and Nicolas refused to speak French: they parried each other's verbal thrusts in two different languages! It's funny to look back on now, but at the time it seemed a weird turn of events which reflected the long rivalry between the different regions of Belgium: the industrial base of the country, Flemish-speaking Flanders, and the farming and agricultural zone in Wallonie, the French speaking part of the tiny nation. It was even weirder given that Patsy was married to a Flemish man, Walter. Now I suspect her bizarre reaction was compounded by Nicolas's family's public profile on the right wing of politics, but Patsy still refuses to go into what she terms 'the insults' of that day.

When Nicolas and I were together, our relationship was electric and volatile. As long as our conversations steered clear of politics, humanitarian causes and ethnicity, we were fine! Nicolas had a tendency to be inscrutable, a trait I found at odds with the openness of his letters and phone calls, and although our private time continued to be passionate, he had difficulty understanding my growing commitment to humanitarian projects.

I was greedy or sensible, I can't decide which, but I did know that my lover had to at least accept my convictions as well-founded and more than just a diversion. On paper or in the bedroom Nicolas was sensational; in reality, at close quarters ... well, I began to mutter 'fascist' under my breath – not an ideal sentiment. Intellectual sparring was one thing, the ugliness of prejudice was another.

Just as I was due to fly to San Francisco, things came to a head between us.

That evening we had returned to the apartment from a black-tie dinner at his club, when he began objecting to a working trip to Bosnia (just emerging from five years of war) that I was planning later that year. It was the final straw. I told him it would be better if he didn't join me in New York the following month, that we simply weren't working, and that to continue romantically would be a mistake.

It was all very civilised. We agreed to part – and we both knew it was for the best.

Patsy was inordinately and most indecorously pleased.

'Bravo, Jacqueline!' she exclaimed on the phone. '*Fffoof* to him, what a relief to hear this news! Don't worry about him, he *is* a fascist like you said.'

And so I boarded my plane for the US with no regrets about the time Nicolas and I had spent together. We had been refreshingly honest with each other. After so much hurting in recent years, and such deep disappointments in past relationships, my time with Nicolas had restored my self-confidence and self-esteem as a woman. Walking away now on my own terms made me feel in control. I understood that it is possible to retain your identity and not subjugate it to your partner – I had finally learned this secret at the age of thirty-three.

A friendship was the best Nicolas and I could now hope for, but at least the chocolate had been divine.

Chapter 13
A Finger on the Pulse

New York was proving to be an excellent place to run away from everything that had kept me in a box in Australia. I was still expecting word from Paula and Michael about the interview. I spoke to Paula every day or so and she continued to talk about schedules and picture shoots for the article. I had begun to suspect that she merely liked talking to me about bits and pieces and I didn't encourage her bitterness. I told the magazine editor this, but she seemed not to mind and asked me to stay in the US or Europe in case the interview finally happened.

Meanwhile, since leaving Belgium, the pace had been hectic, which helped me manage my yearning for my children. San Francisco had been stimulating, informative and fun: the bayside city is beautiful and the hospitality shown by the conference hosts was warm and genuine. At the World Congress conference, I had enjoyed catching up with old friends and colleagues from around the globe. My paper had been well received and I made many new and valuable contacts. The various forums, moot courts and discussions with judges and practitioners, as well as human rights advocates, gave me a broader picture of international responses to parental abduction, and enriched my list of resources and contacts.

Hooking up with my great friend Sally Nicholes was an enormous bonus. We attended a few of the lectures together and snatched time to shop and explore the city. Sally and I shared a room and stayed up until all hours comparing notes, laughing and raiding the mini-bar. We had met originally when she was just a young intern. She is now considered one of the foremost experts in international parental child abduction and the Hague Convention. We had clocked up a lot of hours together, working on other people's abduction cases from all around the world.

Now, in Washington, we also got together with one of our former clients, Jim Karides. We had met Jim when he came to Australia in search of his infant son. An accountant from Virginia Beach, Virginia, specialising in sports management, Jim had twice used my house in Melbourne as his local base during the almost year-long search for baby Adam, who had been abducted by his mother.

Jim had proven to be the perfect houseguest, even though he was going through a hellish experience at the time. Downcast after months of private investigations, police and fruitless media campaigning, Jim had gone back to the USA empty-handed after his second trip to Australia. Sally had pulled out all the stops to convince him to stay just a little longer: 'Just a few days longer, Jim, don't go yet, I feel something's going to break.' But to no avail.

Six days later, Sally and I were shouting down the phone

to him: 'Adam's been found, get back here as fast as you can.'

Following a hearing in the Family Court of Australia, beaming father and baby son were allowed to return home, to begin a proper life together. Sally and I saw them off at the airport, but we had not had any real time with baby Adam.

The little boy was now approaching three years of age. While we were here, he was going to experience the descent of the Australian aunties.

Sally and I had rented a serviced apartment in downtown Washington so we could get around with ease, and it was there we met up again with Jim and Adam. We took little Adam to the National Zoo in Washington and, on days off, for walks in the park. It was amazing to be holding this little boy's hand, for the last time I had seen him he was a baby in arms at the end of a very long and traumatic odyssey. It brought home to me how much my own children must have changed physically and I felt an uncontrollable pang of loss. But I wouldn't have missed this reunion for the world as I was very fond of Jim and felt so pleased to see him well settled into the role of primary carer and all-rounder Dad. Then, when our commitments with the State Department were over, Sally and I piled into Jim's car and headed for his tranquil home town, Virginia Beach, to meet the extended family.

It was wonderful and humbling to be with Jim's big family and circle of friends. They threw a barbecue to thank Sally and me, and we were even treated to a VIP night with Jimmy Buffett and the Parrotheads – an experience in one type of American music from which I will never recover! Box seats, I was told to expect at the concert, so I dressed in a black lace cocktail dress, only to find the rest of the audience clad in

Bermuda shorts, Hawaiian shirts and straw hats decorated with parrots and exotic flora!

After Sally had to leave, I delighted in babysitting Adam so Jim could have a bit of a break. And I discovered the local delicacies – soft-shell crabs and crab cakes – and took long walks with Adam down picturesque country lanes. Being trusted with a small child and being allowed to be a vaguely surrogate 'aunt' afforded me some very private moments of maternal comfort. Spending time with Jim and his parents and sisters reinforced my confidence in Jim's devotion to the welfare of little Adam and made me understand, even more, that good parenting means quashing your prejudices in favour of what's good for your child. Adam's mother was encouraged to visit her son, and Jim bit his tongue and did what was morally and emotionally right for Adam.

Anthony (silent 'h' please) Williams had been a literary agent and powerbroker on the international publishing circuit well before I became his client, and friend. Formerly head of the British literary agency William Morris, he had decided to return to Australia, after an absence of many decades, to launch a branch of that prestigious agency there. Tony wasn't by any stretch of the imagination a blood-sucking, percentage-hungry agent like those in the movies; instead, he was urbane and immaculately turned out, with a droll and cutting sense of humour and a fierce loyalty to those he chose to be his friends. In his mid-60s, Tony collected interesting people as well as exquisite recipes – and enjoyed throwing the lot together in an entertaining melange. His eye for detail was intense and his management of my adventures around the globe hysterical – he resembled nothing so much as a cross between mother hen, fashion stylist and wedding planner.

Questioning me closely before each trip overseas, Tony would consider the nature of the journey and whether or not I had any acquaintances at my destination. He would then broadcast my arrival to his close friends with an imperious fax, directing them to take me under their wing. Meanwhile, he would give me their potted histories and all the inside info, foibles and fabulousness.

Tony had decided that my professional and social lives could be combined during this trip to New York, by a proper meeting with the William Morris Agency, and also with one of his very good friends, Sonny Mehta, head of Random House Publishing. Tony duly forwarded me a list of telephone numbers, appointment times and engagements, along with instructions to call Sonny Mehta and his other good friends, the Averetts, once I got to New York.

'My dear, Sonny Mehta is the god of publishing in New York,' Tony had emphasised. 'He is also an utter gentleman and a very good friend of mine.'

After checking into the quirky Wyndham Hotel, where Tony had been adamant I must stay (it being reasonably priced and the haunt of many British writers in New York), I set about following Tony's itinerary to the letter: a breakfast meeting with my American agents at William Morris; and in the early evening an invitation to a publishing function with Mr Mehta.

The breakfast meeting at the William Morris Agency on the Avenue of the Americas proved to be nothing more than a painfully polite courtesy extended to me because of Tony.

It became uncomfortably clear that the two agents, a man and a woman, were thoroughly unimpressed by me and my Australian origins and were not keen to offer more than a stale Danish pastry and an instant coffee. But three-quarters of the way through this excruciating session, the office phone rang and it was Tony, for me.

'Just listen and say yes or no,' he started. 'Have they asked for another meeting or shown any interest in what you are doing in New York?'

'No,' I answered, reflexively glancing in the agents' direction.

'In that case, in a few minutes volunteer that you have to get on with the rest of your day as you are out this evening. Casually say the following: "Sonny Mehta is sending a car for me at 6 p.m.," and watch the condescending little shits turn bright green.' He chuckled maliciously, and hung up.

'Err, yes, right, shall do, bye now,' I squeezed out to the empty line.

Handing the receiver back to these clearly uninterested agents, I resumed the thread of our conversation, then did exactly what Tony had recommended. It was amazing – as he predicted I noted a definite colour change in their complexions and they even came up with a hurried invitation to take me to lunch the next day, at the famed Four Seasons – if I was free? A little perversely, I promised to get back to them when my schedule was clearer. My stakes on their client list had risen.

Chapter 14

A New York State of Mind

I simply wanted the earth to open up and swallow me. A cluster of New Yorkers gaped. I was firmly wedged in the revolving doors of the department store Bergdorf Goodman! Shopping bags, left hand and wrist still firmly inside the shop, and pale-blue-clad body and beetroot-red face straining to emerge onto East 58th Street.

Fifteen minutes and a shattered Raymond Weil wristwatch later, I was free.

Savvy bystanders crowded around and offered advice. 'You should sue,' seemed to be their consensus. I simply wanted to slink off to my hotel and attempt to pull myself together before the car arrived to carry me off to the hallowed orbit of New York's god of publishing.

After finally collapsing through the door of my hotel room, the telephone began to ring just as I was heading toward the shower. It was Tony once again. Glancing at the bedside clock, I realised that it was the middle of the night back in Sydney. What on earth could he be calling about?

I should have known better, as his unmistakable drawl opened with, 'Hello, my dear; now, what are you wearing tonight?'

'Err, umm, I thought my black lace Dinnigan and a pair of black-silk evening pumps,' I volunteered tentatively.

'Yes, that will do,' Tony stated in an imperious tone. 'But for goodness sake don't even try to compete on the jewellery front. Gita, Sonny's wife, has the best collection I've ever seen and you'll just look like a poor relation.'

Nothing like a 'Mr Williamsism' to cut to the chase!

'Well, actually, I just thought my nanna's jet necklace and my hair out,' I said, seriously wondering at this bizarre scenario.

'Perfect,' Tony pronounced. 'Have a lovely evening, dear, remember the posture and just play your history up to the hilt,' he chuckled and rang off.

What would my nanna have made of all this? She was such a quiet and joyful soul, with a bit of pessimism thrown in to keep her level-headed. Her first trip overseas had been to my royal wedding the idea that her granddaughter was now hopping on and off planes like commuter buses and was actually trotting down the Holy Grail of musicals, Broadway, would have left her speechless. The pinnacle of success in Nan's mind would have been to shake the Prime Minister's hand and I had done that a number of times.

Sonny Mehta greeted me with an outstretched hand at the door of his apartment after the town car he had sent for me dropped me off. A man of medium height and mellifluous tones, his eyes projected a piercing intelligence that had me wishing I had spent the day rehearsing witticisms or brushing up on the classics. I felt like a fraud standing in his foyer, insinuating myself into his presence by virtue of association.

But it didn't take me long to realise that Sonny was warm and welcoming and thought nothing odd about his old friend Tony Williams sending him someone to look after. We chatted for a while and I stole glances at his wonderful collection of books in their floor-to-ceiling shelves. Sonny told me we would be attending a cocktail party for Condé Nast publishing, which he hoped wouldn't be too boring for me. Later we would dine with a few of his friends he thought I would find amusing. Gita, his wife, was overseas and so wouldn't be joining us.

Arriving at the cocktail party and treading the red carpet was a *Sex and the City* moment – flashbulbs going off and photographers demanding my name from Sonny, as we made our way inside.

'Watch this,' Sonny murmured with a mischievous gleam in his eye, and he turned to answer a reporter: 'This is Princess Yasmin, she's a writer.' People stared, openly evaluating me as we continued towards the inner sanctum.

Inside, Mr Mehta showed impeccable manners, introducing me to people and providing me with conversational partners as he worked the room and greeted acquaintances, always keeping a gentle hand in the small of my back or on my arm. My head spun with all the names and I felt gauche and out of my depth, but determined not to embarrass my host.

Dinner that evening was at an uptown restaurant owned by fellow-Australian Nell Campbell (of Nell's nightclub fame) and her partner, Eamon. We were joined at a large table by Susanne Bartsch – a glamorous Euro-Gothic identity who apparently rose every day at 5 p.m. to prepare for the evening's excursion, make-up artist on hand – as well as her husband, David, and a number of others. The conversation was fun and much more relaxed than earlier in the evening. Names flew around the table like tear sheets from literary reviews and *Vanity Fair.* Márquez, Leibovitz, Vidal, Clinton and Sontag. Each was uttered with a familiarity that spoke of close acquaintance. I was now the acquaintance of a friend who actually knew these people – it was a surreal six-degrees-of-separation moment.

Nell decided to take me under her wing, and came up with suggestions and dates for me to meet her friends. And as we chatted in his car on the way back to my hotel, Sonny advised me to take up Nell's offer. I thanked him for a stimulating, funny evening, inwardly agreeing with the words that the author Joan Didion had once spoken of my escort: 'he projected . . . a kind of irresistible gallantry and intelligence'.

New York provided me with much-needed insight into myself and what I lacked in terms of bravery and confidence. The artistic Australian expatriate horde never questioned me about Iddin and Shahirah, just allowed me to exist in the city for a time almost anonymously. I learned the knack of taking a book to a small French restaurant on West 58th Street to fend off unwanted companions. And I trawled the Metropolitan and Guggenheim museums for days on end between my appointments. Freelance writing for Australian Consolidated Press helped pay the bills and kept me busy as I waited for that Paula Yates and Michael Hutchence

Iddin aged seven, me holding our puppies, Jock and Strap, and Shahirah aged five on our back veranda in Hawthorn.

On Fifth Avenue, New York, filming the documentary *Empty Arms – Broken Hearts*.

Walter and Patsy in their garden in Ambly. One of the very rare occasions I managed to get camera-shy Patsy to stand still. Walter was an amazing bear of a man, full of laughter and insight.

The wonderful Averetts, Jack and Ros, on their rooftop terrace in Beekman Place, New York. Friends of Anthony Williams, they took me under their wing and made sure I had a homey place to visit.

Me with Pamela Green and her children in Surrey. It was wonderful to finally see the whole family reunited.

Ernie Allen, President and CEO, National Center for Missing and Exploited Children, and Lady Catherine Meyer, wife of the (then) British Ambassador to Washington and a 'left-behind' parent and lobbyist, with me at an international conference in Washington.

With one of my closest friends, Deb Gribble. If anyone could get me to grin during the hard times it was Deb, with her dry wit and speedy quips.

In Washington with my friend and attorney, Sally Nicholes, the day after I gave a presentation at the US State Department. We're with little Adam, a kidnapped child we had helped reunite with his father.

Filming *Neighbours* in Kenya with the Maasai. Pictured are Brett Blewitt and Jackie Woodburne. Holding the camera is Harmon Cusack, my friend and enthusiastic pilot.

Operation Book Power at work in Maasailand.

Rasoa, one of my foster children. I hadn't seen her for several months so our meeting in Kenya was tentative at first, especially because of the cameras.

One of my favourite photos of Naipanti and me together. It's amazing that a common language isn't really needed with children if there is a hug involved.

With the US Army Lieutenant who was assigned to escort me in Bosnia. When I first put on the flak jacket, I almost toppled over with the weight.

Bosnia, 1997: Jasmin, my interpreter, with young Elvis Pivic, who lost his fingers when playing in a fruit tree that had been booby-trapped with explosive detonator caps.

The dreaded mattress distribution at Stenkovec II, a refugee camp for Kosovars during the war. I found it terrible having the power over the comforts of the children and the infirm. The yellow inflatable French field hospital is in the background.

At dawn atop a hillside overlooking the Cegrane refugee camp (by noon, temperatures rose to 45 degrees in the shade), where 57,000 souls lived under canvas all pegged out with German military precision.

Kushtrim, my twelve-year-old shadow, and me in the
International Committee of the Red Cross clinic tent
at Stenkovec II. I'm holding the frail baby I had just
resuscitated, hoping for the best.

exclusive. I endlessly walked the streets of New York and every day gravitated to St Patrick's Cathedral and its bank of votive candles. Afterwards I'd always write Iddin and Shahirah a postcard, seeking out the most amusing ones I could find. I'd kiss the stamp as I affixed it, trying to imprint my missive with never-ending love.

Sonny Mehta, along with his extended circle of friends, made it possible for me to meet some fascinating people and to experience a wide range of events. One memorable night I danced at a salsa club with four or five principal artists from the New York City Ballet and two male dancers from the Dance Theater of Harlem. Unashamedly, we took up the whole floor and revelled in the moment.

More sedately, Tony's dear friends Ros and Jack Averett, who resided in Beekman Place, kindly took care of me too, and ensured that I had lunch or dinner with them regularly. A charming couple in their late 60s, they were witty and very 'old' New York. Their penthouse had an amazing rooftop garden and views over Manhattan and Roosevelt Island. Since then, Ros and I have maintained a friendship; I will always remember her hand over mine and the tears welling up in her eyes, as she told me that if she was twenty years younger she would 'go get your babies back myself'.

I fell in love with New York, its pace and vibrancy, and never felt apprehensive or unsafe when out alone. And often I was accompanied by a male friend whom I'm sure Nell Campbell and Sonny had decided might be right for me, and to whom they had engineered an introduction.

At over 6 feet tall, with shoulder-length hair flecked with

grey, swarthy skin and large hooded eyes looking out from behind spectacles, David Rieff was a towering presence. His cowboy boots, large nose, sharp intellect and big laugh really made him stand out in a crowd. A respected journalist and writer on human rights issues and international conflicts, his stories on Bosnia were powerful and insightful, and of particular interest to me as I was due to travel to the Balkans in a month or two. His company was easy and not threatening. I think I amused him with my fervour for aid work and he probably thought me rather naive and idealistic, for he had been at the heart of the bloody conflict in the former Yugoslavia, living in the besieged city of Sarajevo.

The famous photographic exhibition that was mounted by Annie Leibovitz had come about because David had challenged her to accompany him into the war zone and record the devastation and its human toll. He also took her to Rwanda to record the humanitarian disaster there, he told me, as we sat in his chaotic living room and went through boxes of never publicly released photographs taken by Leibovitz. My impression was that the photographer had been overwhelmed by the human misery in Africa; the sheer enormity of the carnage had not allowed her to focus closely on a person or a moment as she normally did, and for once her artistic confidence had wavered.

David's quirky living arrangements were something to behold. Dark, almost devoid of natural light, his tiny apartment was full of books, and every available surface was covered with newspaper clippings yellowing with age. Lined up in front of one immense bookcase was his collection of cowboy boots and a bowl full of the turquoise and silver jewellery he was never seen without. A sleeping alcove was in one corner of the room, a closet served as a mildewed shower and toilet, but I don't recall ever seeing a kitchen. Across the hall, he kept another small apartment as his writing studio; I was allowed only a snatched look into that sanctum.

The only child of writer Susan Sontag and her former husband and college professor, Philip Rieff, David had been educated in French and English, attending *lycées* in America and France.

In the midst of all this activity, I had to fulfil my public speaking engagements too, which seemed to be ever increasing following Operation Book Power. While still in New York, I received word that I had been given an award by the National Center for Missing and Exploited Children for my work on child abduction and child protection. I was very pleased to be honoured by this American institution and to be told I had made a difference. The overseas success of *Empty Arms – Broken Hearts* also meant more frequent requests to give briefings and lectures, all of which were unpaid but played a prominent part in my quest to explain and reduce the impact of parental child abduction.

While in the US, I travelled to Hong Kong – soon to be handed back to China – to assist in the briefing of family law practitioners following Hong Kong's ratification of the Hague Convention – an important international step which gave the treaty a foothold in a formerly intractable jurisdiction. And there was a lightning visit back to Belgium, where it was imperative to convince the Belgian government to sign the Hague Convention. Amazingly, Belgium was one of the few members of the European Union to refuse to sign the Convention. So many children were being affected by this stance that lobbying governments to ratify the Convention became a focal issue for me.

One piece of good news came through around this time. The United Kingdom decided to close a loophole that had made child abduction from the UK to other countries too easy. Children of any age would now require their own individual passports and travel documents; a parent could no longer simply pen the name of a child into an adult passport and slip across international borders. This was a huge win to celebrate.

But it wasn't all plain sailing and an exciting whirlwind of activity. I fell into a bit of a heap emotionally, never quite able to escape my reality. It was simply too great a strain to constantly act in a professional manner and maintain my composure while discussing child abduction, statistics, legal strategies and political machinations – when my insides would be screaming out with all their might for Shah and Iddin. Some nights I was barely able to sleep, I missed the children so intensely; other times I wagged the proverbial finger at myself in the mirror, lecturing the reflection that this course was one the children would approve of.

Even so, at the first opportunity when I returned to Australia, I crawled into bed and stayed there for a few days, pushing the world as far away as I could. I was weary with feeling the void of my children's absence, and exhausted by reminders of my inability to champion Iddin and Shahirah as I was championing others. Tears came and wouldn't stop for hours. They bore no resemblance to my Kenyan tears – these were tears of grief and loss.

I wanted to sleep for years until the day I could see my children again. But there was still more work to do.

Chapter 15
'I'm a Hungry Pickle'

Bosnia was next. Yet even there my children would be with me.

I had hooked up with a couple of large aid organisations and would be looking at their work and filming some of their rehabilitation projects with a view to the footage possibly being used for a documentary or fundraising. I also planned to investigate whether the Book Power programme was suitable for children in the region. I wanted to establish which educational resources would be needed by kids who must learn to recreate a safe and happy fantasy world amidst a reality where innocence had been smashed. The figures for the Bosnia–Herzegovina region were horrific in terms of child trauma. One in three children had lost a parent or a close relative in the war, witnessed the detonation of a landmine, been maimed by a landmine explosion or had witnessed the death of another person.

Only weeks earlier, Diana, Princess of Wales, had been working in the region and now, tragically, she was dead. The world was saddened and concerned for her young sons – I felt so devastated that her boys would never have the opportunity to know her adult to adult. She and I had both had difficult royal marriages and had been thrown in at the deep end at a very young age. But despite her difficulties, her bright personality had struck a chord with so many people around the world and her dedication to anti-landmine campaigning had brought its horrors before the world, and had garnered her true respect.

She'd phoned me not long before, just days ahead of her famed dress auction at Christie's in 1997, when we had both been in New York, and I remember her good-natured laughter. Now I was setting off for Bosnia, a place we'd talked about, and would be spending time with some of the people Diana had been with so recently. On the day of her funeral, I was in transit on my way to Bosnia. In a nondescript hotel room I, like millions of others around the globe, watched her farewell on the television with deep sadness for her children and for the many charities I knew she was committed to on such a personal level. She and I were born two years apart, and our birthdays were separated by only four days. I had married my prince in early 1981 and she in July of the same year. Our children had been born at similar times and we had both struggled to find our way amidst very rigid royal families. Ultimately, we had both lost our children, except I still had hope I would one day see my own. It was an eerie feeling.

My time in Bosnia would affect me more deeply than the work in Africa had done, or at least it affected me in a very different way. Being from a Western first-world nation allows one a certain detachment in Africa. There's an unspoken, almost subconscious safety net of superior technology, economics and architecture that sets aid workers and visitors apart from the people with whom we work and mix in Africa. A touchstone of difference for those from the first world. The topography and squalor bear no resemblance to home. In Bosnia, though, prejudice and intolerance, suspicion and hysteria all reflected the ugliest sides of Western nations. The bombed-out buildings and the pockmarked walls of mortar-shelled homes could have belonged to any town in any first-world country. I saw evidence of war in situations I could equate to my own nation and my own life: to transpose these scenes to Melbourne's suburbs wasn't such a great leap to make. To finally understand what it had been like in Belgium or London after bombings and war. Any of the villages we drove through or walked around could have been places I loved in my own safe and peaceful country. The terms and conditions of war were such an alien concept for someone of my age from a country that had never witnessed mechanised conflict on its soil.

In Bosnia, this hell on earth had been the result of extremes of jingoism and inverse xenophobia aligning in a feeding frenzy akin to that of sharks scenting blood. And the rest of the world had stood by and remorselessly allowed genocide to occur.

With the signing of the historic Dayton Peace Agreement earlier in the year, a fragile peace had descended on the region, enabling a real evaluation of what these most vulnerable and displaced people needed in terms of humanitarian assistance and I felt passionately that I wanted to find a small way to contribute.

At the point on the map marked as the major crossing of the Savva River and the route into Bosnia from Croatia were massive pontoons upon which a giant raft had been constructed, in lieu of the bombed-out bridge which lurched to the side – two sad halves smashed to smithereens. Vehicles queued here to make the crossing. The wait was tedious, but all seemed resigned to it for a turn on the raft as it ferried passengers, cars and the odd lorry in either direction.

In the inevitable Toyota four-wheel drive, the trip to Tuzla, our first stop, took seven hours over mountainous terrain and winding roads damaged by landmines and neglect. Often single-lane and blind-cornered, the road ran through scenery of incongruous beauty in the midst of mindless vandalism. Abandoned and partially destroyed homes bore racist clichés, the marks of automatic weapons and posters of wanted war criminals – most prominently Radovan Karadzic, a former wartime leader of the Bosnian Serbs who had been indicted on charges of genocide, crimes against humanity, murder and multiple breaches of the Geneva Convention. Karadzic had been a doctor and a practising pyschiatrist. Some say that much of the pyschological torture and ethnic cleansing of the war was designed by this man, with an eye for the finite details, and a true understanding of the long-term impact of mass rape camps that had held over 50,000 Bosnian females aged between three and eighty-three. A by-product of this war crime were scores of unwanted pregnancies which the women were forced to carry to term. Those women whose minds were so damaged by their experiences often committed suicide or abandoned their infants for fear of social ostracism.

The Republic of Bosnia Herzegovina is a patchwork of opposing territories and demilitarised exclusion zones. My experiences there were also a patchwork, one of tears and laughter, culture and brutality, gentleness and strength.

I had taken pains to attempt some fluency in the local language by listening to a tape made for me by my friend John Udorovic, whose family had migrated to Australia from the former Yugoslavia when he was a child. My basic phrases, and apparently Croatian pronunciation, would get me by I hoped.

Tuzla itself is a small town, with its business district of eight or nine streets nestled at the bottom of surrounding hills. The architecture has a distinctly Italian flavour, in the way the piazzas with coffee shops and archways worked outwards from the now-notorious civic centre. It was here that, during a supposed ceasefire, a mortar attack had killed scores of young children one summer afternoon.

Food was still being supplied erratically, so there was an overabundance of some things and a distinct lack of others. Shelves in stores were often beautifully arranged and stacked, but with only one or two lines of grocery items. One supermarket might sell only detergent and instant coffee, another condensed milk and salt.

The residential areas of town climbed the steep hills. Most of the roads were in terrible condition and I found that it was often quicker to climb them on foot, rather than sit in a car as it groaned and jolted up the almost vertical terrain. Affluent middle-class residents had lived on the hillside where I was billeted; three-storey homes pockmarked with the ubiquitous bullet holes hugged the inclines and sported satellite dishes the size of small nations. This was the side of Tuzla that had taken the most punishment from Serb artillery placements.

Shortly after my arrival in Tuzla, I had been contacted by Sandra, a young woman of Bosnian–Croatian extraction who had been told by a mutual friend to expect me. Very tall and slim, with lively blue eyes and blonde hair, Sandra had worked as a translator with the International Red Cross during the war, and later with Norwegian People's Aid. One evening, as she and I walked around her garden, Sandra tried to explain what the siege conditions had been like. Sandra spoke of her father and his death during the war, and how she and her mother had survived through sheer tenacity, refusing to leave their home even when the shelling shattered windows and mortars lobbed into the garden beds. They had hosted Princess Diana on her short overnight visit there as their home had one fully intact bathroom and bedroom. Both women had very fond memories of Diana and her innate ability to simply muck in and be a normal house guest. Sandra laughed as she told me she had found the Princess up to her elbows in soap suds at the kitchen sink as she tackled the dishes. 'Fish and house guests go off after three days,' Diana had apparently joked.

The women of Tuzla were a sight to behold: many were stunningly beautiful with clear complexions, and their hair colouring ranged from white-blonde to raven. Great pride was taken in appearance and fashionable clothing was worn by all. Eyebrow-raising miniskirts and long boots were favoured by teenagers, and blue jeans were de rigueur for young women and men. Tuzla had been designated a Muslim town by the warring factions, even though most of the populace had intermarried with other faiths. Slashes of bright lipstick adorned the local women's lips and the contrast between the women who were permanent residents of Tuzla and those more conservative refugees from other parts of Bosnia was marked.

The poverty of those living in the semi-permanent refugee communities was dire. I worked with some of the children for a short while and heard their stories and sat beside them as they drew images of nightmares and bloodied limbs and lost fathers. The largest group among them were the women of Srebrenica, who had been herded at gunpoint from their village, taking only what possessions they could carry in their arms. All males over the age of seven – the entire male populace of 7,000 human beings – were subsequently slaughtered and consigned to secret mass graves in a ham-fisted attempt to cover the massacre.

(This forced ethnic cleansing was observed by a contingent of UNPROFOR, United Nations Protection Force, soldiers from the Netherlands, who did not lift a finger as the Serbian forces separated families and marched the Bosnian men and boys into the forest, never to be seen again.)

One day, a pale woman, accompanied by her young son, who could have been no older than seven, came into the office where I was discussing aid distribution with some colleagues.

'Excuse me, I was wondering if you have some soap, as I would like to wash my children?' she asked politely. I replied that we were only an administrative office and the warehouse was some distance away. I offered a biscuit to her little boy and he took it but refrained from eating. This seemed odd in a child of his age and just as I was contemplating his behaviour, his mother swayed on her feet and collapsed to the floor.

When she came to, we prised her story from her. Her dignity and reticence were humbling. Over a cup of tea, the woman explained that she and her three children were living rough beneath a bridge, her husband was dead and the small family had been itinerant for nearly eighteen months. Awkwardly I thrust the remainder of the biscuits at her child, and made plans to find some proper accommodation for her and the children.

Two things will always stay with me about that day. First, for all the difficulties this brave woman was encountering, her dignity and self-respect had not allowed her to lose her sense of pride in cleanliness for her children and herself. Secondly, her little boy did not nibble a single crumb from the packet of biscuits until he shared, with great gravity and restraint, the treats with his younger siblings.

The Organisation for Security and Cooperation in Europe (OSCE) and the United Nations Stabilisation Force (SFOR) had accredited me to observe and report on the first elections since the end of the war. Having been assigned to one of the largest contingents of the US military forces stationed in the Balkans, I was to make my way from Tuzla to Eagle Base, an army camp just outside the town of Brcko.

Street signs and highway postings were few and far between in those days, so it was rather a tense trip as I navigated to instructions scribbled on a scrap of paper, such as: 'Turning for left around white pole exactly 7.8 kilometres south-east of last highway road, then looking for big rock.'

In contrast, the army base was an advertisement for the might of the American military machine. It was as if everything had been done to ensure that a slice of downtown USA had been lifted and deposited in Bosnia. The accommodation for the infantry units was mostly in tents linked by above-ground wooden duckboards to keep the soldiers out of the mud. I was housed in a secure and private tent adjacent to mostly female soldiers. There was a chapel, a library, two huge canteens offering Coke and fried chicken, a pool hall, computer centre and cinema, all constructed from demountable materials. The jewel in the crown for any under-resourced aid worker was the company 'PX', a one-stop shop and home-away-from-home convenience store where you could buy anything from Tampax to T-shirts, shampoo and CDs. (Strictly speaking, it was for the exclusive use of serving US personnel, but with loads of eyelash batting and begging I was allowed to tick off my shopping list – a copious one filled with requests from aid workers around Tuzla who had gotten wind of my foray into US military territory.)

As part of my assignment with OSCE, I travelled with the infantry units out of Eagle Base in tanks and armoured Humvees. Always travelling in a convoy of four vehicles and armed to the teeth, the peacekeepers patrolled the surrounding areas every hour to ensure that the democratic political process was not impeded by harassment or gunfire.

My first 'insertion' into a Humvee was quite disturbing. Wearing the mandatory flak jacket, I was seated hard up against the legs of a soldier who stood for the entire journey facing backwards, his head and arms poking out the top of the vehicle as he manned a machine gun to cover our rear. And anchored to the central column of the Humvee, pointing more or less into my face, were the soldiers' M16s, long-necked and deadly. More disturbing, though, was that after the first frightening day of such casual exposure to firearms, I became quite nonchalant about the guns that were always everywhere.

Every now and again, the patrol would pull over and check on the situation in a village or at a polling booth. Sometimes the soldiers bent their non-fraternisation rule and talked to children and handed out sweets. It was fascinating to watch the young Americans throwing basketball hoops with refugee children in the middle of an aid camp. Despite being dressed in full battle fatigues, helmets and flak jackets, for ten minutes these soldiers would seem little older than the children with whom they played.

It was during one of these stops that a quirk of fate brought me my only first-hand news of Iddin and Shah in many years.

We had halted the convoy to inspect a small town just outside Serb territory. Intermittent rain was falling from a grey sky and the sides of the road were sludgy and uneven. The tracks from our vehicles made deep impressions and my feet slid awkwardly in the mud. No building here was unmarked by the war: the facade of each house had been sprayed with shrapnel and no glass remained in any window. The weather was kept out with old flour sacks and sheets of plastic stamped with the United Nations emblem in blue. Many roofs were missing and walls were riddled with gaping holes. Very few trees remained; most had been cut down for firewood for the rickety camp stoves of the largely refugee population.

Four armed GIs surrounded the Captain and me as we made our way towards the partially bombed-out building housing the polling booths, which were staffed by volunteers from all over Europe. Suddenly, a member of the United Nations International Police Taskforce hailed me – in Malay!

The man seemed dumbfounded to see me amidst an official SFOR escort and wearing a flak jacket in the middle of Bosnia. Under the circumstances, I was no less surprised to hear someone address me in Malay.

'Do you want to know about your children?' he asked. 'The prince says you aren't interested and don't care about them.'

In quick order, I felt stunned, mocked, then elated – and then determined to focus, to obtain as much information as I possibly could.

After some gentle pleading, the Malaysian police officer finally relented and looked me full in the eyes.

'So you really want to know?' he sneered intently.

I quashed an impulse to slap his face for his condescending arrogance and focused on remaining calm.

'Yes, of course I do, I want to know how tall they are, I'm desperate to know anything about my children. Have you seen them in the newspapers?' I spoke in Malay, but not daring to hope.

And then he told me.

Before coming to Bosnia, this man had been seconded to the Terengganu police contingent, and had spent quite a lot of time at the Badariah Palace, on royal detail. I had to suck my stomach in and lock my knees to stop from falling over when he said, with just a hint of a smug smile, 'I looked after your son, Prince Iddin, a few times.'

Forcing myself to keep calm and quiet, I struggled to avoid grabbing him by the collar and shaking more information from him. I just had to allow his contemptuous power play; I had to allow him to feel his superiority over me. And finally, he did volunteer a little more.

'Prince Iddin is very tall. He's at least 6 foot, maybe even 6 foot 3.'

The man could tell me no more and knew very little of Shahirah.

In the end I took my leave with as much dignity as I could, and made my way around the corner of a bombed-out building, the bewildered GIs surrounding me closely. They hadn't understood a word we'd said as the entire conversation had been conducted in Malay. Out of sight of the Malaysian policeman, I bent over double and began to dry retch and sob.

Trying to compose myself, I managed to blurt out an abridged explanation of my distress to the American soldiers. Then, removing his helmet and scratching his head, the sergeant, whose name was Larry – a beefy guy of twenty-five from Indiana – drawled out a question that made me laugh and shrug off my gloom.

'Do you want us to go fix him, ma'am?' he asked solicitously.

I wasn't sure if Larry meant the UN police officer or my ex-husband, but for a split second I allowed myself the luxury of imagining what Bahrin would do if a platoon of American soldiers turned up on his doorstep!

I thanked Larry, but declined the offer.

For days following this incident, my thoughts swirled around my head and pulled me in so many directions. I was thankful that I'd had a snippet of vaguely first-hand information on Iddin, but I was also despondent and incensed that these details had to be learned from a stranger with dubious goodwill. But this was what my motherhood had been reduced to – tabloid-like observations.

The rest of my time in Bosnia was filled with vividly contrasting events. One day I'd be singing songs about kookaburras and doing bizarre Australian animal calls with children in the shell of a school partly destroyed by bombs, then I'd be meeting teenagers who had lost limbs to landmines and seeking their opinions about disarmament. I'd spend time with the bereaved refugee women from the devastated village of Srebrenica; and I'd talk with Serbian, Croatian and Bosnian Muslim youth workers in their 20s, who refused to be defined by their ethnicity and harmoniously worked together at a crisis centre in the town of Banja Luka for Serbian families in need. By the shores of a crystal-blue lake nestled in the hills surrounding Tuzla, I sipped Turkish coffee and listened quietly as four of my young male colleagues, some of whom had been soldiers, explained what had happened to the women in their families, to girlfriends and female colleagues who had been amongst the 50,000 women subjected to the rape camps. The next day I'd lead a conga line of children on a kangaroo hop, just 10 metres from the uncleared minefield beside their school, as they whooped with joy. These were all contrasts of situation and logic that left me simultaneously confused, elated and distressed.

Once, when our convoy of aid vehicles was left unattended for a brief time, it was robbed of its cargo of children's books, luggage and money. Another time, during my second trip to Bosnia, my vehicle was pulled over and the driver and I were robbed at gunpoint. Stupidly, I had declined an escort for the short trip between Serbian and Bosnian territories. The butt of an AK-47 being bashed into the back of your head serves as a good reminder of your folly.

I also witnessed another event that was history-making and uplifting for a myriad of reasons. Filing into Sarajevo's battle-scarred Olympic Stadium on a clear but chilly evening, I made my way past rings of NATO tanks, barbed wire cordons and fully armed UN troops. AWACS (Airborne Warning and Control System) airplanes circled above to exclude a missile attack by zealots. The need for security was very real as a cowboy mentality still prevailed. Searchlights lit up the sky as I underwent two security pat-downs by burly Italian soldiers (quite enjoyable actually – I was tempted to go through again) before gaining admittance to Sarajevo's most eagerly awaited event since the ceasefire: an amazing rock concert by Irish band U2.

There was a mood of intense expectation as the 45,000-strong crowd waited for the group to take to the stage. The concert was a symbol that the formerly besieged city was living in the 'normal' world again. People aged five to fifty-five leapt to their feet as the first guitar riff filled the stadium. Thousands of cigarette lighters flickered and swayed in unison and the crowd began to sing. Bono, U2's vocalist, had tears streaming down his face as he exhorted the audience to *fuck the war and celebrate peace*. For one night, the people of Bosnia became a force united around one goal – to hear one of the biggest international rock bands from a small island with its own history of internal conflict. Sarajevans were cemented together that night by the one thing that transcends language and hatred: music.

I will always count that as one of the most unforgettable nights of my life. My respect for U2 and Bono's activism turned me into a fan – the band had fulfilled a promise made during the height of the bloody war and never wavered from the commitment.

Yet another evening, I found myself in the grounds of a fort. Built atop one of the hills overlooking Sarajevo, it had served as the perfect vantage point for heavy artillery and snipers. Looking down, I saw a cemetery nestled at the base of the hill. Hundreds of simple white headstones marked the graves. I descended the hill and saw that the majority of the graves were quite new. A fragile gate set into a green picket fence opened into the cemetery. Other people were inside, trimming grass and tending plots, but it took me several minutes to realise that all of them were elderly. The natural order of life and death had been disrupted by the war – parents and grandparents were tending the graves of the young. Lives full of promise had been obliterated by civil conflict and religious demarcation.

I paced slowly up and down the rows of headstones until I noticed that the dates in one portion of the cemetery all related to one particular day. All twenty-six graves were those of children killed in an apparently calculated mortar attack. These children had been the same ages as Shahirah and Iddin.

Looking more closely, I suddenly felt as if the oxygen had been sucked from my lungs and time jolted to a halt. I hurried now from one grave to the next. Two graves carried the same first name as Iddin's: Baharuddin; three others were the graves of little girls – one was called Shahirah and the other two Aishah, Shah's middle name. It was so wrong, so terrifying! Children aren't meant to die before their parents and children are not supposed to be the targeted victims of bloody conflict.

None of us in the world outside that strife-torn territory can escape responsibility for what happened to the children of Bosnia. How many of us watched the coverage of the war on CNN or the BBC over dinner or aperitifs, changing the channel when it became too graphic? Where was our loud united voice demanding strong intervention and peace? Why are we so scared of pacifism, of peaceful and humane political will? Why, even today, as we watch military actions around the world and the carnage of terrorism grips us by the throat, do our political leaders not listen to our calls for peaceful solutions to conflict? This is not just a failing in Westernised societies, it is an obscene crime perpetrated by all those who advocate religious intolerance, violence and cultural supremacy, and hide behind religion or politics.

War can never be the answer to our problems.

Transferring my base across to Banja Luka in the Serbian territory of Bosnia, I was assigned to observe the work of the United Nations Mine Action Centre. UNMAC was responsible for overseeing and implementing the safe defusing and removal of landmines, as well as conducting landmine-awareness education programmes.

One cloudless warm morning, I accompanied an UNMAC team of sappers into the field on a de-activation mission. The military personnel were mainly British, save for an Australian army major on secondment, with the rest drawn from a number of regiments: the 21st Field Squadron of Royal Engineers, the 3rd Armoured Engineer Squadron, and the 38th Engineers Regiment.

A search for an active landmine starts with the sapper donning a rather scanty protective apron, slipping on a large pair of gloves and a helmet with perspex visor. He then picks up the tools of the trade: a long, slim metal prod and a small hand shovel. The sapper drops on all-fours and crawls to prod and scrape every square centimetre of a small field, for three dangerous months.

Painstaking, unnerving and delicate.

At the time of the Dayton Peace Agreement, when the fragile peace had arrived, there were an estimated three million landmines in Bosnian soil. Landmines do not degrade. Made of plastics and other modern wonder materials, landmines maintain their deadly blast power until defused, which means they can sit passively in the earth for decades just waiting to inflict their deadly payload. In current economic terms, it costs less than US$3 to produce a landmine but US$1,000 to locate and safely remove one.

At that time in the Balkans, every month eighty children left their homes to play or go to school and were killed or maimed by a landmine. Young kids were even targeted, in an obscene campaign of terror: explosive detonator caps were used to booby-trap fruit trees, playground equipment and musical instruments. Children lost fingers, eyes and hands.

Even in such a brief time with the UNMAC unit, I lost partial hearing in my right ear. A cocky Serbian soldier, under orders from UNMAC to detonate an anti-tank landmine, thought it would be hilarious if he did so two minutes ahead of schedule, before the area was fully cleared of personnel. It was meant to be a joke to get up the noses of the British engineers; a bit of rebellion. The blast, processed through the audio headphones I was wearing for filming, knocked out my ability to hear certain sounds in my right ear, and has left me with difficulties in dealing with ambient noise and conversation. Oh well, I always fancied an ear trumpet, but it does make sweet nothings a thing of the past.

Completely exhausted and absolutely ravenous one night, having not had time to eat for twenty-four hours, I devoured an entire jar of local pickles and fell into a heavy slumber. By early morning my complexion had turned a fetching shade of green and I had the body temperature of a tropical heatwave – ptomaine poisoning.

'I am a hungry pickle,' I shouted desperately in garbled Bosnian to the doctor leaning over my bed, trying hard to explain that I really didn't need an appendectomy! This was made very difficult as, despite my protestations, I had been given a hefty shot of pethidine upon my arrival at the hospital, rendering me incoherent.

I kept my appendix, and learned some valuable lessons: never eat pickles as the only meal of the day; never attempt to speak a foreign language in a strange hospital after a dose of pethidine; and always wear decent underwear in a war zone.

Chapter 16

Keep on Running and Don't Look Back

The often-talked-about interview I was meant to write for the *Women's Weekly* never happened, though both Paula and Michael talked with me about it intermittently. Only a couple of weeks earlier, before Michael's death, I received a garbled phone call from him from New York – upset, but very protective of Paula. He wondered if she and all four of her daughters could use my house in Melbourne as a bolt hole if they followed him to Australia in the coming weeks. 'You've got a pretty normal big old house, haven't you?' he queried. 'It might be a solution to our problems.' He ended the call by saying Paula would be in touch soon.

Paula never called and I didn't speak to her until after Michael's funeral, where she'd sat in the front row of the church, cradling their daughter, Tigerlily, and weeping silently. Around her were Michael's glamorous ex-lovers, including singer Kylie Minogue and model Helena Christensen. The atmosphere was simultaneously maudlin and fashionable, an incongruous mix, but understandable given the circumstances. The who's who of show business and the fact that the funeral was being televised live ensured a confusion of media and mourning. I sat next to an old acquaintance, writer and commentator Richard Neville, as members of Michael Hutchence's family reflected on their loss.

Paparazzi and tabloid media hounded Paula after the funeral, sliding notes underneath her hotel room door trying to provoke a comment on Michael's death. She was forced to go into hiding in a hotel-cum-serviced appartment in Sydney – inconsolable, and adamant that Michael had not deliberately taken his own life. I managed to reach her on the phone and we spoke twice in the days after the funeral.

'He didn't fucking kill himself,' Paula sobbed and sobbed. 'He wouldn't do that to us. Why won't anyone listen? It was a fucking accident.'

'I don't understand how it happened either, darling,' I offered inadequately.

'You saw how he loved us, he did, he did, aren't I right?' She pleaded over and over for my agreement, which I readily gave, bewildered by what had transpired on the night that Michael had been found dead in the Ritz Carlton hotel. Michael was talking about the future when he had called me that night, weeks earlier. I didn't know what I could do for Paula and Tiger; I knew she had a friend travelling with her, but I offered to help with the baby, though I had no choice but to leave it at that

After the trip to Bosnia, I often found myself thinking of the women I had met there who were living in such difficult conditions. My mind's eye kept returning to the woman who had asked for a piece of soap with which to wash her children, and to the other women who'd approached me – not asking for food, but seeking feminine hygiene products, wondering if I had any left over from my personal stock. I couldn't think of anything worse for a woman already beaten down by volatile and degrading circumstances than being without sanitary pads or tampons to deal with their menstrual flow, and it wasn't as if there were alternatives available. Toilet paper was an expensive commodity and often missing from the shelves in stores, so it wasn't even possible to stuff wadded tissue in one's knickers. And money, if the women of Bosnia had any, was for food and fuel to cook with, not commodities that most women in first-world countries take for granted.

So I developed a project called Operation Angel, which aimed to assist women and children caught in the middle of conflict. Donations were not a focus of the project: I was after goods and help in kind that were practical and appropriate.

The main project in 1998 was to collect hygiene and sanitary products, from the Australian public and businesses, to give to women and children in the volatile Balkans. A funky television commercial promoting the idea was made with the help of members of the film industry, many of whom donated their services. Richard Lowenstein did an amazing job directing, and Michael Hutchence's band, INXS, really showed friendship and support by giving us the song 'Mediate' as the theme music for the commercial. Shoppers were urged to help by doubling up when purchasing one of the nominated Johnson & Johnson hygiene products; and for every two purchased the company generously donated one to Operation Angel. As an added incentive, consumers could clip a coupon from women's lifestyle magazine *New Idea* and enter a competition to win a range of prizes. Airlifting a huge shipment of sanitary pads, soap, deodorant and shampoo seemed a feasible and practical way of restoring a little bit of dignity. The campaign collected more than A$600,000 worth of goods which were sent to refugees from the Kosovo war.

In hindsight, I was pushing myself too hard. I'd been to Vienna to meet with executives of (the now defunct) Lauda Air to get a Boeing 777 aircraft for an Operation Angel airlift to the Balkans. Then, in quick succession, I lectured in Scandinavia, Belgium, Hong Kong, South Africa, Paris and Washington.

I could be accused of running away, I suppose, when I travelled outside Australia, even though the attempt would be futile and escape itself unachievable. But travelling made the hollowness in me moderately bearable for a short time.

So when the granddaughter of a prominent family in Hong Kong was abducted and taken to Columbia via London, I agreed to help.

The father of the child was desperate to see his four-year-old daughter again, and very concerned by the unsavoury connections of his former wife's new boyfriend. Luckily for this particular family, money speaks, and with unlimited resources to back up legal claims and counterclaims, the case was soon resolved using specialists in international law from four countries and without resorting to counter-abduction. A family of more modest means could never have managed such a quick resolution. But I didn't begrudge the financial wherewithal that made this outcome possible – a child in peril deserves any legal action that is available to protect them.

Occasionally, when attending conferences on human rights issues or international law, I was asked by other delegates about my own children. Many meant well, but some were dispassionate academics out to make a name for themselves in a newish field – it irritated me that they treated left-behind parents as a species to be studied and regurgitated for intellectual merit, ignoring the humanity of their terrible situation.

I always felt a churning of nausea in these situations, and I would excuse myself at the earliest opportunity to escape to the nearest loo, to gather my breathing and quell the tears that always threatened. It was imperative that I kept my self-control. My children were constantly and continuously on my mind, they weren't shoved into a safe space in my head and summoned forth as and when I wished to be a grieving performance act. I had not been allowed even a single phone call with my children after so many years. But I was ineffective if I showed too much hurt; at all costs I wanted to maintain a distinction between myself and the often tightly wound left-behind parents who sometimes turned up at these conferences with only personal barrows to push. To behave in anything but a professional manner would have been a huge disservice to the cause as a whole. My view was the bigger picture, for every contact and scintilla of intellectual respect I garnered I had the potential to help other children and their parents. And maybe, just maybe, my own children would benefit in the long run.

In Washington for a week-long conference organised by the National Center for Missing and Exploited Children, I met a new player on the international parental child abduction scene, the dynamo Catherine Laylle, newly married to Sir Christopher Meyer, Britain's Ambassador to the United States. Lady Meyer was an elegant and sophisticated blonde woman of French and Russian heritage who had previously worked in London as a commodities broker. Foremost though, Catherine was a mother, who, like me, was a left-behind parent. Her struggle to secure the return of her two boys, Alexander and Constantin, who had been kidnapped in 1994 by their father, a German national, had proved as futile as my own.

Until the time of their removal from Catherine's custody, the boys had been living with her in London, where she had rebuilt her life following the marital split. The children were nine and seven when they were retained in Germany following an access visit. When Catherine and I met, neither boy had been allowed more than a cursory form of contact with his mother. Ten years older than me, Catherine had exhausted every legal avenue open to her to gain her boys' return, and nearly beggared herself in the process. But still she had lobbied and doorknocked.

One day this odyssey had brought her to Christopher Meyer's office, in his capacity as British Ambassador to Germany. Several months later they married and she found herself on a plane and in a new role – as first lady of the British Embassy in the US.

Thrust upon the diplomatic circuit by her marriage to Christopher, Catherine quickly made her mark on the Washington scene with her style and erudite conversation.

Soon active with the National Center for Missing and Exploited Children, the Meyers had offered to host a black-tie dinner at the Embassy for the conference delegates, as well as an afternoon tea.

During pre-dinner small talk, Catherine and I had gravitated to each other, for we both seemed to view our predicaments and the pain of being separated from our children as part of a bigger global picture. Comparing notes and discussing our cases in private was a natural progression. When it was time to go into dinner, I remember the tall figure of Christopher approaching us; he placed a solicitous hand on his wife's shoulder and murmured a very gentle and heartfelt 'Darling' into her ear. She answered with a dazzling smile and a slight bending of her head towards her husband's hand. It was the one time I remember feeling a pang of loneliness that had nothing to do with my children and everything to do with being a woman alone. For as much as I appeared to be independent, the solidarity and obvious romance shown by one of Washington's most glittering couples made my solo struggle seem, for a split second, pitifully solitary and desolate.

Catherine and I farewelled each other at the end of the week with a warm embrace, and a comic exchange of our books on the abduction of our children – there were some things that were just too raw to voice in person. Neither of us were quitters and both of us were determined to work within the system to obtain the best outcome for the most beloved beings in our lives, our children. We were more than capable of looking after ourselves; it was the emotional and psychological impact on our little ones that most concerned us.

Chapter 17
Just a Little Bump in the Road

It was almost 1998 already; time seemed to pass at breakneck speed. Inwardly I raged at the ageing of my children and cursed the hours, days and weeks that took me further from them.

I'd come back to New York, after a trip to Kenya, to write some articles – anything to keep me out of Australia on the triple-whammy month I loathed. My birthday was 5 July, Shahirah's was 7 July, and 9 July was the anniversary of the kidnapping. Reporters always diarised the anniversary and would approach me for comment, attempting to persuade me to cooperate with articles or television stories they could use to make a name for themselves. Everyone hoped for an exclusive that would serve no purpose in getting the children returned home. The annual black cloud of this period was overwhelming and I would do anything or go anywhere to avoid it.

But then my agent, Tony Williams, rang, tracking me down at the quirky Wyndham Hotel where I always stayed at his insistence. Seemingly satisfied that I was keeping out of trouble as I wandered Manhattan's museums and galleries, he launched his next campaign. In a spate of phone calls, he asked me to meet him in Los Angeles, issued instructions, and made sure I had suitable attire for California.

Informed that I had fashioned independent plans of my own in LA, Tony went about reorganising my hotel bookings and meetings with the William Morris Agency. Discussions had begun again about optioning my first book, but I was singularly unenthused – knowing as I did that Hollywood likes a happy ending, I thought it would be another futile discussion.

The whirlwind of social activity arranged by Tony swooped me up the afternoon I flew in from New York. A drinks party at his dear friend Pamela Godfrey's was overflowing with the writers, directors and talented people Tony knew in Los Angeles. We sat around a huge wooden table in the garden, and there was much laughter from everyone when they heard about the blind dates I'd been set up with in the preceding months. I made light of these embarrassing dating disasters, with embellished stories of encounters with a British Queen's Counsel, an American film producer and the scion of an aristocratic French family.

Suggestions were then volunteered as to whom I should be introduced to in Hollywood. I shuddered at the thought and begged off – an erudite dinner companion was one thing, a date with expectations was quite another.

Next day, I had a whale of a time with Tony as we stormed the hallowed halls of the Los Angeles offices of the William Morris Agency, and then took on the world over lunch on the rooftop at Barney's department store, the famous Hollywood sign visible on the hillside to our right. Later we strolled Rodeo Drive as Tony picked out clothes for himself and made cutting and hilarious asides about various walking examples of plastic surgery dos and don'ts and age-defying attire.

I'd not spent much time in La La Land before, and was curious to press my nose up against the window. Some of the glass for this exercise had been organised by an icon of mine, Miss Jackie Collins, whom I had admired for many years. Jackie and I had been introduced during one of her book tours to Australia, lunching together and generally 'hitting' it off. She'd been very kind to me during our encounters, and had done a lot to encourage my writing.

Jackie said she thought her friends would enjoy meeting me – I only hoped I would live up to their expectations. Lunch was scheduled at the famed Le Dôme restaurant on Sunset Boulevard. I shamefacedly changed my dress three times before going, settling on a grey silk-jersey sheath and black suede accessories.

As I was shown to a huge round table at the rear of the restaurant, I mentally straightened my shoulders and told myself to go with the flow. Immaculately coiffed and wearing a stylish but casual suit and eye-catching jewellery, Jackie now rose to kiss me on both cheeks, and made the introductions. The guests included the exceedingly beautiful Shakira Caine, David Niven Jnr and Joanna Poitier.

Jackie had always struck me as highly intelligent and incredibly droll, a savvy woman who had found her niche as a novelist and knew exactly how to deliver entertainment to her audience. And her friends today were kind and chatty, interested in my aid work and the issues of child abduction. They, too, had ideas about whom I should be introduced to as part of the Hollywood dating game, but I politely and firmly declined. What my nanna would have thought of all this was beyond my imaginings, I just felt a little bit of a fraud holding my breath before being caught out.

The rest of my sparkling LA sojourn passed in a blur of dinners and lunches – Spago, The Ivy and Le Dôme were the popular places to be seen, and I enjoyed every minute of it – but couldn't help feeling completely out of my depth.

On my last day in LA, the film producer David Giler had kindly offered to take me to the airport for my evening flight to Australia. We spent the afternoon by his pool, barbecuing steaks, sunning and swimming – a relaxed and make-up-free day.

As I was showering after the swim, I suddenly felt a shiver, as if someone had just walked over my grave.

'That can't be right,' I muttered as I ran my fingers over my right breast close to the armpit. A small lump the size of a pea was there. 'Bugger,' I swore.

I had felt a lump when I was in Kenya weeks earlier, then it had disappeared. But my breasts had been so unpredictable in recent times – I had even at one stage begun spontaneously lactating due to an excess of oestrogen, a by-product of grieving for the children. Lumps and bumps had become the norm.

Well, there was nothing I could do about this one here and now in Los Angeles, not when I was due to hop on a flight in a few hours. So I swallowed my panic and carried on dressing.

Later, at the airport, I was so distracted as I said goodbye to David that I didn't notice he'd arranged an upgrade for me, to first class, and I hardly acknowledged the man, Wes, to whom he introduced me and who was also travelling to Melbourne. Although we would chat later during the long flight, all I wanted was to sleep and wake up with no stupid little lump making a nuisance of itself.

During transit in New Zealand, Wes lay down on the floor of the VIP lounge and went through the most limber-stretching routine I've ever seen a man achieve. People began to point and a couple of flight attendants asked for an autograph, managing to slip past his bodyguards. Through my haze, I realised that this Wes was Wesley Snipes, the action-movie star.

He was travelling with his entourage, to promote his latest film. When we parted at the airport in Melbourne, Wes extracted a promise from me that I would attend his premiere later that night, and come to the after party.

Out of curiosity I went along, and quickly realised that all I had seen in Hollywood had been as tame as a nuns' picnic compared to this moment in my reportedly staid home town! Deafened by the music permeating the closed doors of the private room of the nightclub, I took stock of my surroundings and felt like an extra in a bad parody of the lifestyles of the spoilt and tameless.

In the end, I beat a hasty retreat when the 'refreshments' and 'entertainment' provided by Wes's entourage were brought out. Nevertheless, it was a surreally funny scene that I could call up in the coming weeks, one that would never fail to deliver a giggle when I really needed one.

'Drink this,' said Mandy, my neighbour, as she held out a

bowl of miso soup. For days, this was all I could keep down. It turned out that the little lump was more insidious than I had first imagined. A speedy lumpectomy had been performed, and to my immense relief the surgeon believed I would be one of the lucky ones. But as a follow-up, I was having radiotherapy at a nearby hospital, in the very early hours of the morning to avoid any media attention.

Getting over the illness as quickly and as efficiently as I could was the goal that I doggedly fixed my mind upon. I was determined to see Iddin and Shahirah again – dying was simply not an option. For the most part, I closed down emotionally and only had contact with close friends, who kept me going during this time; my focus was on making my body provide the best long-term outcome.

My great regret was that my commitment to Operation Angel had to be wound back. It was tremendously hard to admit that I wasn't able to bring the project the energy it needed, but I simply had no other choice. Fortunately, *New Idea* magazine, the major sponsors and promoters of the programme, stepped into the void and kept the project on track, and not a single whisper leaked out about my condition. Bunty Avieson, Sue Smethurst and Laurelle Duffy kept my health an absolute secret and made no attempt to turn it into a story or abrogate my privacy in any way. Their help and friendship was an amazing watershed in the cut-throat business of women's magazines.

Twelve months later, following some discussions, the magazine became an active fundraiser for breast cancer awareness and research, and I agreed to discuss my (by then) positive outcome publicly in *New Idea*. Someone up there was obviously looking out for me.

Chapter 18
A Whole lot of CARING

Though seven years had gone by, my longing for Shahirah and Iddin had never lessened. I missed their scent, the tantalising mixture of odours unique to one's own children. I even pined for the little irritations, the tangible childhood grime of living in close proximity with your own flesh and blood. Intellectually, I understood that Iddin and Shah were no longer little children, but the memory of their grubby little hands wrapping around my face as their lips came in for a kiss still had the capacity to stop my heart beating and shred my carefully constructed composure. My yearning for them was intransigent and constant, but so too was my anger on their behalf. The fact that Shahirah and Iddin had been possessed and carried off like trophies, to be stripped of independent will and reasoning, made me furious. Unilaterally depriving them of their right to know both of their parents was such an abrogation of the most basic tenet of self-awareness and development and I was fearful of how this deficit would manifest itself in their adult lives.

As for me, I knew I was more than the sum total of the abduction of my children. I never wanted to be mired in the tragedy of their kidnap. Since the earlier days following the loss of the children, my mind has matured and stretched; I've learned to embrace life's vagaries and become more comfortable in my own skin, less worried about others' perceptions of me and more at home with my reflection in the mirror and with my inner strengths.

I recognise though, particularly since my brush with breast cancer, that much of my strength has come from my friends, my loved ones, and from all that I've had the good fortune to experience and witness around the globe. This element of life has enabled me to contextualise my response to the bombardment of media images that affect society's common conscience.

It is this insight, combined with my irritating and innate stubbornness, that I learned to channel into projects and causes about which I felt passionately – it kept me from going mad and also reinforced to me, at my darkest moments, that getting on with life is what we are all meant to do. That, and creating change if we believe there is a wrong to be righted. I believe that an openly voiced opinion is a way to change the world – the complicity of silence can be as obscene as the injustice itself.

I *know* that one person is able to change the world – it may not be a seismic shift, but simply a shift of heart or a contribution to humankind that can make the existence of another human being more tolerable.

When the situation in Kosovo began to flare up, around the

time I became a Special Ambassador for CARE International – one of the world's largest independent emergency relief and development agencies – I hoped I could create a tiny niche from which to make a difference in a complex and diverse forum. The deal breaker when I was discussing my appointment as Special Ambassador with Charles Tapp, then the CEO of CARE Australia, was that I be allowed to work in the field, in conflict and emergency zones. (Fortunately, we'd known each other for years and Charles was used to my 'out of left field' aid ideas, so he didn't view me as entirely demented.) I didn't want to be some token 'rent a celebrity' wheeled out for photo opportunities. I needed assurances that I could continue to get my hands dirty and stomp around in the mud with the people CARE was trying to help. That way, when I participated in public lectures or discussions involving CARE's work, I would not be regurgitating a press officer's briefing: I would be speaking with first-hand experience.

To put you in the picture, the CARE International Federation consists of twelve member states – USA, Denmark, Germany, France, Canada, Japan, Austria, Netherlands, Australia, United Kingdom, Norway and Thailand – and is overseen by a Secretary General based in Geneva, Switzerland.

Each individual nation manages stand-alone projects in various regions and areas of expertise, as well as supporting programmes in conjunction with other CARE Federation members. CARE is completely non-sectarian and non-political, an important factor to me as I wanted no religious affiliations which would dilute the purity of the aid work in which I was involved, and no distracting agendas based on gender, race or politics.

During times of emergency, like earthquake, war or famine, the deployment of a CARE International Emergency Response Team (ERT) is rapid, usually within forty-eight hours. These specialists in emergency relief simply drop everything, obtain leave without pay from their normal place of employment, grab their bags and jump on a plane. They partner with CARE staff already working in that region, and are specially trained and experienced people drawn from around the world with backgrounds as diverse as engineering, logistics, nursing, infant welfare, media, accounting and military. The pay is minimal for ERT members, just enough to keep the bills at home vaguely covered and to buy food in the country where they have been sent.

CARE was first established in America in 1945 as a grass-roots response to the aftermath of the Second World War; life-saving 'CARE Packages' were sent from the more bounteous USA to the survivors of the war. These packages contained tea, tinned meats and other food staples, with the addition of warm blankets as the programme evolved. CARE Packages often meant the difference between survival and death for whole families in need. Over the first two decades of CARE's existence, over 100 million CARE Packages reached people, first in Europe and later in Asia and other parts of the developing world.

CARE's work expanded over the years, addressing the world's most threatening problems. The 1950s saw the organisation begin working in emerging nations and using the USA's surplus food to feed the hungry. In the 1960s, CARE pioneered primary health care programmes, and in the 1970s and '80s, CARE responded to massive famines in

Africa with emergency relief and long-term agriculture and forestry projects that integrated environmentally sustainable land management practices with specifically designed farming initiatives. CARE began to emphasise the importance of microeconomic projects in the late 1990s to the current time, projects such as improving the lives of women through financial independence and education as a core element of eradicating poverty and childhood mortality.

With more than 14,500 staff worldwide – most of whom are citizens of the countries in which CARE operates – a major focus of what CARE undertakes is programmes that work to create lasting solutions to the deeper causes of poverty. It's estimated that CARE's relief and development programmes touch more than 50 million people globally on a daily basis.

CARE stands for Cooperative for Assistance and Relief Everywhere, Inc, although ask most staff who work outside of CARE's main offices and the majority will simply answer, 'Don't know, we're just CARE.' Frankly, from my perspective, the simplicity of the name without the meaning always worked for me, as the word 'CARE' translates beautifully in most languages. That is the primary value for me.

President John F. Kennedy said in 1962: 'Every CARE Package is a personal contribution to the world peace . . .'

I believe that every single time CARE assists another human being, we are furthering the promise of a better and safer world for our children.

I had an enormous feeling of hope inside my chest as I agreed to take on my new role. More than anything, I wanted my children to be proud of me and to one day share in my convictions. I felt as if I was somehow starting a job that could build a bridge over which Shahirah and Iddin might walk one day.

To prepare, I took an advanced first-aid course, so that I wouldn't be at a loss in a difficult situation and could handle resuscitation and bleeding. I also studied the treatment of psycho-trauma, which in some ways was a natural extension of my work in the field of child abduction and its aftermath.

I also had to fulfil further commitments first, on the Hague Convention and child-abduction front, flying to France for meetings with representatives of the European Union, before attending a conference in London on EU policy changes on international parental child abduction that coincided with the release of my book in Britain.

In Paris, I had two half-days off from scheduled appointments and used those to catch up with friends, including the designer Martin Grant, whose studio was in the funky Marais quarter of the old city. Martin had started in Melbourne, studying sculpture before branching out into fashion design and eventually ending up in Paris, where he has made a name for himself with his elegant and classic designs. Supplying stores such as the exclusive Harvey Nichols and Barneys, Martin creates garments that emphasise the curves of a woman's body. Now he conjured up suitable attire in which I could face the barrage of press scheduled for me in the coming weeks. It was comforting to be around Martin; his attention to detail, his demeanour and love of fabric and stitching reminded me so much of my nanna. He had a way of slightly narrowing his eyes whenever I emerged from behind the fitting-room curtain wearing one of his dresses that made me feel seven years old again, with Nanna fussing and re-pinning a creation she had fashioned for me from leftover curtain material.

Everything Martin produced for me was simple to slip on and propped up my confidence enormously; I had never worn such beautiful and well-fitted garments. All just another piece of my armour – for all my bravado, I was quaking in my shoes at the thought of a tour to promote my book in the UK.

I travelled on to London during what was becoming a tumultuous time for CARE. The war in Kosovo was spiralling out of control and scores of refugees were flooding across borders into Albania and Macedonia, seeking sanctuary. NATO had waded into the conflict in an attempt to bring order, and was running bombing raids over Belgrade. Compounding the humanitarian emergency, three of CARE's aid workers, Peter Wallace, Branko Jelen and Steve Pratt, had been arrested in Serbia as alleged spies and were being detained by President Slobodan Milosevic on espionage charges. I arranged with Charles Tapp to speak about CARE's work in Kosovo and also fundraise during my publicity tour, dovetailing my old life with my new.

In London, the next fourteen days passed in a blur: the EU conference, interviews, the odd cocktail party and myriad book signings. I also became a spokesperson for the Kosovo Crisis Appeal in the United Kingdom and used every opportunity during live-to-air broadcasts to exhort people to donate to the very sensibly centralised fund, which covered the Red Cross, Oxfam, Save the Children, CARE and other agencies, and cut out competitive fundraising in a time of international emergency.

It was a whirlwind of mismatches. Train trips up to Edinburgh to do press; a quick flight to Dublin to appear on a talk show; 5 a.m. starts, and a car picking me up and depositing me at the headquarters of BBC Radio for twenty back-to-back interviews in a windowless bunker for regional radio. Emerging like a mole into the light, I remember feeling confident that I had talked about the crisis in Kosovo and deflected a few questions about myself onto a more important topic.

And there was a gruelling interview with Tim Sebastian for the BBC World programme, *HARDTALK*. Nausea churned my stomach about this interview, for, as Mr Sebastian reminded me just before the camera began to roll, I knew there was a possibility that Iddin and Shahirah might see, or hear of, this particular television piece. *HARDTALK* was broadcast around the globe, with the same episode aired numerous times in the one day, so as I tried to answer Mr Sebastian's probing questions, I imagined the children seeing me for the first time in years. My heart was ready to jump out of my chest with hope and trepidation.

It was fascinating entering the House of Lords and being ushered by a uniformed page to an enormous leather wingback chair that made me feel like a Lilliputian escapee. Baroness Patricia Scotland QC, whose acquaintance I had made during the European Union conference on the Hague Convention, gave me a quick tour of the building, then we retired to the bar for atrocious sandwiches and very good vodka. Patricia was the first black woman Queen's Counsel and life peer in Britain – quite a trailblazer. (She is now the

Minister of State for the criminal justice system and law reform in Tony Blair's Labour Government.) There in the hallowed halls of the House of Lords I sat with two peers, for I was also introduced to Waheed Alli, another recent addition to the peerage. I wondered if Nanna was doing a double-take in heaven.

Nanna had never been very impressed by the title of my first husband; to her, royalty meant British or European titles and suits of armour – there's nothing like a grandmother to rightly bring you down to grass roots.

My real treat for the evening was being able to catch up again with Shakira Caine, whom I had previously met in Los Angeles. Intelligent and sophisticated, this was a woman who was so much more than a famous husband's trophy wife. Shakira invited me to dinner at a restaurant she and her husband, actor Sir Michael Caine, owned at Chelsea Harbour. It was a great evening with good conversation and amazing hospitality, a good counterpoint to the previous fortnight of intense regurgitation of facts and figures to the media. The company was good too, and very relaxed. I had asked a friend, Salah Brahimi, to escort me, and along with Patricia Scotland, it made for an interesting dynamic at the table.

A luncheon meeting with the British managing director of Polaroid was a late addition to the schedule, but I'd had an idea for a relief initiative for the Kosovo crisis and wished to discuss my proposal with him and he'd readily agreed to meet me.

As we sat in Café Orsino, in Covent Garden, ironically with delicious food before us, I outlined the conditions in the refugee camps. Small, lost children, I explained, were often incapable of recounting their proper names or those of their parents, so getting little kids back into the arms of those who loved them was fraught with problems. Photographs would speed up the process enormously, but there was no electricity in the refugee camps, so no way to process film quickly. Polaroid agreed to donate one hundred cameras, and thousands of packs of film stock, to assist the Red Cross and other agencies in the reunification process for families who had become separated in the flight to safety. It was a lunch that I would bless in the weeks to come.

Chapter 19

Bond, Boots and Bastards

Feeling the pressure of a hand grasping the back of my airline seat, I half turned to see who it was. 'Roger Moore,' the throaty deep voice said, in tones familiar the world over. I blinked as he extended his hand to shake mine. A frivolous voice in my head quipped, 'Moore; Roger Moore,' in a bad imitation of the classic James Bond line, and I swallowed hard to focus my attention on the dapper, bespectacled gentleman towering above me. He explained that he had seen me on the BBC recently and was familiar with my background.

The flight from Zurich was taking us to Skopje, the capital of Macedonia and the central command post for much of the humanitarian relief effort during the ongoing war. Roger and his Swedish wife, Kristina (Kiki) Tholstrup, were travelling to Skopje as part of his role as a long-time UNICEF Goodwill Ambassador.

Roger asked if he could introduce me to someone. I was aware that I couldn't have looked less like a 'Bond girl'. I'd tucked my oversized CARE T-Shirt into black cargo pants and cinched them in tight at the waist to keep them up, and my enormous Belgian paratrooper boots took up most of the aisle. But now was not the time to be worrying about elegance – a couple of minutes passed and Roger returned with a smiling black-haired man, who he introduced as Toni Popovski, Minister for the Environment and Urban Planning for the Republic of Macedonia.

'Your Excellency, may I present Special Ambassador for CARE International, the former Princess Yasmin,' said Roger with a resonance so familiar from his films. 'She prefers to be known as Jacqueline Pascarl,' he added, almost as an aside. Cringing inwardly, I smiled and raised an eyebrow at Roger over the minister's shoulder. An almost imperceptible shake of his head was all Roger gave in return. Obviously, Roger knew the non-government organisation (NGO) ropes better than I did. Excusing himself with a smile, 007 turned and took his seat beside his wife, leaving the minister to clamber over my feet and into the vacant seat beside me.

Talk about being thrown in at the deep end! Although I knew the value of being acquainted with a Cabinet member in a host country, I wasn't well prepared and understood none of the political dynamics of Macedonia, but I winged it.

Popovski was in his mid-30s, I gauged, and determined to be charming. He questioned me closely on my role with CARE and the organisation's work with the Kosovar refugees flooding into his country. The Minister said he recognised me from the cover of my book, which he had seen in an airport bookshop. Did I have a copy with me, he asked, as if I was on a promotional tour!

We talked for the rest of the flight and Popovski was insistent that I attend a few of the government and diplomatic functions, scheduled over the next few days, as his personal guest. Well, you never know when a private telephone number will come in handy, I thought, as he pressed his business card into my hand. Under his protection I cleared Customs and Immigration.

Walking into an established clique of people is always a hard ask, triple that if it's a group of aid workers with a determination to make the interloper sweat a bit of blood. The first couple of days at the official 'country office' of CARE International were pretty isolating. Many of the Kosovar staff were traumatised by the arrest of three of their colleagues, particularly as a number of them had worked closely with Steve Pratt and Branko Jelen before the war broke out. They felt that they might also be at risk, and their family members left behind in Kosovo during the evacuation. They were refugees themselves, who were trying to function as relief workers in a foreign country. As well, the office director had been called away for operational meetings, and morale was very low.

There is a distinct division between the administration staff at Headquarters and the Emergency Relief Team working in the field. One is about dotting the i's and crossing the t's, and the other is more worried about food rations for their charges and the supply of potable water at the location they are working.

I straddled the two in a weird grey area that confused everyone not privy to the parameters of my role with CARE

International. Sometimes *I* was even a little perplexed, as I always felt more akin to relief workers. I was there to represent CARE with the media, work in general camp management, attend any UN or host-nation gatherings, film enough material of CARE's work to utilise for publicity purposes and generally find a niche for myself. Add to the mix further instructions from CARE's Secretary General, Guy Toussignant. He'd repeatedly impressed upon me the importance of my role as Special Ambassador and the focus he wanted me to put on diplomacy and public image, drawing on any lessons in deportment or conversation I had used in my old life as a royal.

The two sides of aid work needed their counterpart; one without the other is a recipe for chaos. This was not Hollywood or a theoretical exercise, only idiots and cowboys would lob up to a relief zone with no infrastructure or plan in place. No effective aid agency is able to undertake a firm commitment to operate under such difficult conditions, for weeks and months on end, without the back-up of a diverse and skilled set of people handling the nuts and bolts. The logistics of such an enormous aid operation were complex and many. Everything has to operate like a domino effect. Money, transport with a reliable fuel supply, national staff (as local employees are called), power, paper, computers (or at least pens), accounting, *in situ* accommodation – they all have to bubble away before you even start on the more 'sexy' side of helping rebuild shattered lives.

Cynicism is what I expected to encounter – I would have been naive to expect otherwise. I knew that I would have to earn my stripes, and I wanted the opportunity to do so.

A population of 450,000 normally resided in Skopje. Now

the city was reeling from the influx of NATO troops, hundreds of United Nations and other NGO aid workers, a gaggle of international media and a huge number of Kosovar refugees, who were sheltering with distant relatives in basements or on living-room floors around the city. Along with all the people confined to the refugee camps that had sprung up in outlying areas, this was a city bursting at the seams.

Many local residents had chosen to move out of their homes, renting them out fully furnished to a gaggle of international relief workers – a windfall for the locals, and an arrangement that suited all concerned. The local economy was flooded with cash. But the strain on the Macedonian infrastructure was immense and heated up unspoken ethnic tensions in this former state of Tito's Yugoslavia.

Over the centuries, Skopje had been plagued by earthquakes, so the architecture was an incongruous mix of Roman and Ottoman ruins, terrible Soviet-influenced tower blocks and pseudo-Mediterranean villas. Roads were broad and well surfaced and the people friendly, although the Macedonian word *ostavime*, meaning 'leave me alone', proved to be handy every time I was wolf whistled at or approached by young men with more bravado than sense.

There was a CARE house in Skopje, but it was already full. So my billet was the Roza Diplomatik, a small hotel in a very quiet location near a Catholic church and within walking distance of the CARE office. Roza Diplomatik was a quirky little place – four storeys high with only twelve rooms, a twisting staircase and an open-air courtyard at the rear, it was more of a family-run pensione than a hotel. With my own bathroom and a working air-conditioner, I could retreat to my room on the top floor when I wasn't on duty or sleeping at one of the refugee camps.

Breakfast was available at the Roza, and drinks and coffee, but otherwise food had to be found at one of the little cafés or restaurants that dotted Skopje. I seldom saw my fellow guests as I had to leave the Roza by 6 a.m. to be on time for the 6.30 a.m. shuttle, and the thirty-minute drive out to Stenkovec II, one of two camps CARE was running and that currently sheltered over 27,000 refugees.

The standard joke around town was that the US government foreign-aid agency (USAID) people staying in my hotel were really CIA operatives. Needless to say, I always checked my cornflakes box for hidden cameras!

Shading my eyes from the sun, I looked up at the UNHCR flag flapping from the flagpole overhead. Danish Fred, one of the UN staffers working at the camp, would finally be satisfied, I mused ruefully; all he had done for the past few days was badger CARE people to have that flagpole erected. Frankly, there were other more pressing matters to deal with but, in the end, a minute's peace was worth it.

I had driven up to the vantage point of Skenkovec II's highest hill for a fifteen-minute break from the fetid air in the alleyways between the tents in G sector. I chugged water from the bottle I kept in my pants pocket, next to my Leatherman multi-tool, and pulled off my neck scarf and hat. Twenty minutes earlier, I'd been staring down a bulky and aggressive man with a knife and I do admit that it takes a bit out of a girl mentally. It was a bugger too that my walkie-talkie battery had gone flat so I couldn't call for assistance even if I had wanted to. This particular man had taken exception to my asking him and his family to share their tent with another influx of refugees, and he had drawn his knife, saying he was going to slit my throat before he would be forced to share the accommodation. It wasn't the first time – and it wouldn't be the last – this had happened. It seemed standard procedure that men would 'try it on' with me and not one of the blokes with whom I worked. I suppose some of the more macho and traumatised refugees thought they could scare a woman into agreement, but I knew that their bluff had to be called. I calculated that they wouldn't risk committing a crime in which the Macedonian police would inevitably become involved. More importantly though, I knew that if I didn't stand my ground, word would get around and it would be open season on the other aid workers in the camp. The knives would then truly come out to settle disputes and the result would be unrestrained aggression and chaos.

The small hill on which I now sat allowed me to survey the barren camp below. Devoid of trees, it was a swirling dustbowl when any wind was about. Inside each gully of the former quarry, hundreds of tents clung to the rough terrain. The broad high walls created by the old excavations served as makeshift roads that we drove along at very slow speed to avoid accidents. We were without sewerage, running water or electricity – nothing was simple or easy about providing the creature comforts to our refugee inhabitants. Each sector of the camp had been assigned a letter of the alphabet as its designation, and stencilled in red on the side of each tent was this letter with numbers. The system allowed us to allocate resources and count heads in each enclave. Every sector had a representative chosen by the inhabitants to liaise with CARE staff on all matters pertaining to the running of the camp, from bread deliveries to petty grievances. This was important to ensure that the people we were there to help were active participants in decisions affecting their day-to-day existence – there is no room for a patronising attitude in such situations.

The water supply to each sector was sketchy at best, but critical to maintain, especially for the thousands of children and elderly for whom we were responsible in the 40-degree summer heat. Every sector had a hosepipe supplying a water source for the scores of families dependent on the corrugated water tanks from which gravity fed the taps. These massive tanks had been an amazing feat of engineering which our designated water and sanitation experts, the charity Oxfam, had constructed on the hill behind me. The tanks were replenished by trucks which ran into the camp twelve hours a day. If the trucks didn't run, the taps wouldn't either, so I had a special dislike of visits from perceived VIPs as water deliveries would be halted for these.

On a smaller hill adjacent to the one on which I sat, a huge yellow form sprawled like some alien spaceship. This was the French Emergency Hospital, an amazing structure that had been inflated like a gigantic children's jumping castle. Powered by diesel-operated generators, it was without a doubt a feat of modern ingenuity and the best design for a field hospital I had ever seen. Fully air-conditioned, it came with sleeping quarters for medical staff, an operating theatre, X-ray department, three wards and a pathology laboratory. As the nights could be very cold in the old quarry and the days blisteringly hot, the hospital was truly a godsend for newborn babies and surgical patients. Staffed by a mix of military doctors and nurses, and paramedic-trained fire-fighters, or *pompières*, the hospital would be with us for just 30 days, the maximum deployment allowed by the French government.

Supplementing their specialist medical care was a small outpatient clinic down on lower ground. Run by International Medical Corps (IMC) and staffed by a handful of volunteer doctors and nurses from around the world, this was the front line in most medical treatments and evaluations. Dentists Without Borders and Pharmacists Without Borders also operated between the three main camps in Macedonia – the other two were Stenkovec I and Cegrane, where I worked occasionally.

Although the UNHCR banner flew over the camp, the United Nations' presence was minimal. CARE International had been officially tasked and contracted by the UN to handle the day-to-day running of Stenkovec II, with an allocated budget for the provision of food, water, shelter and national staff drawn from the population of the camp. (This is the normal procedure in many disaster and war zones to ensure that the expertise of the different aid organisations are fully utilised.) CARE's staff slept in the camp and were responsible for all aspects of its management, and security as well. We were also in charge of the Mother and Baby Units, an expression of CARE's belief that little ones need to be protected and nurtured through tough times by a dedicated nurse educator and staff. These units, dotted around the refugee camp in specially provided tents, ensured that mothers could bathe their children, and had access to baby food, formula, potable water and disposable diapers – all essential in maintaining a disease-free environment under very harsh conditions. Women giving birth in the camp were encouraged to breastfeed for their own health and that of their babies. A special nutrition-monitoring programme was also operating to keep up the health of the many children living in this less than ideal situation.

The other agencies working within Stenkovec II and Cegrane camps were the International Committee of the Red Cross (ICRC), who undertook the mammoth task of tracing lost children and adults and reuniting families, and UNICEF, who set up shop in the relatively fresh air on this unimpressive hill. Here they ran a kindergarten, playgroup and school for the children of the camp, but still in very dusty conditions – most of the land was denuded of grass.

During daylight hours, in a caravan set up opposite the converted shipping containers that served as our camp management office, IOM (International Organisation for Migration) operated its service. Here displaced people queued for hours to apply for temporary humanitarian relocation to places all over the globe. Every agency present in the camp interfaced and worked together without rivalry – this scenario bore no resemblance to the outside worlds of Australia and the USA where humanitarian organisations routinely compete for positive publicity and the donor dollar. Emergency relief was an entirely different kettle of fish; that we all pulled together was one of the things I most enjoyed. That and the camaraderie.

The tents provided for the refugees were a hodgepodge of ex-military surplus and donor-provided shelters. It always amused me that the tents in Stenk II seemed to have been erected anywhere in odd clusters and at strange angles to each other – the wonderful and constantly good-humoured pompières and French soldiers had done most of the grunt work – while at Cegrane, German military engineers had laid out the camp with Teutonic efficiency and precision. Global Positioning Satellite beacons in hand, the Germans had striven for exactitude, and as a result their perfectly aligned canvases stretched unswervingly as far as the eye could see, housing 57,000 displaced souls on what had been a rubbish dump.

Overflowing with people from different walks of Kosovar life, time at Stenk II proved challenging. Gypsies, teachers, factory workers, farmers, musicians, college professors, housewives, shopkeepers and plumbers were forced to exist cheek by jowl in stifling conditions devoid of privacy and autonomy.

Fire was a huge and dangerous problem. Candles were prohibited inside the pitch-black tents at night, but this rule was frequently flouted. Cooking fires were another hazard. There was no central kitchen to dole out food in 'wet feedings' (the term used to describe pre-cooked meals) to the inhabitants; instead, a two-day food ration of canned fish or meat, onions, a loaf of bread and some fruit was distributed from a designated point in each sector and recorded on a ration card. There were so many fires in or near tents as a result of cooking fires getting out of control, I still can't believe no one died.

When I flip back through my diary from that time, I realise just how diverse my duties were. The team worked each day with little complaint. The one thing I detested was distributing mattresses, for they were as valuable as gold and as sought after. This job often fell to me because I spoke Bosnian and had picked up a smattering of Albanian, the

Kosovar tongue. Slabs of foam the size of a single bed, they were released according to very strict criteria. Essentially, they were reserved for pregnant women, the elderly and the very sick, although if a family had numerous children we could sometimes justify the allocation of one mattress to the entire family group. All the other refugees slept directly on the tent floor, only a groundsheet separating them from the granite beneath. Blankets were given out upon arrival – one each. No pillows were available.

I hated the power I had over the refugees' comfort; I hated that I couldn't offer them more. Most of all, I hated the clamouring and the pleading when the appointed hour for applications rolled around – the desperation shown by young men on behalf of their womenfolk overwhelmed me. They seemed to link their self-esteem as males to their ability to provide a comfortable bed for Grandma or their younger siblings. In a refugee camp, I learned, men are the ones stalked by depression and disenfranchisement.

Day after day, I would enter tent dwellings and find dozens of men lying with their faces turned to the canvas; their hopelessness was almost palpable. They had lost all they possessed materially, but worse, many of them had been unable to protect their female relatives from sexual abuse, rape or torture at the border crossings controlled by the Serbian forces. This humiliation sometimes manifested itself in the form of aggression, knife-wielding and threats. It was the one thing they could do for their abused women – stake a claim on a tent and refuse to allow interlopers a foot in the flap. Women, by the circumstances in which they found themselves, didn't have the luxury of mourning or solitude; their extended family depended on them to collect rations and water, wash clothes and care for the children and the elderly. The gender division was enormous and the responses to the trauma of displacement, violence and war were markedly different.

One of my duties was to inspect every tent in my designated sector for that day, and ascertain numbers of people and available space. Stenkovec II and Cegrane were officially transit camps, which meant many of the refugees were awaiting immigration processing and evacuation to temporary safe havens being offered by nations around the world.

The inhabitants of Stenk II could spend as little as five days with us, or as long as several weeks. Our population ebbed and flowed to such an extent that it was imperative we keep track of head counts and of the spaces becoming available in tents throughout the camp.

In any given twenty-four-hour period, six buses of fifty people each could be processed to other countries and depart the camp. At night, when the Macedonian government opened its borders – the prime hour being 1 a.m. – an enormous convoy of incoming buses would arrive at our guarded gates, escorted by NATO military or Macedonian police. A snapshot of human trauma and misery was crammed into these convoys with buses meant to carry fifty-five people practically bursting with 120 passengers. On the other side of the border crossing, in the full summer heat, the buses were loaded by the Serb paramilitary when the sun was at its highest. Then the doors were closed. If the refugees were not carrying water, then there was no way to slake their thirst.

I hadn't been prepared at all for the night of my first large arrival. Faces were squashed up hard against glass, people standing and reaching hands through the small sliding windows near the roof of the bus. Tiny children were held up to the slits for some fresh air. Condensation dripping down the glass made it obvious how stiflingly hot the buses were. The Macedonian authorities would not let us open the doors to the buses en masse – we could only process the buses one by one. I wanted to smash windows and pull everyone out, but we couldn't antagonise our hosts.

Our radios had crackled to life just before twilight, warning us that buses would be coming across the border tonight. We had heard rumours all day and I'd had the tents in A sector prepared and the people who had been in them relocated to G sector and throughout C. I was warned to get some rest, but to sleep with my clothes on. At midnight the wail of the police sirens started in the distance, and grew nearer as I pulled on my boots and reached for my miner's lamp.

As the first bus approached with its interior lights on, we could see the shocked and weary faces of the people crowded into it. We watched as one, two, three, four, five, six buses followed in the wake of the police vehicles, straight past Stenk II's gates and on to Cegrane, three more long, hot hours' drive away. Seven or eight minutes later, a police car swung through our gates followed by eight buses lumbering under the weight of too many passengers. The most immediate need was for water, and we ran up and down the length of the parked vehicles like people possessed, tripping over rocks and tufts of grass, pushing bottles of water through small window openings as the desperate cries for *vodu* – water – sounded from the souls locked inside. The outside temperature was still at least 30 degrees. My frustration was rapidly turning to tear-suppressed anger that we were forbidden to simply fling open the doors to the buses and process everyone in the cooler outdoor air.

Finally, a half-hour or more after the buses had trundled in, we were allowed to direct them around the rabbit warren of our camp to A sector, where we would release the new arrivals. I plunged cross-country, dodging guy ropes and potholes to get to the offloading area fast. The pompières were frantically resetting the arc light that ran off a car battery, and repositioning trucks to illuminate our working area by the headlights as we had no generators to provide electric light. Residents of the camp gathered to help us or in the hope of finding a lost relative or friend.

It was organised chaos, a tragedy of human suffering and shock. Finally opened, the first bus disgorged its cargo – in an explosion of dehydrated, exhausted, weeping and soiled humanity, clasping whatever was most precious in a tight grip. Moments went by before I realised that some of the stiff bundles were tiny babies swaddled in the traditional way with layers of wrapping and string. Overheated, the fragile mites were pale and glassy-eyed. Traumatised toddlers clung to their parents' legs and wailed.

Immediately, paramedics and aid workers made their way rapidly along the lines of squatting and collapsing people, trying first to assess medical requirements.

A woman in her mid-20s holding a baby began to scream. I ran to her, trying to decipher the cause of her distress. Checking the child, who appeared to be no more than a couple of months old, I realised it was barely breathing and had poor skin tone.

'Too hot,' I said to the mother as I pulled the knife from

my belt and began frantically to slice away the string and the swaddling around the child.

Sinking to the ground, I placed the baby across my legs and stripped away the last layers, including a putrid plastic shopping bag which had been serving as a nappy. It was a girl and she lay limp in my lap. Pulling off her bonnet, I saw a tuft of blonde hair.

'Come on, sweetie, take a big breath,' I urged her, as the mother wept and pulled at one of my arms.

The baby was terribly thin and covered in a heat rash. I began rubbing her limbs and body, as I yelled to a pompière-paramedic, Jean Paul, for help. Then, taking a chance, I gently blew into her mouth and nose – her pulse was barely registering. After a fraught few seconds, she took a big gasp of air that seemed to inflate her flaccid wee body, and letting out a feeble whimper, she nuzzled for food. At that moment, Jean Paul arrived by my side. Looking at my face, he put a hand on my shoulder and pronounced, '*Aucun probleme, Jacqueline, c'est OK, n'est-ce pas?*' (Is there still a problem, Jacqueline, seems it's OK now, isn't it?) and quickly moved on to a gunshot wound that had just been identified.

The mother gratefully took the tiny girl from me, and I told her in sign language and rudimentary Bosnian that it was too hot to wrap her baby. She nodded, beginning to free a breast for her daughter.

Obscenely, human dignity was reduced here to whether I could find a nappy for a baby and a shelter for them both. How could the perpetrators of this ethnic cleansing allow tiny children to lie in excreta, fight for oxygen, and be denied the right to grow up in safety, surrounded by family?

The team were flat out. So many of the new arrivals had

been sleeping rough in caves throughout the mountains, or under bushes, as they tried to get to the safety of our camp. Parents were dazed and kids exhausted; all had a haunted look in their eye, an insecurity that transcended the underlying grief, and a bone-weariness shaded with suspicion about their new surroundings.

Making my way up and down the lines of families, I continued to slit open swaddled bundles to cool down overheated and distressed infants. One baby was convulsing, and the pompières transferred it to their truck for the trip to the hospital on the hill. Then a man with a gunshot wound that was still oozing blood and pus was loaded into the truck with the baby and mother.

Group by group, the new arrivals were ushered into the enormous tents that would be their home for the next few days. Tentatively, they followed us into the darkness, where they would have to sleep like sardines against the torsos of strangers, in the most rudimentary conditions. We distributed ration packs, explained the no-candle rule and asked that people use the latrines and not relieve themselves inside the tents.

We left the refugees blinking in the dark. I could hear whimpering and moaning as we walked away. Misery, fear, grief and desperation sound the same in any language and are somehow worse in the dark.

The next night it began all over again.

An intense groan of pain, guttural and exhausted, escaped from the woman's lips. Pushing the damp fringe back off her face, I glanced at my companions. Three concerned sets of eyes caught in the light from the miner's lamp on my head.

A single arc light was set up 6 metres away, illuminating the night and the line of buses stretched out in front of us.

'*Oui*,' Jean Paul nodded to me, '*le temps pour pousser*' — it was time for the woman, just unloaded from a bus, to push.

'OK,' I said turning back to the woman who was gripping the edge of my T-shirt in a twisted bunch. Her back was propped against the tyre of the bus, and her pelvis was on a sterile pad that the pompières had placed over my waterproof jacket, to keep her from the bare ground. Looking her in the eyes, I urged her in throttled Albanian to push. Switching to Bosnian, I encouraged her, '*guranje*', adding sound effects for good measure. Slipping my right arm around her, I mimed a huge breath in and pushing down. Thank goodness her primal instincts took over. The pompières were taking care of the birthing end, but I took a quick look after she gave two enormous pushes and saw that the baby's head was beginning to crown.

'*Attendez une seconde*,' came the sharp command from Jean Paul; he wanted to avoid any tearing as the head was delivered and had to slow things down.

'*Poor marlo*,' I told her in bad Bosnian, 'slowly, wait', and breathed shallowly for her to copy.

Getting the nod once more from Jean Paul, we all urged her, in a multinational cheer squad, to push. With a guttural wail, the woman concentrated all her strength, and in one gargantuan push the baby slithered out into the waiting hands of Jean Paul.

'*C'est un garçon!*' — a boy — beamed Jean Paul with tears in his eyes. He showed the newest member of the human race to his mother, and the tiny creature let out his first protesting cry of indignation.

There was no beautifully warmed bunny rug for the babe,

no delicate clothing, no downy soft towels, just a sterile pad on which the tiny boy was laid while the pompières tied his umbilical cord and cleared his airways. As soon as Jean Paul and the others had finished, I whipped off my CARE T-shirt, turned it inside out for cleanliness, and gave it to them to swaddle the baby, blessing my luck that I had a utilitarian tank-top bra underneath. Once the boy was safely placed in his mother's waiting arms, I helped her unfasten the front of her dress and got the baby to latch a slightly lazy mouth onto her breast. Tears had welled in my eyes and were now beginning to run down my face. By this time, a stretcher had been fetched, and mother and son were transferred to the pompières' truck, to go to the French hospital where the pair would be properly checked and the placenta could be delivered. I climbed up on a tyre, hoisting myself over the edge of the truck, and kissed the woman's cheek gently.

Stepping back, I watched the tail-lights bob unevenly over the rise and then they were gone. I wiped my jacket on the grass as best I could and pulled it on over my tank-top. A few hundred refugees still had to be processed, and my job was to help get them under shelter for the night.

A couple of hours before dawn, I sank onto my sleeping bag laid out on the floor of the shipping container with as much relish for its embrace as I would have evinced for a feather bed at the Plaza Hotel. Mashing my knapsack into an acceptable repository for my head, and still fully dressed, I reached out a hand to make sure my boots were close by and shut my eyes. Around me, I knew my colleagues were equally as horizontal as me, and mostly snoring. Three of us lay shoulder to shoulder and another fellow was propped up on a row of boxes under the window. With a stifled groan, I

Paula Yates and my
dear friend and partner
in crime, Judith Curran.
Paula lit up the room
on the day we met but
her fragility was evident
as well.

At Le Dôme restaurant in Los Angeles. Me with Jackie Collins, Joanna
Poitier (wife of Sidney, second from right), David Niven Jnr and Shakira
Caine (far right). That day I wondered what my nanna would say to all this
Hollywood royalty.

Translating in East Timor whilst recruiting staff. Ten positions available and three hundred applicants. Chris 'Geeb' Allen is just visible behind me.

At Dom Bosco camp, where I was tasked with converting the burnt-out buildings into a temporary transit camp.

East Timor: we had just driven a truck convoy across a mountain range to deliver urgent food supplies and this little baby girl simply ended up in my arms – she's grinning because she's just about to pee on me!

One week before
Verity was born,
a bit of levity
was needed. This
picture was taken
by cinematographer
Peter James.

Verity at four weeks,
wearing the leopard-print
suit that Paula Yates sent.
Verity was soon to fill
up the fabric and it now
adorns her favourite teddy.

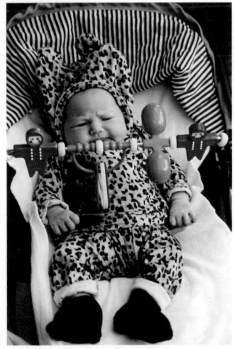

My beautiful daughter, Verity Isabelle (aged eight months). That afternoon we saw a double rainbow in our garden.

Verity, me and Bill on our wedding day.

Verity gives her baby brother, Lysander, his first bath twelve hours after his birth. She'd been practising on her dolly for this moment and has been a fiercely loving and protective big sister ever since.

Verity, Bill and Lysander, who was so chubby as a baby, and I can proudly say that, like his older siblings, it was all due to breastfeeding.

Verity's fifth birthday party and Shahirah's homecoming.

A family holiday at the foot of the Victorian snowfields. Verity, me, Shahirah and Lysander after a wonderfully fun Easter egg hunt.

The best of times with family and friends: Sally (and three of her five dogs), Shahirah, overjoyed to be around dogs again, and an equally happy Verity and Lysander.

It was quite amazing to be sandwiched between, and hugged by, Shahirah and Iddin. I seem destined to be shorter than all four children!

Lysander watches in awe as his big brother, Iddin, dives with the sharks and stingrays at the Melbourne Aquarium. Diving is one of Iddin's passions and he was so at peace in the water.

My greatest wish had been to one day introduce all my children to each other. Blessedly, that day had arrived.

prayed that my bladder would hold out for a couple of hours and promptly plunged into a deep and exhausted sleep – it had been a long seventy-two-hour stint.

When I awoke, it was to the dual reveille of a rooster crowing in the distance and the loud explosion a human fart can make in a confined space. Pulling my arm over my mouth and nose, I half-opened one eye and hazarded a guess at which one of my male colleagues had serenaded the rest of us.

As a rule, aid workers had to be genderless in terms of interaction within the framework of their own organisation. That was the thing about often being the only woman present on an emergency relief mission, it was imperative to be one of the 'boys' and not be viewed as a woman at all. Judging from the fart, I had apparently been successful, although I drew the line at competing on that playing field. I grinned to myself as the others awoke around me – to think, just ten days ago I was dining in posh London restaurants with wall-to-wall celebrities and sporting designer gear. It's amazing how quickly you can get used to the whiz of overhead air-to-surface missiles, helicopters and pit latrines!

'*Bonjour, Jacqueline,*' came the exuberant greeting, as I raised my wet head from above the bucket of water where I had been doing my early morning ablutions behind the shipping container. 'You must come to the hospital,' Jean Paul said when he arrived from the adjoining French compound. 'It is the Abanian custom: the new *maman* wants you to give the baby his name.' With a broad grin and a salute, he was gone.

And that is how it came to pass that a small Kosovar baby was named Baharuddin, in honour of my missing son, Iddin. Fortuitously, it was an appropriate name for a Muslim child and not too unusual within his culture.

Holding the precious mite, I whispered his new name into his ear and blessed him with all the love I could muster. His mother lay back on her stretcher bed and beamed, while visions of my Iddin as a tiny baby flooded into my mind.

'Stay safe, little one, and grow up safe and strong with your mum; be a good and gentle man,' I cooed to junior Baharuddin, his hours-old eyes blinking at me wisely and his face a solemn study of concentration.

Excusing myself then with a hug and a last kiss, I withdrew quickly, afraid that these tears of joy might change to grief.

Chapter 20

The Truth about Emergency Sex

id workers are a funny bunch, most of us deeply flawed or carrying some sort of chip on our shoulders that makes us want to do better. We feel compelled to work hands-on in areas rife with death, disease and distress.

Certainly aid workers are deeply committed to a better world and the resolution of human suffering – but are they holier, more noble than the average person on the street? Absolutely not.

Aid work strips away all the defence mechanisms of a person's character and leaves them naked and exposed. Human frailties are unmasked but, more importantly, tremendous human strength and depth of character come to the fore. It's possible to know exactly where you stand with another emergency relief worker within seventy-two hours. That's the time it takes for the real person to appear. Without a doubt, I know that the handful of really close friends I have made during aid assignments are the most reliable, trustworthy and dependable people I have ever met. The best of them can look at a problem and see a lateral solution in no time. Hesitation is not in their lexicon, though caution should be. In the best of them, intelligent caution combines with dogged determination. I would not hesitate to trust these people with my life, as indeed I have on several occasions.

The difficulty for most aid workers is reintegration into normal life post deployment. For weeks after getting back to Belgium or Australia, I would feel physically ill at the sight of all the food overflowing on supermarket shelves and have to quash down my contempt when witnessing the stupidity of road rage or unconscious greediness. I felt my detachment and isolation intensely after I returned, my experience more intense because it also added to my unquelled desire for Iddin and Shahirah.

Comparing notes with other aid workers on 'civilian' dinner parties they'd been invited to, I realised that we all come up with similar tales. 'Tell us what it was really like,' is the stock request. Urged at the dinner table by friends and acquaintances to describe Sudan, Bosnia, East Timor, Iraq, Afghanistan or New Orleans, a newly returned aid worker can go one of three ways.

The first, usually preferred by seasoned veterans of emergency deployments, is to provide a heavily censored vignette with a good outcome involving child/mother and clean water or medicine. One nods sagely and shrugs when someone says, 'Well, I think you are wonderful for doing that work, I don't think I could,' and changes the topic swiftly.

The second option is to tell the uncensored truth, describing tortures and rapes, the suppurating wounds and starvation. Then for good measure, relate how it felt to have a child die of measles in one's arms, or what it was like to see the eyes of a child roll back in their heads as they pass away from starvation. You can attempt to describe how inadequate words are to a woman who has lost everything, and people begin to shift in their seats. A glazed look in their eyes takes hold and silence falls over the dinner table. Someone will then make a light-hearted attempt at praise and then offer to open a new bottle of wine to cover the awkwardness. And all the while the aid worker sits with a fixed smile and seethes at the glazed eyes and realises that no one really wants to hear what it's like.

Following the lead of one International Red Cross nurse to whom nurse I spoke is the final option. She routinely lies about her profession to any casual acquaintance, becoming a secretary or a dental technician – she gets too angry at the glib remarks and the inevitable glazing of the eyes if she says what she really does.

These are hugely contentious observations to make, I know, but the honesty in no way detracts from the genuine and passionate dedication of aid workers around the globe.

The human mind and soul have their limits, and sometimes a short circuit is needed to avoid a meltdown precipitated by severe trauma and the continual witnessing of man's inhumanity to man, or the indecipherable cruelty of Mother Nature.

In emergency zones, quiet and unremarkable pairings sometimes occur. Each week, staff from different aid organisations might get together to let off steam. These are no dress-up-and-preen-to-disco-music affairs; instead a precious bottle of Baileys might be shared from tin cups outside a tent, a local café might see fifteen aid workers gather for a meal and a drink, or a small low-key party might be organised, with a few military personnel who have provided direct logistical support as guests. These get-togethers are not a prelude to an orgy or anything of that nature, and any pairings that result are distinct from the drunken snoggings seen in corners of rowdy parties the world over. The interactions I silently observed at these functions often began with a quiet and intense conversation away from the main group, usually about work problems, frustrations with head office responses, and exhaustion.

Somewhere in the midst of shop talk, the dynamics would change just a little – suddenly the pair would both feel safe and utterly devoid of bullshit. Two oddly genderless creatures needing respite devoid of ego and games.

Who better to comprehend the human suffering and barbarity you have witnessed and waded into that day, but another aid worker? Where else could you find another person who could see the black-humoured side of unwittingly squelching through human remains? How else to obliterate those images and the memory of the sounds another human being makes as they plunge into the bloody abyss of their tragedy?

Rob and I had met at a United Nations cocktail party to honour a visiting celebrity to Macedonia. We'd been given the dubious honour of attending as the representatives of our respective aid agencies and were each mindful of the politics involved. It was also a fascinating chance to see how the flashy side of international aid carried on in a conflict zone when a VIP comes to town; the incongruity of the celebrity 'meet and greet'. An enormous part of me detested these kind of events; I understood them to be a necessary part of my job, but I inwardly railed because I knew the people inhabiting our camps wouldn't recognise me gussied up and sipping chilled wine only a few kilometres down the road from their shattered subsistence.

For me, this evening had been the third soirée in as many days for the same VIP. After my 5 a.m. start and a day working amidst the sweltering heat of a refugee camp, traipsing up and down the dusty tracks in temperatures topping 103 degrees, I had been dirt-caked 20 minutes before the scheduled start of the reception. I'd just managed to snatch time to peel off my filthy combat boots and grubby CARE T-shirt and cargo pants, hurl myself under the shower at my billet in town, the Roza Diplomatik, and wriggle into the one dress I'd had the foresight to cram into my backpack along with a pair of stiletto-heel Gucci sandals. Adding a dab of lip gloss, a slash of eyeliner and mascara in the back of the cab on the way to downtown Skopje, I shook my hair from its plait and walked into the cool of the air-conditioned building. The last thing I felt like doing was making small talk – I'd had a shit of an afternoon trying to find a way of moving an elderly woman around the camp to the latrines without a proper wheelchair. Topping that off, apparently I needed to speak to some guy at the other camp, Stenkovec I, about her predicament, but no one had his mobile number or radio call sign.

Realising I was the last to arrive, and having the bad luck to walk in right smack in the middle of what would prove to be a tedious and long-winded speech, I scouted the room for a familiar face. Not a single one, bar the UN Country

Director and the celebrity. Resigning myself to a dismal and dutiful evening, I caught sight of a very tall and lean bald man on the other side of the room who seemed to be finding all the wordy sentiments being expressed as amusing as I did. Dressed in a pale-blue polo shirt and jeans and aged somewhere in his mid-30s, he leaned against a pillar and glanced around the space at regular intervals. Eventually we made eye contact and exchanged wry smiles.

Later, mercifully released from our listening posts, we found ourselves in a group who were discussing the latest sanitation problems at our respective refugee camps. I began relating my difficulties meeting the needs of the elderly lady, and adding a few expletives about the elusive 'fixer' at the neighbouring camp being un-contactable. I trailed into silence when I noticed that Rob had broken into a wide grin.

'Do you think all this is funny?' I challenged him.

'No,' he replied, 'it's just that I'm the arsehole you're cursing.'

Sheepishly I apologised, feeling about 2 feet tall, but he seemed to think it was hilarious.

Looking round the room, I realised that the crowd was thinning and my feet were aching – my stomach was also growling furiously and very audibly. One rumble obviously reached Rob's ears, and he guffawed and asked me if I wanted to grab a bite to eat. Accepting thankfully, we exited the building and I climbed aboard his vehicle, the ubiquitous aid worker transport, a white four-wheel drive.

Minutes later we arrived at a local café, apparently known for its fresh Greek salads and local roast meat dishes. Over dinner, which thankfully arrived swiftly, we chatted about conditions in the camps and the state of our charges in our respective domains. The meal and the conversation went down easily, we used the shorthand peculiar to relief workers around the traps and kept away from the gritty, less palatable topics of the job stresses, our emotional states and the inevitable anger and despair that so many of our ilk carry around just beneath the surface.

Twilight was still to fall as we arrived back at my hotel. Opting for a drink in the open-air courtyard downstairs, we talked some more and when they closed the kitchen we eventually found ourselves upstairs in my room as night fell. It was not love at first sight, or even lust. There was no huge frisson of attraction, it was what it was – comfort and escape in a tumultuous world of crappy war and tragic human consequences – a night off – no thoughts of riding off into the sunset together, no complications, or romance, or expectations. And when it was over, when we'd sweated and laughed together, we made the first move towards a friendship and a mild curiosity about each other. This, as far as I was concerned, was the minefield to navigate, and the item of conversation I was so overly prepared for as to seem too pat and glib. I dreaded trying to explain my background.

'So, what number war is this for you?' I ventured with a pre-emptive strike.

'Err, let's see,' he began, as he reeled off some locales. 'Bosnia, Somalia, Northern Ireland and a couple of places I can't discuss, and here. How about you?'

Pulling myself up on one elbow and tugging the sheet higher, I countered with my list. 'Bosnia just post-war, dabbled in Rwanda and here, Macedonia. Before that, East and South Africa in straight development aid.'

Out of the corner of my eye I noticed Rob shoot a quick look at my CARE International identity card and security name badge which lay on the nightstand.

'So Jack, what's with the alternative name on the official ID?' he quizzed me. 'I know that you're CARE's ambassador, but all the talk tonight was about your work in the field. The title ambassador and now this,' he said jerking his head at the IDs, 'don't exactly scream dirty hands, luv,' he ventured in his southern English accent.

Inwardly I cringed, feeling defensive and exposed as I always did when I had to talk about my past and the reality of my life and its complications. How to pot a history for a lover one hardly knows, and who doesn't have the foggiest about one's background? Should one rise from the bed, wrap oneself in a sheet and grandly declare, 'Once I was a princess, and there aren't a lot of jobs around for us fallen ones.' Or should I spill my soul by ripping open my carefully constructed facade and explain that I had once married into an Islamic royal family as a teenage bride and many years after the marriage was dissolved, my former husband, the Prince, abducted both my children in a fit of revenge and cultivated religious fervour. Either way, each of these solutions would leave my emotional composure the worse for wear and my coping mechanisms in tatters.

Leaning over the edge of the bed, I mentally steeled myself as I fished an oversized T-shirt off a pile near my backpack and pulled it over my head. Turning to Rob who was leaning back against the headboard with his hands behind his head, I began to speak. 'Better you hear this from me rather than from the gossip that'll eventually start floating around the aid workers network.'

I folded myself into a cross-legged position facing him on the bed and continued, my arms crossed over my chest defensively.

'On the 9th of July, 1992, my two children, Iddin and Shah, were kidnapped and I haven't seen or spoken to them since – that's six years, ten months and a couple of days.' Before Rob could form a question I was off, outlining all that had passed and all I had lost. I could hear myself talking rapidly and realised that I was like a battleship by this point, steaming ahead at full speed and too raw to draw a breath or pause for comment for fear I ran aground.

'Since the day they were kidnapped by my ex-husband, Bahrin, that's the abbreviated version of his name, I haven't been allowed to see or speak to Shah and Iddin at all – zilch, nada. It all made international headlines at the time, and since. The whole battle was pretty ugly and I was gutted – still am actually, life just fell apart, and if I'm honest, that's a bit of why I'm here. Anyway, I've also written a book about what happened, which has just come out in London, so I schizophrenically arrived here fresh from a huge publicity tour and an international conference.'

Taking a deep breath, I shot my companion a quick look and added, 'CARE appointed me as their Special Ambassador, but only on the criteria I insisted upon. So there you have it, a precised life story.'

Expelling a huge breath of air, Rob opened his mouth, 'Well, bugger me – that makes some of the things I've heard in my travels sound like a walk in the park. My turn then. I'm ex-SAS, did a long deployment in Bosnia before I left the regiment – stuffed up a bit and just got tired of being on the armed side of the fence, so here I am, heading up an NGO mission in a war zone. My mob are here with minimal funding to try and help the refugees who fall through the cracks . . . the disabled, intellectually and physically, as well as the elderly.'

With a flip of his eyebrow he added, 'S'pose that's why I came up in the conversation when you needed a wheelchair for the old lady at your camp. I've got funding for that, and over at Stenk I we've set up a corner of the camp to deal with "special needs" people – you know, the ones at risk and with no families to look after them.'

Scratching his pate, he queried gingerly, 'So just how well known are you in the UK?'

'Enough to have the London *Times* journo, Danny McGrory, who's posted here want to speak to me while I'm about, and NBC from the US, etc.,' I answered as I saw him wince.

'Hhmmm, great, look, I'm not married or anything, I'm single so there's no worry there, but I loath the tabloid press. I can just see the headline now . . . "The Princess and the Paratrooper".'

I laughed tightly and shrugged. What else could I do? He was right – on a slow news day, a story like that could possibly get up. It would also take the focus off the work CARE was doing in Macedonia and the rest of the Balkans. To risk a headline for something that wasn't even yet defined as a full friendship, let alone a proper love affair, was just unnecessary, and frankly would use up too much energy.

'Hey, I make a bloody good friend and colleague,' I said as I switched off the light. 'Night.'

'Yeah, you too, Jack.'

We saw each other through work as he moved between

my camp and his, Stenkovec I, a couple of miles down the road. Sometimes I would hitch a lift to town, or work with him, and we occasionally ate together. Sleeping and sex were just extensions of deep conversations. In the desolation of this place, tenderness was a huge factor in our friendship. Both of us had to be so hard and so focused in our duties that physical and emotional letting go when we were in each other's company often brought us to tears at the strangest times.

We guarded our friendship fiercely, keeping it private and casual when around others. We were watchful against media interest, too.

As the weeks went on, I came to love Rob as a friend with whom I occasionally had sex – or more often than not, someone with whom I wept and slept minus any sexual contact. It was about trust and respite, being emotionally naked and frank together in a very lonely situation. Even now, from a distance and over thousands of miles, we speak by email every so often and we have shared the happiness of our subsequent marriages, and joy in our respective children with goodwill. As the song goes, 'but most of all when snowflakes fall I wish you well'.

Flirtation for food was a whole different kettle of fish and was enjoyed with a huge sense of humour by all involved.

One day as evening was approaching, there was still no sign of the car from town which brought our lunch – bread, cheese, fruit and salami. Our stomachs were rumbling, and we would be on duty till late that night. Nearby, the immense storehouse was crammed with rations, but it was out of the question that we would touch food meant for refugees. So we munched on a stash of melted Mars Bars that a donor had dispatched from London as a treat for us, and chugged water to quiet our hunger.

Around us, the camp cooking fires were lit, and from the nearby French encampment came laughter and appetising aromas.

Rummaging in my backpack, I withdrew two packets of dehydrated miso soup that I prudently carried with me. Waving them in front of the four other CARE team members, I told them I had an idea.

Shaking my hair free of its long plait, I pulled out my small bottle of perfume, applied a smudge of lip gloss and announced I was heading off to the French field kitchen to forage and beg.

'Go get 'em, Jack,' was my colleague Michael's mirthful reaction as I began my walk.

Along with the wonder of the inflatable hospital, the French had brought with them a fully equipped kitchen to cater for their entire contingent. With a cast-iron stove and oven, pantry, wine store and proper cutlery and plates, I'd never seen anything like it before or since in the world of humanitarian relief. The mess tent was filled with a long dining table that could accommodate thirty, and there was a fridge and freezer in the annexe. Trust the French to bring the creature comforts of good food and wine into a war zone!

Fluffing out my hair before rounding the corner, I entered the camp to joking wolf whistles and greetings. Taking the bull by the horn, I approached the captain and put my request. Could they spare a couple of eggs, I asked, fluttering my eyelashes exaggeratedly and murdering the French language. '*Certainment*,' was the beaming reply, but surely I could stay and eat with the French contingent and share a glass of *vin rouge*? I would be the welcome rose among the thorns, they laughed good-naturedly as they crowded around me while I tried very hard to avert my eyes from the torsos of the pompières emerging from the shower block.

No, I thanked them, the rest of the CARE people were hungry, and I had to share with them.

Graciously handing over three eggs to add to my soup mixture, the captain insisted that all the CARE team return the next evening to share a properly cooked meal and a good bottle of wine. With a laugh I played up to the invitation and the spirit in which it was offered and excused myself.

As we slurped up our soup and bread, the rest of the team agreed that it had been worth the spray of perfume. Hunching over in the light of a single candle as night fell, we would have been a comical sight: we were all leaning forward in an attempt to hear the music from a pair of tiny earphones attached to a Discman and resting on top of an empty drink bottle. Small luxuries meant so much in the middle of nowhere.

The time had come again. I must use the latrine in the CARE compound. I had learned to value my bathroom at my billet extravagantly, and this was a moment I always dreaded. So putrid was the facility that I would hold on for hours longer than was physically good for my bladder!

Approaching the building, I undid my belt and drew a small bottle of Diorissimo from my pocket and sprayed myself liberally. Taking a huge intake of air before lifting the latch and stepping into the cubicle, I tried not to look down, and was able to hold my breath for the entire procedure.

Emerging with comically bursting lungs, I heard my name called. A CARE worker was approaching with a delivery man proffering a huge beribboned bouquet of carnations. Another utterly surreal moment! I'd already had enough of these off-kilter episodes that day, as a distraught and barely coherent Paula had managed to track me down on my mobile phone.

Handing the bouquet to me with a slight bow, he departed in a government car. This was the second bouquet of flowers I had received that week – in the middle of a refugee camp!

Attached to the flowers was an admiring note from Toni Popovski, the Macedonian Environment and Urban Planning Minister. It was all getting too much. He had already turned up unannounced for a tour around the camp – but at least that had given me the opportunity to ask for more water trucks and an extension of Cegrane camp into the nearby forest.

I had even begun to suspect that the minister was keeping tabs on my movements. One evening, when I was just about to throw myself into the shower at the hotel, the front desk telephoned and announced he had arrived to see me. I met him in the courtyard and spent an awkward half-hour with him, sipping the local liqueur, slivovitz, before pleading exhaustion.

Another time, when a few of us were sharing a meal at a local restaurant, he suddenly popped out of nowhere and asked if I cared to go for a drive to see the ancient parts of town. When I demurred, he promptly sat at another table and penned an amorous note to me, and had a waiter bring it over.

Good relations with a host government were one thing, having a Cabinet minister as a suitor was quite another! I ended up phoning Antony Robbins, my brilliant and helpful minder in the London CARE office, for instructions. All I can say is that the conversation Antony and I had sent me into fits of hysterical laughter and helped not one iota! Of course Minister Popovski had been immensely helpful, and as Special Ambassador I had been taken by him to meet both the Prime Minister and the Macedonian President, but this was a delicate situation I wanted to exit from gracefully.

Now, heaving a sigh of bewilderment, I resolved to make the best of the situation. Gathering all the empty plastic water bottles I could find, I drove up to the hospital on the hill. Dividing the carnations (not my favourite flower at the best of times), I made up small arrangements for all the female patients in the hospital. The French medicos looked at me as though I was slightly demented, but I reasoned that women the world over deserve flowers for having a baby or surviving surgery, and especially in the middle of a refugee camp, far from home.

Chapter 21

Bread, not Circuses

An uglier form of unwanted male attention can be found anywhere. But this time it was provided by a new member of my own organisation.

He was one of those utterly dysfunctional, weird aid workers that you sometimes encounter, a war-zone junkie, and he seemed to have decided that his mission was to take a former princess down a peg or two.

His first stunt was to make sure there was no vehicle available late one night to take me from a café where all the CARE staff had been eating that night in a nearby town to the house CARE had rented for staff in Cegrane township, forcing me to walk 2 miles alone on the back roads of rural Macedonia with only a miner's lamp to light my way.

'Bastard,' I muttered under my breath as I walked along the rutted track with my knife open in my hand. But worse was to come.

After a couple of weeks, during which he made it very difficult for me to function in the camp, I found myself alone with this man in the back room of the Cegrane site office, where I had been sorting through boxes. As I straightened up, my back against the wall, he placed his hands either side of my shoulders and began to speak.

'So, if I had a castle, would you shag me?' he leered, his breath hot against my face.

'Not bloody likely!' I retorted.

'You jumped-up bitch,' he hissed as he tried to grope my breast and bring his mouth down onto mine.

Fortunately, Rob had taught me a few self-defence tactics earlier in the week, and I can confidently say that I caused my unpleasant co-worker a significant degree of discomfort. I doubted he would attempt to bother any woman over the following few days or want any sort of 'emergency sex'. Not all aid workers are saints, and occasionally you can come across an utter bastard.

The celebrity visit to an emergency relief zone is a double-edged sword. On one hand, it has the potential to throw a spotlight on tragic circumstances, bringing attention to desperate situations and fuelling the public's financial response. On the other hand, relief workers stationed in conflict and disaster zones often view the intrusion of a celebrity and trailing media pack as a necessary evil they have been directed by head office to facilitate, and they may quietly resent the disruption to the finely calibrated daily routine of the camp.

And disruptive these visits are. During my time in Macedonia, a circus of celebrities came to town: Richard Gere, Bianca Jagger, Hillary Rodham Clinton, Vanessa

Redgrave, Roger Moore, the German Foreign Minister and the Dutch Prime Minister and his wife, to name but a few, all on fact-finding trips, and all, I am sure, genuinely concerned by the human suffering they observed.

But whenever a celebrity pays a lightning-fast visit to a refugee camp, at least three aid workers attached to the charity with which the celebrity is affiliated must swing off normal duties to act as ushers, answer queries and generally help wrangle the celebrity's entourage, photographers and other hangers-on. With most camps chronically short-staffed, the disruption to normal schedules is huge, and many daily duties in the camp go out the window.

When Hillary Rodham Clinton visited Stenkovec I camp, for example, water and bread deliveries were suspended for the day, for security reasons, and some residents simply didn't get fed. Many of the vital services in the camp ground to a halt as secret service agents swarmed through the old quarry and cleared an area, specially sanitised for Hillary's viewing. I don't believe she got a realistic view of the camp at all. It was hardly her fault that the security and media requirements were so disruptive, and, of course, the political influence Hillary could wield was important. But I often wondered whether VIPs knew what being deprived of bread for a day did to a refugee family with an already tenuous quality of life, would they still be as determined to observe the woes of humanity at close quarters?

Certainly the movers and shakers of the world, the decision-makers who hold the purse strings, should see first hand the suffering of others and carry those images and the pungent smells of misery with them as they make determinations on life-and-death issues. But surely it's unnecessary for actors and models to have the same level of access for what is often a glorified photo opportunity.

If the celebrity arrived without fanfare three days before the media phalanx – and without a publicist, bodyguard or entourage – to unpack aid shipments, distribute food rations and live alongside the relief workers . . . if they were exposed to 72 hours of reality before fronting a media conference – I wonder how many would opt to send money instead?

Cegrane camp held 57,000 displaced and emotionally shattered people; a rubbish dump converted to a refugee camp, its white granite tiers cut into a steep hillside now bore row after row after row of barely weatherproof tents, as far as the eye could see.

Before the Dutch Prime Minister, Mr Wim Kok, came to Cegrane, workers of various aid organisations ran around trying to clean up the camp and briefing all and sundry on proper behaviour. Watching everyone buzzing around like big blowflies, worrying about their T-shirts being stained, made me incredibly pissed off. Medical treatments slowed to a snail's pace, while the putrid pit latrines were cordoned off from the areas designated fit for viewing by the Prime Minister. They were deemed too filthy for his sensibilities.

On the day, the official welcoming party stood in an orderly line to greet the PM, who had just inspected the medical clinic and some tidied-up tents. Standing there as CARE's Special Ambassador, I felt rather grubby: a sudden downpour earlier in the morning had quickly begun to flood a row of tents and I'd had to dig out an overflowing drainage ditch with my hands and the lid of a tin can. Now, dried mud stained my clothing, although I had done the best I could to wash my hands.

When he reached me in the line, the Prime Minister checked that I was actually the CARE Ambassador, then called to his wife, Rita, to join us. By coincidence, she had just finished reading my book in Dutch. We made chit-chat about the work in the camps and the conditions – until the devil in me took hold.

Catching Mr Kok's eye, I boldly asked whether he and his wife would like to see the real refugee camp.

'Absolutely,' he replied emphatically, and to the horror of their entourage, Mr and Mrs Kok followed me as I cut through the cordoned-off area and steered them in the direction of the communal latrines, a few hundred metres away.

As we got closer, the stench was almost overpowering and I explained that each block of five latrines accommodated the needs of almost 2,000 people. With no flushing mechanisms, the latrines were large holes in the ground surrounded by wooden duckboards. There were no showers in the entire camp, I told the stunned couple.

Walking away, we moved to a row of tents that through their open flaps revealed humans at their lowest ebb – their faces defensive or blank, distressed and humiliated by the state to which they had been reduced. The tents were designed to hold six people but each accommodated twenty desperate souls.

Mrs Kok stopped in her tracks and turned to me.

'You know, after the war, when I was a child, I was a refugee,' she confided with tears in her eyes. 'What do you need from us, how can we help?'

'Well, we desperately need the mattresses and funds the government of the Netherlands has pledged to us,' I told her.

'Not in a month, but now. The granite is too hard for the sick and young to sleep on.'

'Wim,' she said, turning to her husband, 'it has to be done.'

The Prime Minister looked me in the eye and took my hand. 'I promise you that I will see what can be done quickly,' he said, and with that his entourage was upon us.

A lot of glares were directed at me from some UNHCR people, but they didn't dare utter a word of rebuke. It was one of those out-of-kilter moments when being a fallen princess really paid off and boundaries of etiquette were blurred for a good cause.

Twenty-four hours later the Dutch money was in the bank, and the foam mattresses arrived forty-eight hours after that.

Driving around Stenk II in the battered old blue utility truck we used to carry refugees and supplies around the camp, I would pull over if I had a few minutes up my sleeve. Time for some fun.

Over the past few weeks the children and their parents had become used to me jumping from the truck and starting up a game in the handiest dusty clearing. Often as I was driving around in the middle of a task, children would run beside the truck and beg me to stop and play. They knew the drill by now.

'Kangaroo, kangaroo,' they shouted excitedly as they hooked into a long conga line behind me and I sang 'Skippy the Bush Kangaroo' at the top of my lungs. 'Hokey Pokey' came next, then 'Kookaburra Sits in the Old Gum Tree' – which ended with my ear-splitting rendition of the mad

Aussie bird's call, much to the delight of the adults looking on. I didn't give two hoots if I looked foolish; the children loved a game and I loved watching their faces split with laughter.

Smiles and laughter were such rare commodities in the terrain in which these children were marooned. They needed to have fun; I didn't need my dignity. And every time I made a solemn little face crack into a grin, I blessed my own children and hoped that someone was making them laugh in their captivity. I saw Iddin and Shahirah reflected in every small face that looked up at mine, and longed for them more than ever. For now, the children of the camps were the closest I could come to being with my own children.

One morning, the renowned British photographer Tom Stoddart arrived in our camp and asked if he could photograph the doings of the day. Even though it was part of my job to shepherd the media around Stenk II, I was heartily sick of unscheduled film crews traipsing through the camps and getting in our way, often with little respect for the human tragedy going on around them. On guard, I watched him carefully as he followed aid workers around on their regular tasks. I was surprised to see him first obtain the permission of a chosen subject before he took any photographs. It was a refreshing change, as so many members of the fourth estate came in, shot their footage and departed as if they'd been to observe animals in a zoo. Tom, though, talked to everyone, squatting on his haunches in the dirt, and giving some dignity to people living in very undignified circumstances. This was a man to trust, and admire too.

Tom and I shared transport if our destinations were the same. He seemed to avoid the bulk of the hungry media pack and instead wandered around on his own, trying to discover the human spirit of his subjects. The photograph that appears on the back cover of this book was taken by Tom. Without good photo-journalism that respects the subject matter, so many moments of social injustice, violence and need would go unrecorded and the world would remain in ignorance. One of Tom's photos, in my opinion, was worth more than the visits of a thousand celebrities.

Kushtrim, a slim young boy aged twelve, was our youngest Kosovar volunteer. A pensive and gentle boy, he had brought his elderly grandmother into Stenkovec II on wheelbarrow, hauling her over mountainous terrain to reach us. They were the only ones to have survived the brutal slaughter of their entire family and had been forced to hide beneath the bodies of the dead for two days before escaping into Macedonia. If ever an adolescent had a justifiable reason to become taciturn and sullen with an enormous chip on his shoulder, it was Kushtrim. Instead, he had decided he was my protector and had taken to following me around the camp as I worked.

Someone had reported a 'mad' couple and some 'feral' kids in F sector, and I was sent to investigate. With Kushtrim in tow, I found a man in a catatonic state lying in a pool of urine and his wife, who was probably schizophrenic, defecating in the tent they shared with other people. Their three-year-old daughter was filthy and hungry and was scavenging food from other refugees. The woman seemed oblivious to the barely breathing baby lying on the bedding

241

beside its father. Other refugees said the mother hadn't fed the baby for three days at least. According to passers-by, the couple usually ran a newspaper kiosk in Pristina. Upon arrival, they had slipped through the net at assessment time and were now without the medications they normally took to keep their mental illness in abeyance.

I had to make a rapid decision. Snatching up the non-responsive baby and running to the truck, I handed the flaccid baby to Kushtrim and drove towards the French hospital, but it was too late – it had already been deflated and packed up ready for departure. I diverted our vehicle to the clinic on the lower level and was halfway there when looking up at me with petrified eyes, Kushtrim told me the baby wasn't breathing. I pulled over and began to give the baby CPR on the front seat as Kushtrim tried to help. Blessedly the little one took a small breath and we drove on to the clinic. Once there, the International Medical Corps doctor from California set up a drip for the baby boy and I fed him a bottle of paediatric rehydration as Kushtrim hovered close by. Under the circumstances, the doctor said he could only keep the baby overnight as a favour to me. The small child must return to his parents in the morning. There was nothing more I could do other than arrange a medical visit for the baby's parents and extract a promise from the International Committee of the Red Cross (ICRC) to find medications for them. I knew that without help for the sick parents, the baby would probably die. Just another day in the camps.

A couple had stumbled off a bus into our camp, the husband barely supporting his wife's weight in his own distress and grief. Their two little girls had been separated from them at the border crossing in the mêlée caused by aggressive para-military guards. The parents had protested violently, to no avail. The mother was so severely dehydrated it was nearly impossible to find a vein in which to insert an IV drip. She was almost speechless with worry and shock. I had to bite down on the inside of my cheek so as not to cry with her as I could so easily understand her physical and mental anguish.

Four days passed with no word about the children. I knew the parents' pain: I was looking into my own reflection 10,000 miles from home and seven years on from Shah and Iddin's disappearance.

With one of the Polaroid cameras, I headed to the medical tent where the mother was still being treated. I took three shots of the parents, and organised for Tom to drop them off at the ICRC tracing centres at Cegrane and Stenk I.

Two days later, two little girls at Cegrane, just three and four years old, pointed to their mum and dad's picture — success!

The next day, with tears all around, the family was reunited. I felt relief so sharp my sternum seemed split. I only wished I could conjure up more happy endings.

Chapter 22

The Fine Line Between
Pleasure and Pain

I left Macedonia in June 1999, just as an official ceasefire
took place in Kosovo. I felt ambivalent about returning
to Paris and London – the *real* world was where I had
been working. I had commitments on behalf of CARE to
attend to, but it didn't make my departure any easier, or the
goodbyes any less distressing. I had wanted to remain and
work on the repatriation of refugees; I wanted so much to
see Pristina, the Kosovar capital, and help put the homes of
some of my new friends back together. But I was needed for
fundraising and publicity duties, and knew that if I stayed in
the camps, I would be dangerously close to burning out. I
was sick to my stomach with worry about some of the kids
in the camps whose parents had been killed and who now
found themselves in charge of siblings and elderly relatives at
the tender age of twelve or thirteen. Kushtrim was of
particular concern, but I made arrangements with another
family for him and his grandmother to travel on their tractor
when the time came to go home.

Arriving back in Melbourne in July, it took only three days before the nightmares about Iddin and Shah kicked in. It seemed that the familiar surroundings precipitated their return to my subconscious. Nights were no longer a time of rest – I came to believe I slept better in a war zone than at home.

Awakened at night by what sounded like the children's voices calling for me, I would have to get out of bed and look around the house. I knew that it was just some kind of trick that my nightmares played on me, but the longing for Iddin and Shahirah that surged through my body, the ache I felt in my womb, told me that the bond between them and me wasn't broken.

Like Pavlov's dog, I jumped when an email pinged into my box. Could it be true or another hoax? It was from Iddin, the heading told me. But it was an Iddin who didn't seem familiar with any private family history. I could explain that away to myself though, in my desperation to believe my children might be trying to contact me – after so many years, perhaps the children had only hazy memories of what life had been like at home in Melbourne. I held with all my stubbornness to the kernel of hope that pushed its way to the surface even though my rational side told me not to wish for the impossible. I felt physically sick as my head and heart slugged it out for ascendancy.

Every time I did some media in Australia – as I did when I came back from Macedonia – fresh interest would be sparked in my family's case. Either a junior reporter would decide to do something new on the abduction of my children, approaching the 'tragic mother' like a loyal friend; or a twisted stranger would pretend to be one of my children contacting me via the Internet.

Back home, going through the motions, I replied to the latest 'Iddin' as guardedly as always, asking a few questions – and then spending days compulsively wondering and waiting for a reply.

Four days passed before I heard anything, and then 'Iddin' implored me to 'get us out of here. Hire some guns and muscle and rescue us'. The hoaxer then gave themselves away: 'You asked me if I remembered Granddad – yeah, of course, really worried to hear that he isn't the best. Get me and Shariah home so we can hug him. Just get us home. Love from your son Iddin.'

The children's grandfather had died before they were born – I was only fourteen when my father died in Singapore from throat and nose cancer. And Shahirah's name was misspelt.

There was no way for me to tell if this was a journalist, or a kid hoping for money. A story about me contemplating an armed retrieval of my children would make a good headline. But I had neither the time nor the inclination to allow this sicko any more of my attention. Move on and regroup had to be my attitude or I'd never survive.

One thing never changed, though: the concept of what, and who my children were – precious rare gifts, individual spirits whom I loved with all my heart and soul. I hoped and prayed that one day they would find their way home to me.

Chapter 23
A Crocodile and a Bullet

With an eerie green glow the television screen showed a baby being tossed by a frantic mother over high barbed wire, and by sheer luck falling into the arms of a UN official. Eyes, terrified and pleading, shone in the night-vision lens of network video cameras – the sheer terror of the East Timorese people. All the while, gunshots and frantic screams came from off-camera.

Friends from around Australia began to telephone me, each distressed by what they had seen on television, and incensed that this violence was unfolding on our doorstep, just two hours' flight from Darwin in Australia's north.

Next day on talkback radio farmers called in, teachers, truckers, elderly veterans, teenagers – oddly aligned in their reactions, regardless of age, political persuasion or economic position: 'not on our bloody watch, not at our back door, we have to stop this'.

The unfettered violence the world was witnessing via satellite broadcast had come about as a result of a ground-breaking plebiscite coordinated by the UN on 30 August 1999 and designed to allow East Timor's people the right to call for independence and autonomy from Indonesia if carried by the majority vote. The Indonesian President of the day, Mr Habibie, had pledged that his government would abide by the results of the vote with good grace. Even though Indonesia had invaded the former Portuguese colony of East Timor when the Portuguese withdrew in 1975 after more than 300 years of colonisation.

During the twenty-five year period of Indonesian dominance in East Timor, a virtual terror had reigned – people disappeared for speaking out against the occupiers, and an active resistance movement sprang up to combat the oppression of democracy. The resistance lived in the hills and were sustained by a network of brave villagers who passed food and communications to the fighters in the jungle.

The Indonesian language had been installed for all day-to-day administrative and educational dealings (whereas before, Portuguese and Tetum had been the lingua franca), and a forced migration policy was undertaken by Indonesia to eliminate unruly and uncooperative local elements and to build up an ethnic Indonesian population in this predominantly Catholic territory.

By 4 September 1999, when the then Secretary General of the UN, Kofi Annan, declared that a resounding 75 per cent of the Timorese population had voted for their right to be self-determining and free of Indonesian rule, anarchy and chaos had broken out across the territory. Fuelled mainly by pro-Jakarta militia and with the suspected cooperation of the Indonesian military, East Timor's gun-toting, machete-wielding thuggery was in a state of vengeful aggression and violent dissent. One-sided rioting prevailed, armed vigilante militia roamed the streets unchecked by the Indonesian authorities, pro-independence supporters were being abducted and probably murdered, and the towns torched.

Australian-based aid organisations, including CARE, began to plan for a relief effort, if and when the opportunity arose.

A full-scale evacuation from Timor to Darwin of all UN officials and many Timorese fearful for their lives was organised by the Australian Defence Force. A huge tented city sprang up and local motels and caravan parks were overflowing with refugees; scores of humanitarian relief workers flocked to the northern capital to assist the displaced and traumatised.

Australians had a very close rapport with the people of East Timor, one that had endured since the Second World War when East Timorese freedom fighters had assisted Australian and Allied troops against a Japanese invasion, at great cost to themselves and their families. Later, in 1975, a number of Australian-based journalists who'd been attempting to report the invasion and occupation of East Timor by Indonesian troops, following the withdrawal of the colonial ruler, Portugal, were slaughtered by Indonesian forces in a small town called Balibo. And a considerable number of East Timorese, vocal against the Indonesian annexure of East Timor, had settled in Australia and were known and respected in our country. Now tens of thousands of Australians took to the streets to demand that our government take action, to restore order and bring humanitarian aid to our tiny neighbour.

Disembarking in Dili, the tropical heat washed over me, taking my breath away. Sweat and humidity drenched me in seconds. It was day eight of INTERFET, the UN-sanctioned peacekeeping 'International Force in East Timor'. A couple of goats and a horse wandered across the tarmac. For a moment I had a flashback to my time living in Malaysia, and I wondered how Shah and Iddin were coping in the intense and constant heat.

Only one building in the whole of the city had glass remaining in the windows – the residence of the ousted Indonesian Governor. Every other piece of glass had been shattered by the retreating Indonesian forces and the sewers filled with tar and cement to wreak maximum havoc. Power stations were destroyed, schools demolished and water supplies poisoned. The city was reduced to burned-out buildings, caved-in roofs, and walls daubed with obscenities directed at INTERFET and Australians. Even the crops had been torched in the mayhem of revenge.

At CARE's offices in Darwin, Canberra and Melbourne, we had planned and stocked up, for distribution of humanitarian relief aid and reconstruction materials. Now we passed INTERFET checkpoints at regular intervals, and Australian soldiers on foot patrol with weapons cradled in their arms.

Chicane roadblocks secured the entrance to the central city area, the most secure point in the capital. Identity checks were carried out every few hundred metres by diligent Gurkha soldiers, part of the daily influx of international forces that would eventually include soldiers from twenty-two nations. The Gurkhas' fierce reputation was legendary, and they had secured many of the positions nearest to the remaining contingents of Indonesian military, who had been confined to barracks until their final, and hopefully peaceful, evacuation.

Bored and hostile, a number of Indonesian troops had carried a tiered set of bleachers to the perimeter fence of their barracks. Seated with their red berets firmly affixed to their heads, they were making a big show of sharpening large combat knives as we drove by and they mimed dragging the blades across their throats. It was good to know they were now outnumbered by our protectors, and that at least three checkpoints would have to be crossed before they could reach the UN compound.

Occupying four classrooms in the burned-out shell of a high school next door to the UN compound, CARE's Dili base was mostly roofless and carpeted in black ash and filth from the violent rampages that had taken place within its walls. Smashed furniture stood in sad groupings around the perimeter. There was no electricity or running water. Six dome tents had been erected in one of the classrooms, with camp stretchers serving as beds, two to a dome. The tents were a sensible idea as the zippered mosquito netting kept the worst of the bugs out at night. The tropical heat was still and close even after sundown, when small gecko lizards crawled above our heads on the other side of the netting, throwing elongated shadows in the moonlight. Every morning we awoke with a fine dust covering our possessions and it would be six weeks before we were told by an ashen-faced INTERFET Health and Safety Officer that we had been sleeping beneath unstable blue asbestos exposed by the trashing of the building and would need to move.

Cooking facilities were sketchy: a single-burner kerosene stove and a 44-gallon drum. A plastic basin for washing plates and a cupboard full of tuna, sardines, crackers and locally purchased rice. After dark we used torches and a lantern or two, but as the daytime temperatures and the conditions under which we were distributing food would be harsh, most of us turned into pumpkins well before nine. We had to be up just after dawn.

One night, with the miner's torch on my head, I made for the outdoor toilet. Our water and sanitation engineer had managed to construct a septic toilet in the grounds, to be flushed with a bucket of water. There was even a makeshift shower – a bucket of water and a pull chain suspended above an old shipping pallet; our water supply was dependent on an INTERFET tank filled from a fire pumper.

Blinking now to adjust to the moonlight, I made out the figures of perhaps three or four men standing in our compound and conferring in whispers. The faint crackle of a radio revealed they were soldiers. One voice was of CARE's security coordinator, Bob McPherson, just discernible. In profile, the outline of night vision goggles stood out in relief against the night sky as one of the soldiers turned slightly. I wasn't concerned by their presence: INTERFET troops were on patrol day and night and were concerned also with our protection.

Catching sight of me as they turned to leave, the soldiers nodded a greeting then disappeared silently into the still and breezeless night. Bob explained that Indonesian soldiers had been apprehended in the next-door compound. The Indonesians had been playing a game of incursion and see. I didn't ask if they had been armed; I really didn't want to know the answer.

Fluent in Indonesian, I'd joined the team as interpreter, Assistant Shelter Coordinator and Special Ambassador. My other primary duty was to liaise between CARE International and CMOC (Civilian Military Office of Coordination) at daily briefings to ensure we were aware of safe travel zones and military and militia activity.

The work in Dili seemed never-ending as we were very shorthanded, so it was all hands to the wheel but it was uplifting and the rewards came with seeing people getting fed, their lives improving bit by bit. There were times when I watched the faces of displaced people light up as we successfully reunited their families and I had to quash the temptation to transpose my own family into that situation. Personal thoughts were almost too distracting, although I was constantly aware that geographically I was so close to Iddin and Shahirah. I had hoped that news of my presence in East Timor might filter through to them in Malaysia, as the conflagration was obviously big news in the region, but I may as well have been on the moon. There was still no breakthrough in my quest for contact.

The coastal road, along which I drove a small truck of supplies, was narrow and rock strewn and had a sheer drop onto the cliffs below. We were on our way to the eastern province of Bacau as part of a safe INTERFET convoy. This route had been the target of hit-and-run militia activity and was therefore deemed unsafe to travel without armed guards. Our military escort wanted to undertake a training exercise whilst with us – it would be a mock ambush to show CARE staff how to handle themselves.

Swiftly pulling my vehicle over when the radios crackled with a pre-arranged signal, and under direction of the officer in charge, I jumped down from the cabin to proceed to a protected position. Hitting the rocky ground I felt a snap and searing pain in my left knee and couldn't help yelping out in shock, but I picked myself up and limped on. When the drill was over, I hobbled back to the vehicle and hauled myself in again. By the end of the day, the pain in my knee had worsened, probably aggravated by the three-hour drive in both directions.

Back at the compound, an American army medic whistled at my swollen knee, which by this stage resembled an overripe melon. A self-cooling field pack from an army med kit was applied to my knee and I strapped it up for good measure. I would need crutches for a few days as I had torn the cruciate ligament in my knee.

Everyday was a hard slog in East Timor, the humidity made moving around exhausting, and the sheer scale of what needed to be done to restore society to a functioning community was immense. Our national staff were living in the same conditions as our refugees and it was inspiring and poignant to be surrounded by colleagues who were so committed to moving forward and building a new nation from ruins.

Little by little, conditions were changing for the better and new staff were arriving. Steve Gwynne-Vaughan, a seasoned aid worker who spoke Portuguese, English and French, had come from Canada to become CARE's Country Director in East Timor. His 6 foot 6 frame caused great mirth amongst our local staff over whom he towered. Endowed with laconic good wit, he was great at cutting to the chase and looking at problems with a lateral eye but did not suffer fools gladly.

We also acquired a new Head of Security, Chris Allen, a retired army major, clean-cut and well built with a crooked and funny smile and a dry sense of humour. He'd been part of the elite 3 RAR Parachute Battalion and had been seconded to the British Airborne Forces in Africa and Central America. Following a few injuries sustained in the parachute battalion, he had left the military to study at university. Chris had been motivated by the media coverage of East Timor to approach CARE, and apply for the role in Dili. We had a couple of heated run-ins during our time together in East Timor, but that only seemed to serve as a strong basis for a friendship that endures to this day. I put my life in Chris's hands a number of times while on deployment. He backed some of my more hair-brained schemes and never once patronised or treated me like fragile crystal. I doubt if he thinks I'm female, nicknaming me Peej. Insisting on pulling his bivouac across the open-air entrance to the sleeping quarters, Chris kept watch over all of us at night. Personally, I suspected it was more a ploy to avoid the pronounced grunts, groans and wind problems our diet of crackers and canned food produced in all of us.

As Assistant Shelter Coordinator, I was supervising the setting up of a camp for thousands of demoralised refugees, many of whom were very ill from spending weeks in the jungle with little food and no sanitation. Our main shelter was to be the ruins of a Catholic boys school, Dom Bosco, that had seen a lot of militia activity.

Preparing the burned-out buildings was a mucky job: the somewhat unstable walls had to be checked and the floors of the buildings had to be cleared of rubble. Weatherproofing with UNHCR tarpaulins was imperative, as the rainy season was fast approaching. I designed a series of lashings with old water bottles filled with dirt to weigh down our temporary roofs. The Canadian sailors from the ship HMCS *Protecteur* and US Marines detailed to assist me proved to be invaluable, climbing precarious roof ridges to secure roof joists. Although I would have preferred if they had been unarmed as I narrowly escaped a bullet that accidentally discharged from a sailor's rifle during one of our rest periods and went whizzing past my head into a spot on the wall where my head had just been! That aside, together we wielded hammers to get the job done as quickly as possible accompanied by a lot of laughter.

Pushing and shoving with all my strength simply wouldn't budge one charred door, to the side of the main hall we were clearing out, so I called over a couple of burly US Special Forces soldiers, otherwise known as Green Berets, to help. A mighty thump from them sent the door flying off its hinges.

Entering the small side room with a shovel and broom, I calculated how long it would take to clear the collapsed roof and began to move debris, assisted by one of the sergeants. We worked for five minutes or more before my shovel struck something that rolled. It was the blackened remains of a person. Reeling back, I half squatted at the doorway and peered at the charred pile that was partly covered by ashes and muck. I unclipped my radio and made a call to INTERFET headquarters, trying to keep my language as innocuous as possible as this was an open frequency. The last thing we wanted was to have a huge crowd of local people descending, trying to identify the morbid discovery. And it would be too distressing for the people whose loved ones had disappeared.

What divides us from those who can snuff out another human being's life without compunction? What provides the impetus to propel a person forward to strike the first blow when anarchy breaks out? I believe that a mob mentality buoys up a deranged absolution of collective guilt, allowing people to act in ways that they would never usually have enough moral fortitude to do so. It is cowardice of the greatest magnitude.

When the crime investigation unit arrived, we withdrew sombrely to another part of the complex and allowed them to work undisturbed. A number of local priests and nuns were still unaccounted for and this was a place some of them had taken refuge. In my mind, there was no doubt that this was the site of an execution. Two body bags would later leave that small room. I was never to find out whose resting place I had disturbed, but I made my way that afternoon to the large white church near central Dili and lit four candles. One for each of my children, and two for the poor souls who had died amidst so much violence and terror. This time I prayed that my children would never know war first hand.

The open-sided gymnasium at Dom Bosco became the initial processing point for the thousands of displaced persons about to flood back into Dili, and it was here that scores of people disembarked in October, November and December of 1999, from all manner of vehicles, including a fleet of Timor's garbage trucks into which the elderly and children had been crammed.

Late in the afternoon of our first day as a functioning transit camp, a commotion broke out. Dozens of people were suddenly swirling in a mêlée around two bobbing heads. Bloodthirsty howls rose from the crowd. 'Militia, militia!' came the screams of anger.

Pushing my way through, I saw two men being kicked and punched where they lay, quite close to the CARE vehicle.

Two New Zealand INTERFET soldiers with whom I had been speaking minutes earlier arrived quickly on the scene, and I told them as calmly as I could what was happening. Whether or not the blokes on the ground were really members of the detested militia I would never know, but we had to act swiftly to get them out of the crowd before they were torn to shreds. Back-up was at least 15 minutes away.

I clambered onto the running board of the four-wheel drive and shouted in Indonesian and bad Tetum, the local dialect, for the crowd to calm down. INTERFET was here, I told them, and would take the two accused back to headquarters for interrogation.

While the soldiers hauled the two men into the tray of the vehicle and bravely placed their own bodies and weapons between them and the fist-shaking crowd, I begged the people not to behave like the militia themselves. And, fortunately, the respect the Timorese felt for INTERFET won the day – the crowd backed off a couple of steps. I managed to start the engine and slowly steered us through the muttering throng, and towards the military police compound.

Sometimes the sheer magnitude of a relief effort can prove

almost overwhelming and the individuals you are trying to help become one big blur.

Other times, though, you become passionately and personally concerned for a particular person or family. It could be you've made a connection somehow with a single glance, or recognise that this woman or man could so easily, under different circumstances, be a friend you would catch up with over coffee back home. Perhaps one single human being becomes for you the encapsulation of all the sorrow, misery, violence and injustice you have been witnessing on a grander scale. Somehow, you become determined to help this one person and you'll move heaven and earth to do it.

This happened for me twice in East Timor – both times with women called Maria. The first Maria I met as I walked beside the breakwater taking photos, for CARE fundraising, of the temporary shelters refugees had erected on Dili's harbour foreshore. Maria had two small daughters and a son with her. Bright-eyed and smiling, their vivacity reminded me of Shahirah and Iddin. We began talking and Maria told me she had just returned from West Timor. Her husband had been killed by the militia and all she now owned was packed into a striped carry-all bag with a broken zip. Beside her was the standard issue UNHCR repatriation pack of a yellow HDR (Humanitarian Daily Ration), a bucket, a water storage container and a pan for boiling water.

Maria and her children needed a lift for the last stage of their journey home. So in the CARE truck I drove them to the backstreets of a suburb not far from the cemetery. There, Maria's face crumpled, as she surveyed the ruins of her home for the first time. But she remained dignified, determined not to let her children see the tears in her eyes.

The family prospects were indeed grim: Maria couldn't leave her still-nursing baby and young kids to forage for the basics of life, and she had no man or other relative to help.

I hugged her and said I'd be back soon. At the UNHCR warehouse the supervisor knew me, and pretended not to notice as I pulled a tarp from a pile, along with a reel of rope and bits of plastic for windows. I tucked a couple of blankets into my pile of loot too. Tossing everything into the back of the vehicle, I headed next to the CMOC, where I pleaded for two mosquito nets. Back in the cabin of the truck, I heard a thump – two folding army cots had landed in the tray as well. Not much was said; just a nod and a wink from a friendly Major was all I caught in my rear-vision mirror. It was enough that I came to CMOC in need, as I was not in the habit of asking for favours. Next, at the French INTERFET contingent, I scored some extra ration packs, 2 kilos of rice, a loaf of bread and some fresh fruit, including oranges just off the supply barge from Darwin. A broom and extra cooking pot and a sharpish knife came from the Thai contingent, and soap, a torch and a new toothbrush from the US Marines.

Four US Special Forces guys with a ladder and a tool kit lashed to their Humvee came back with me to Maria's. Only 90 minutes had passed. Gobsmacked, Maria watched while the Green Berets clambered onto what was left of her roof and repaired it with the tarpaulins. Then they busied themselves with the windows, and suspended the mosquito nets from the charred ceiling beams. After the floor had been swept the army cots came in. Not content with all that, the burly men squatted against the wheels of their vehicle as the delighted children watched them fashion a windchime from razor wire and steel – which we hung very high above the front door, out of the way of little fingers. It wasn't much, but when we were finished, Maria and the children were weather-tight and had a bit of a head start.

What I'd done was against the rules. But I didn't take anything out of the mouths of other refugees, and there are times when rules just have to be broken.

The second Maria was holding a tiny bundle in her arms in a back room of the Dom Bosco complex, where a priest had given her refuge upon her return from West Timor. A small towel was draped over her baby's head. First asking Maria's permission, I drew back the covering to find a little boy of six months, frail and non-responsive, but suckling at his mother's breast. The child's head was grossly deformed and the size of a basketball. It was obvious the pair needed help, so I contacted INTERFET doctors, who diagnosed the baby as having severe hydrocephaly, or water on the brain — a condition treatable in any first-world nation with surgery and the insertion of shunts to drain away the fluid. The dilemma was that INTERFET couldn't simply airlift a small child out of Timor without a pre-arranged destination and an appropriate paediatric surgical team lined up. All this needed money that simply wasn't available, so after discussing the options with Maria, I set off for the Hotel Turismo in search of a journalist from News Limited to whom I could offer an exclusive in return for a public campaign in Australia to cover the medical and travelling expenses of Maria and her baby. This plan worked out terrifically, and within three days of the story being published in Australia a paediatric surgeon and his team had volunteered to assist, after consultations with the INTERFET medicos. Major Mark McKay from CMOC helped gather all the documents to process temporary travel papers. By the end of the week Maria and her baby were on their way to Melbourne. It was one of those great moments when all concerned felt elated that we had contributed to something truly worthwhile.

But Maria's child had been misdiagnosed. In East Timor proper diagnostic tools simply weren't available, and it was discovered in Australia that the baby's condition was in fact anencephaly – he had been born without a brain. His brain stem controlled his basic bodily functions, but there was absolutely no chance of his developing any higher brain activity. Anencephaly is a birth defect which can often be averted by the simple ingestion of folic acid prior to conception and during the first trimester of pregnancy.

It was a testament to Maria's utter devotion as a mother that she had kept her child alive by simply holding him in her arms virtually without a break and breastfeeding him on demand. Anencephalic infants usually die within a couple of days of birth. There was nothing for the doctors in Melbourne to do, and so, sadly, Maria and her tiny son were sent home to East Timor to be with family and await the inevitable.

The greatest pleasure during my time in East Timor was the morning swim. Rob, a Dutch aid worker with CARE, and I got into the habit of rising an hour earlier than everyone else and driving to a saltwater lagoon east of town. Wading into the shallow water, we would watch the sun come up while fishermen cast their nets at the mouth of the lagoon. It was a rare enjoyment, one that left us refreshed before the grime of the day set in. Even when we learned the lagoon was home to an enormous crocodile we remained undeterred – stupidly, I admit in hindsight, particularly as both of us were short-sighted and even watching for the croc occurred in a myopic fog. But the chill of the water and the natural beauty seemed worth the risk.

After the transit camp was up and running as smoothly as could be expected, it was time to swing onto the distribution of aid to outlying districts. It was imperative that seed for crops was delivered to the rural areas before the rainy season set in and the roads became impassable. I drove with many loads across the steep mountains of the island, though food supplies were unreliable and aid workers, as well as the Timorese, often went short. Most of us lost a lot of weight rapidly, from illness and poor diet. I had arrived in Dili weighing 53 kilograms and would go back to Australia eleven weeks later at 47 kilograms and looking decidedly gaunt.

The tropics took their toll on each of us to much the same degree: one by one we were struck down with all manner of ailments, from pneumonia (I had it twice and was left with a weakened heart muscle), to dysentery, dengue fever and malaria – typical tropical diseases borne by mosquitos and flourishing in the tough conditions.

Eventually, I was sent back to Australia on a deafeningly loud 'Herculces' C130 transport plane to recuperate from my second bout of pneumonia. The break forced me to take stock of the past few years, and look towards the new with a mixture of trepidation and the desire to make changes.

The absence of my children now straddled two centuries.

Chapter 24

Freedom to Love

Friday, 16 March 2001, 3:41 p.m.
Intense blue eyes fixed on my face in grave concentration and, with just a hint of the quizzical, minute rosebud lips opened from a gentle pucker. As I looked into her captivating eyes I finally knew that everything would be all right. The world had righted itself and nothing seemed so daunting any more. We would be OK, this little person and I.

Verity Isabelle, my daughter, was born with a full head of wavy golden hair and a pianist's long fingers. After months of worry and concern, she was rudely healthy and weighed in at 3.71 kilograms (8 pounds 3 ounces); and at 55 centimetres (22 inches) long, she promised to be tall. Her lashes mesmerised me; they lay long and lustrous, sweeping her cheeks and fluttering in her baby dreams.

Turning to my breast just moments after her first examination of me, she began to suckle confidently and with gusto.

'There,' said obstetrician Professor Michael Bennett, 'I told you that you could do it. You know I've never before delivered a babe down on the floor, so you're an honoured party.'

I assured him that his reputation as the feared head of the Royal Hospital for Women hadn't been tarnished in the least! In an amusing cliché, Michael had truly ended up being the man who stood by me through a pretty horrendous time. It had been a very difficult pregnancy – I had been hospitalised several times with complications, premature labour, and spent the last three months of Verity's gestation lying down, medicated for the heart problem I'd developed in East Timor.

During the early months of my pregnancy Paula began to telephone me again; sometimes slurred, her words were full of pain. Shortly after this our contact was only sporadic and so sad, although always full of her love for the girls. Tragically Paula would spiral further downwards and be found dead in September 2000, apparently from an accidental overdose. Her former husband, Bob Geldof, turned out to have real depths of compassion and love, becoming legal guardian to Tigerlily and raising her along with her three sisters in a secure and safe family unit.

A parcel arrived for me a week after Paula's death – inside was a gift-wrapped present containing a miniature leopard-print jumpsuit and matching bootees – a gift from Paula for the baby I was carrying.

Now Sarah Hicks, my gorgeous friend and birth coach, had tears streaming down her face. A friend ever since Judith had introduced us, our friendship had grown and endured. She is the gentlest soul in my circle of friends. Sarah had propped me up as I pushed my baby into the world. My other friends, Valerie and Fiona, were also present at Verity's birth, and now their eyes too were glistening with tears.

All my fears about not being capable of unreservedly loving another child disappeared like evaporating fog on a sunny day. My self-doubt and the emotional trauma of the pregnancy receded into nothingness. I could feel in my deepest core that I wasn't as damaged by the kidnap of my older children as I had feared, and that I still had the capacity for the deep and visceral love one feels for one's own child. It came as a relief and a revelation, for intellectually I knew that the nuts and bolts of mothering would be a breeze, it was in the emotional bonding department that I had been worried I would be wonky.

But Verity was not born to heal my wounded heart. Nor have I ever thought of her as a replacement for her older brother and sister. Children are not interchangeable, they are unique individuals in their own right, not mindless extensions of their parents' egos.

Unthinking people often ventured, after Verity's arrival, that she would make up for the loss of her siblings. How little they understood, and how little they knew of the small and determined 'old soul' that Verity is.

'Verity's herself,' I would find myself retorting forcefully, softening my words with a smile. One child doesn't make up for another, and though I delighted in my new baby, her brother and sister were always in my thoughts – and my heart.

I had loved my Peanut (Verity's nickname until late in the pregnancy) from the moment I had held my breath as her strong heartbeat showed up on the ultrasound machine, only weeks after her conception, as my then partner held my hand in the doctor's office. While I'm definitely pro-choice, abortion had never been an option, even though the pregnancy was a surprise considering my medical history and the risks involved. At first, the medicos were dubious that I could carry Verity to full term, as I had a history of miscarriage at ten weeks and of stillbirth at twenty-six weeks.

Even now I tell Verity that she was my miracle from God and one of life's greatest gifts. I've always, since she was tiny, whispered in her ear as I've tucked her in at night: 'Mummy chose to grow you in her tummy. I love you as much as all the leaves and all the trees in the whole wide world. I love you with all my heart and all my soul and I always will, no matter what.' And later, when she met the man who would become her real daddy, we added him to her bedtime blessing. 'And Daddy chose to be your daddy – which makes you even more precious, and he loves you up to the moon and back again ten million billion times.'

For the truth is that Verity is not the biological child of my husband, Bill, but he is her father and she is utterly and completely his daughter. He changed her nappies from the time she was a few months old, and rocked her when she had her vaccinations and was hot and whingey with the pain. He carried her around in a baby sling and proudly puffed out his chest when complimented on the beauty of his daughter. Sometimes I suspect that he fell in love with Verity well before his friendship with me turned into love.

When Verity was eleven months and two weeks old, and we were told that she might have leukaemia, just eight days before our wedding, Bill cradled her struggling little body as the doctors searched for a vein from which to collect more blood. Tears were streaming down his face. He's been there for the good times and the bad, for the midnight vomit sessions and the triumph of first steps and milestones achieved. So in every way that it matters to a child's peace and security and self-esteem, Bill is Verity's father.

It is such a fraught equation to write about, knowing as I do the potential for gossip and innuendo, and the only reason I do so is because I am aware that certain sections of the media find the essentially private story interesting. Our Verity is still very young, and when and how we chose to speak to our little girl about such intensely private and delicate matters is something I hope those of you who read this book will respect and not turn into some salacious or titillating piece of gossip or tabloid fodder, which is sure to affect her deeply for the rest of her life.

When Verity was conceived, I was in what I believed to be a long-term and permanent relationship with her biological father. We had plans to resettle in Washington after her birth. I had rearranged my life to be with him, at his request. Then, when I was eight-and-a-half months pregnant, he decided to redraw the boundaries of our relationship.

He had re-evaluted his future, he declared. The choice was mine to make, not his, he said earnestly: adopt our baby out at birth, or break up.

As devastating as it was to do, I chose the latter and have never regretted my decision. I loved Verity's father keenly and trustingly, without reservation, and with utter confidence in what I thought was his goodness and his understanding of my personal history. I loved him with the encouragement of some very protective friends and people whom I respected – all were shocked by the outcome, and his feet of clay.

When I asked him why he had begun our relationship in the first place, he explained, in front of friends, that he had viewed me as 'a challenge' and had thought me 'intriguing'. He then walked out of my life forever. I have not seen him since, nor has he ever made a request to meet Verity.

It is one of the most painful and deeply humiliating episodes in my life and one I have tried very hard to rise above and move on from.

But on that warm evening in March as I settled down for an exhausted sleep with newly born Verity nestled in the crook of my arm, I wished for nothing more than a wonderful and fulfilling life for her, and that one day she might meet her big brother and sister.

Chapter 25

Serendipity and Salsa

A quick rest on the comfortable hotel bed, after a shower and a Danish pastry, meant that Bill was behind in his schedule. Therefore he missed being in the restaurant on the top floor of the World Trade Center.

He phoned me in the middle of the antipodean night.

'It must be one of those tourist joy flights I've seen buzzing over the city.' The words had barely left his mouth when a television cameraman captured vision of another plane, a jetliner, ploughing into the second tower. The images went out live across the two time zones.

The Twin Towers collapsed and the Pentagon burned.

We remained on the line to each other. I asked Bill what he was wearing. I had started to function like an aid worker before war.

'Head down to the Australian Consulate to register; they'll help evacuate you if the need arises. On the way, withdraw as much cash as you can from ATMs – they'll probably go off-line soon – and buy some bottles of fresh water,' I urged him. What would happen next?

Dazed and concerned, Bill followed my instructions, walking downtown as a tide of humanity surged past him in the opposite direction. New Yorkers covered in ash, dust and debris, starkly white and in shock, moved like a migrating herd as the skyline darkened behind them and an acrid smell choked the city.

Later, returning to the hotel, he managed to get a line to Australia and this time I answered, holding Verity in my arms.

'When and if I get back, we're getting married,' he insisted and I didn't demur.

On 9 March 2002, in front of a gathering of friends from around the world, I married Bill on a late summer afternoon in a beautiful park in front of a chiffon-wrapped rotunda to the music of a string quartet. Verity, Bill and I had our first dance as a married family to the strains of Van Morrison's 'Someone Like You'. Given the lyrics of the song, I couldn't help but grin at the irony of marrying the boy next door.

We had decided to have exactly the type of wedding we wanted. As a special favour, the priest who had conducted Nanna's memorial service and Verity's baptism, Archdeacon Phillip Newman, agreed to marry us in Alexandra Gardens rather than a church. The ceremony was highly personal, and funny as well; one of Bill's most endearing traits is his warm, generous sense of humour.

I wore a very pale pink, strapless A-line dress of Duchess satin with fresh gardenias in my hair and carried a bouquet of David Austin pale pink roses. Verity, our flower girl, was gorgeous in a pale pink frock and satin slippers. Only four days earlier, she had been cleared of suspected leukaemia – we had reason to celebrate indeed. The reception, also in the park, was a casual and relaxed affair, with endless food circulating on trays. Our terrific friends Jane Allen and Jason McLean had spent all morning in the park making sure the rotunda was decorated with metres of white chiffon and bowls of roses. As night fell, hundreds of candles illuminated the paths, courtesy of our hardworking friends, Dawn and Martyn Bradley. I breastfed Verity under a tree as I watched our family and friends sway and twirl to the beats of the salsa band. For Bill's beloved parents, Anton and Elizabeth, we interspersed the Latin beats with Greek music that made guests erupt in unfettered versions of the Zorba dance – skirts, ties and feet flying in a joyous frenzy. Grannies gripped gorgeous young men, and whoops of enjoyment were punctuated by choruses of 'oopa' as the circle of dancers whirled in the moonlight. It was *My Big Fat Greek Wedding* meets *Barefoot in the Park*. I wondered what Iddin and Shahirah would have made of the day and the eclectic mix of people and music. I would have loved to share such happiness with them; it would have made the day simply perfect.

This was a private occasion that was only to be shared with invited guests. We had turned down monetary offers from magazines for wedding pictures.

But the journalists were determined to gatecrash, jostling a number of our elderly guests out of the way as we were making our vows. As a result, several of our own wedding pictures show us scowling at some presence out of the shot. Eventually, the media were firmly ejected, and the happy day continued in a much more relaxed manner.

Days later, we discovered that hell hath no fury like a reporter scorned. Mean-spiritedly, I was ridiculed in print for remarrying, and wrongly described as wearing a bright yellow dress. I know that women reading this book will understand what a low blow that was, especially as I look truly ghastly in yellow! In another newspaper, a columnist who had not even been present made up a story about the ceremony, for which his newspaper was forced to print a retraction and apology after we took legal action. Bill is an intensely private person and found the press interest in my life abhorrent.

By some odd quirk of fate, Bill and I had attended the same high school in Melbourne, where I was a couple of years his senior. For years we had lived only a block away from each other and had often seen one another on the street and at various events, from concerts to open-air markets. We knew the same places and shared a lot of tastes and experiences, but most of all we laughed together – a lot.

As soon as Patsy got wind of our engagement she had insisted on flying to Australia to put Bill through a torturous inspection, after which she declared I had finally got it right. Each of my wonderfully protective friends in their own ways subjected poor Bill to hours of beady-eyed evaluations, usually behind my back, which he good-naturedly allowed. Judith was particularly gruesome in her tortures of Bill. It's a wonder he didn't just tell all of them where to go!

Bill and I had met after Verity was born. I'd realised I wanted to settle back permanently in Australia. Melbourne seemed the best place to raise a child, and some of my closest friends were there – Verity would only benefit from growing up around a great mix of 'aunties' and 'uncles'.

From Sydney, where I was living, I had chosen a house, sight unseen, from an ad in the newspaper. On paper, it had met all my criteria, and so, trusting to friends to inspect the house and give it the thumbs-up, I took a twelve-month lease via email and a series of phone calls with the landlord, who had sounded pleasant and professional. He had been born in the house I was renting from him and had purchased the derelict house next door and renovated it himself. He lived there now.

The sun was trying desperately to emerge from behind the clouds on the day two moving trucks and my car converged outside the house. A new life was unfolding for the two of us. Taking Verity from her car restraint, I lifted her into my arms and walked across the street, to be greeted by the landlord, Bill, who was standing outside the front gate.

'Welcome!' he said. 'I've taken the day off work in case you needed a cup of tea or a quiet place to change the baby.'

And so, over the following months, Bill became my friend, taking an afternoon walk with Verity and me, pushing the pram as we strolled the familiar streets of Hawthorn.

Still, I'd decided not to expose Verity to any transient relationships. Single, I resolved, was the best stance for all concerned. But sometimes I found Bill looking at me in a way that unnerved me. Finally, one day I told him that I simply wasn't a good bet and that I didn't want to lose his friendship by gaining a lover. I urged him to go on the overseas trip he'd been talking about.

'Go find a gorgeous Swedish blonde, or a bombshell in the Greek islands,' I told him. 'You need a girl without baggage.'

A week later, Bill headed off for a two-month trip, hugging Verity and me warmly, and a little wistfully. Almost immediately we knew it was a mistake!

'I shouldn't be here by myself; you and Verity should be with me,' he said on the phone.

And the rest, as they say, is history.

Chapter 26

Knock, Knock, Who's Really There?

I had never predicated my aid work on religious precepts; rather I had gone out of my way to avoid integrating the projects I set up with religious organisations, as I believe that the most evil of human actions is to define a person's worth by their religious affiliation. In Africa, the Balkans and East Timor, I had refused to label people according to their religious belief and felt appalled at the prospect of a globe divided by creed.

Were we moving towards a world divided along the lines of them and us, Muslim and Christian, and if so, what would be the bridge?

And was a reunion with Iddin and Shahirah now further off than ever?

Then came 9/11. I could only hope that zealotry did not play any part in the Islamic instruction Shah and Iddin would be receiving in their Muslim household.

Christmas came and went. I had relished decorating the Christmas tree, and watching Verity's eyes dance in merriment and excitement as each bauble and ornament was carefully unwrapped and hung in its place. I crowned the tree, as always, with the fairy I had made with Iddin and Shahirah so many years ago.

'Shasha,' said Verity, handing me a little picture frame with Shahirah's photograph inside.

Looping it over a branch, I turned again when Verity tugged at my skirt.

'Iddin,' she insisted imperiously, handing me her brother's picture confidently.

Verity was aware of who they were: pictures of Iddin and Shah filled the house and I had told her since birth stories of their childhood. Now, a deep stab of sadness hit me; it was at this time of year I missed the older kids the most.

Bending over to reach for another ornament, I yelped as the baby in my belly gave a swift kick. I rubbed the little foot pushing against my side. At six months, this was an easier pregnancy than with Verity, but I still had to be careful of my heart. The new baby was due in late April and was a dream come true for Bill and me. We had decided early on that we didn't want Verity to be an 'only child': although she had siblings in Malaysia, they were years older, and even if they were to return tomorrow, they logically wouldn't be playmates for her.

Motherhood this time around was wonderful and amazing – although I admit to being exhausted all the time.

I eased myself into the seat in front of the computer and

logged on. I went into the email account for the Empty Arms Network, a mail box I kept for child abduction advocacy. This account did not have my name attached to it as the recipient.

Reposing in the inbox was an email from a sender with the tag 'loveisanillusion' and the title 'Can you help me find my mother'. Mildly interested, I clicked the Open button, expecting it to be from a victim of kidnapping, perhaps in another country.

I almost tipped my chair over backwards!

The email purported to be from my daughter, Shahirah. Something about it – nothing specific, just a feeling – made it different from the others: the tone was so respectful and there didn't seem to be a hidden agenda.

Was this just another hoax? I read the email again, more slowly this time:

> *My name is Shahirah and I am trying to contact my mother, Jacqueline. I would like to speak to her and hope that you are able to help me contact her. My brother and I were taken from Australia a long time ago and I was given this email address by ★★★★★★★★.*
>
> *Sincerely,*
> *Shahirah.*

No matter how hard I remonstrated with myself, I was almost hyperventilating at the prospect that this time it might truly be Shahirah. I struggled to get hold of my emotions, and the baby somersaulted in my tummy, reacting to my surge of adrenalin.

I called to Bill to come and read the email. Much more

sceptical than me, Bill wasn't convinced. But he thought I should investigate further, if I felt there might be a possibility of it being true.

Shaking, I immediately telephoned Judith Curran, in New Zealand, and told her what was unfolding. For simple self-preservation, I had to remain sceptical, and think carefully about replying to whoever this was.

Judith offered to be the intermediary between this new 'Shahirah' and me. We worked out that she could email an explanation to this person, and also a list of questions to which only the real Shahirah would know the answers.

I set to work on the list straightaway, careful not to include any questions to which I had revealed the answers during the thousands of interviews I had done since Iddin and Shahirah's abduction. None of the correct answers would be found in my first book either.

When I had drafted my list, I checked and rechecked it for foolproofness. These were the questions I settled on:

- What was the colour of Shahirah's mosquito netting?
- What was the name of her reversible doll? (Or please describe it.)
- Can you remember what language Shahirah learned at school in Australia?
- Did Shahirah enjoy sleeping in her bed, and please describe it?
- Can Shahirah remember her last birthday party?

With my heart in my mouth, I called Judith back and had her set up a new account in the name 'Chocolateslab' – I am a chocoholic after all and it seemed like a lucky name – so that she could forward my questions to 'loveisanillusion'.

Goodness, I mused to myself, if it is Shahirah, what has happened to her to make her adopt such a cynical email tag at the age of only seventeen?

I held my breath and crossed my fingers and toes – I couldn't cross my legs, I was too pregnant. Three days went by. I pretended not to fret, but secretly I did, checking my inbox again and again each day.

We were at the end of January, and Iddin's birthday was fast approaching. I wondered if my birthday card and gift would arrive, or perhaps whether the anniversary might prompt him to contact me. I realised I had held off checking my emails for three hours. Once more, with trepidation, I sat at the computer. Judith had emailed me.

> *Darling Jack,*
>   *I received this email this afternoon via the Chocolateslab account. Fingers crossed it's positive. Let me know.*
>   *Love Juju xxxx*

Opening the attachment with trembling fingers and a lot of secret hope, I scanned its contents.

> *To Chocolateslab,*
>   *My favourite doll was a cup-cake doll that smelled like strawberries.*

As I read the opening line I began to shake and an enormous sob escaped from my spinning heart: I could hardly read the rest of the email because of the tears. No outsider could possibly know that five-year-old Shah had gone everywhere with what I always called her 'muffin doll' in her pocket. A miniature freckled figure with a wide skirt made from rubber and resembling a crinoline dress – when Shahirah inverted it, the doll looked like a small cake. It was fruit-scented.

Sloshing tears onto the keyboard, I moved down to the next answer.

My mosquito netting was really bright, a really hot pink and my mum sewed it for me.

The netting had been a source of resigned amusement to me, for at the age of four, Shahirah had stood in the fabric shop and adamantly argued against the delicate shade of pink I was proposing. 'No, Mummy, I want the fluoro one,' insisted my pink-mad daughter. It had been so garish, the family joked that sunglasses were needed to look at it and that the colour would wake Shahirah in the middle of the night!

I think I learned Italian, but I'm not sure.

Italian it was! This whole moment was so surreal: was this truly happening eleven and a half years since she had been snatched from me?

My bed was up really high, not a bunk bed but one with high legs taller than Mum, I climbed a ladder.

No one except someone who had seen this bed would have known how to describe it. Iddin had one the same, but always opted to sleep on a mattress down below so our dog could snuggle up with him at night. No photographs had ever appeared showing its strange configuration, and even if they had, it would have been taken for a bunk bed.

By the time I got to the question about her last birthday party, I was convinced it was Shahirah!

We went to the Plaster Fun House and painted, I think it was raining.

I read the email over and over again, the sobs of joy and relief catching in my throat. Finally convinced I wasn't hallucinating, I searched out Bill and told him. He questioned me closely as I wept. Was I sure no one else could have the answers? No, I assured him, only Shahirah and Iddin.

'That's wonderful, darling, what do you want to do now, and where will we put them?'

Shaking my head, I truly didn't know; Shahirah had made no mention of wanting to return to Australia. She didn't even know it was me. I was a little frightened now; I wanted to make the right impression – it was like a blind date with a child I hardly knew any more.

I decided to email her in the morning. Right then I had to organise Verity's dinner and put her to sleep. Most importantly, I had to collect my thoughts and think everything over.

That night I slept deeply and happily, although when I dreamed of Shahirah I saw a blank spot where her face should be, and a fairly neutral body. But I knew it was her – she held her muffin doll and was wrapped in hot pink.

Chapter 27

Out Came the Sunshine

The opening theme to the ABC children's show, *Play School*, drifted through the study door. Verity was occupied for at least half an hour; the electronic babysitter was a godsend the morning after the night before.

My first step was to open a new blind email address in the name of 'yummy chocolate' which could not be traced back to me – I was aware that perhaps Shah's emails might be monitored and did not want to compromise her security. Then I sat back and felt utterly daunted, staring at the computer screen.

Half an hour to write one of the most important letters of my life, to a child born of my body, whom I knew almost nothing about and who had probably been indoctrinated against me on every level imaginable. Eleven years of pining and hoping and loving to be encapsulated in one electronic transmission.

Mindful that this might be the one and only time I could communicate with my teenage daughter, I took a cleansing breath, and then another. Procrastinating paralysed me. This was the one letter I knew definitely that Shahirah *would* receive after so many long years of being held incommunicado. But rattling around in my mind was the possibility that, even though this letter wouldn't be intercepted, it might still not be entirely private, for I had no idea whether or not Shah confided in her father. In some way, this was a test, but whether I would pass, I simply hadn't the foggiest.

No problem, should be a breeze, no pressure; just make this the best letter you have ever written and get on with it. But still I dithered. 'Out came the sunshine and dried up all the rain, and the incy-wincy spider climbed up the spout again,' came the words of the children's song. I could hear Verity clapping delightedly in the living room. It shook me from my stupor of self-doubt. I had sung this same rhyme to all three of my children, climbing the spider up the drainpipe of my forearm. This was my child I was about to communicate with; she may choose not to answer, I knew, but somewhere inside her must be the toddler who had watched in wonder as her mummy made the rain fall and sun shine just to make her laugh.

Mentally squaring my shoulders I began to type, carefully telling of my love and the joy I had found when her answers to Judith's email test had come through. I felt deeply compelled to tell Shah that I had never given up trying to contact her and her brother, and that I wanted so much to hear her now grown-up voice and to know what she and Iddin looked like.

This was not the time for recriminations against their father, so I remained circumspect on that front.

What did she like to do, what were her hobbies, what sort of music did she listen to, was her favourite colour still pink? Did Iddin still have his blond spot on the back of his head? On and on my questions went.

And then I poured out my emotions.

No matter what, I can't, and won't, pretend to be anyone or anything other than me, your mother – warts and all. I have loved you and missed you with every fibre of my heart and all my soul for so many years . . . I love you millions, billions, trillions and infinities and I always will.

I also wrote that I had no desire for media attention and that I was very worried that our private communication would become a catalyst for a new press circus. Explaining how I had declined to give any interviews on personal issues for some time as I preferred a quiet life, I hoped that she felt the same.

Then I went on to describe the terrace house in which we lived and the garden.

I decided not to include my telephone number, as I didn't want to pressure Shahirah into any situation that might prove to be too emotionally overwhelming for her. I just prayed with every cell of my body that I would receive a reply. Hitting the send button I forced myself to rise from the desk and leave the room with only a quick backward glance at the computer.

For the next 24 hours I did my best to concentrate on the here and now and keep my recalcitrant mind off the electronic ether. Poor Verity sensed my preoccupation and demanded extra cuddles.

To top it off, I had an episode of premature contractions and a trip to the maternity ward in the middle of the night, for a check-up on the condition of the baby. Exhausted and with instructions to rest in bed – always such a ridiculous proposition for the mother of an active toddler – I didn't get to check my emails until late the next afternoon – again, thank you *Play School*.

Closing my eyes, I stilled my expectations, but in my heart I was wishing for a miracle. I told myself to remember that Shah and Iddin lived within a religion and culture so very different to my own. Shahirah might be rebelling on a mild level and the initial contact would be all I got. To even take this leap would be a major initiative for a girl brought up in the royal family that I had known and rejected. Perhaps the first email was just adolescent curiosity that would crumble when faced with the reality of direct contact.

With complex and contradictory emotions swirling through me, I reached out my hand, moving the cursor across the screen and opening my inbox.

My hands began to tremble. There was a reply to my email to Shahirah:

Darling Mummy, yes it really is me, your Shah, and I love you too. I miss you SOOO much . . .

I was gone, I was a weeping mess as I tried to read the rest of this precious communiqué. The stony control I had so often called upon over the preceding decade deserted me and all I could do was hang onto the string as the balloon of hope began to soar skywards. My face began to ache from the broad grin I had, like some sort of idiot, under the tears. She had called me Mummy and she said she loved and missed me – no greeting card could ever top those lines for me. As I sit here writing this chapter I realise that this mental image of the day I had my first reply from Shahirah still makes me break into a happy grin – I can't help it, all the years fall away and I am back in the moment.

I found Bill in the garden; I dared not even whisper the news to him for fear of being overheard. I dragged him indoors and wept in his arms then pulled him to the computer and asked him to read, but illogically wouldn't let him go, so intense was my need to be held at this moment.

It took me several readings of Shah's email to twig that she had attached photographs of herself and Iddin. Overwhelmed again, a fresh wave of tears erupted as I saw my children for the first time in eleven years. Shocking and amazing – here were my little ones inhabiting adult bodies – and to me they were amazingly beautiful. Shahirah explained about each hazy image. Here was one of her without her veil so I could see her hair colour and the way it grew.

Somewhere in the middle of all the text I remember reading that her favourite colour was now green. The knowledge of such a simple preference made my eyes overflow with tears again. I felt a twinge of irritation at my own responses, but then pushed it to one side and just revelled in the moment of happiness.

> *People have secretly told me I look like you and that our hair is the same colour. Do I look like you, I really hope so!!*

A doe-eyed willowy teenager with the luminous beauty of youth stared out of the screen at me. I could see some part of my own face reflected in the photograph, but Shah was very much her own person, and needed no comparison to her ecstatic mother.

Included was a photograph she had made Iddin pose for: it was taken from behind, and yes, he still sported a natural blond spot, the one with which he had been born.

Here was another shock, because at twenty he had been transformed into the image of my father. Gone were the long gangly legs and the stick-thin arms and body; in the gauche boy's place was a stocky young man – handsome, somewhat serious, and fully grown. And he had a beard!

This was better than I had hoped, for even if it all turned pear-shaped and contact was again cut off, I now had photographs – I finally knew what my beloved children looked like, and it appeared that they were both taller than me!

Iddin sent his love, Shahirah wrote, but he was a bit shy and said he would write soon. Could she have my telephone number so she could give me a call when she was able?

'Of course,' I wrote in my reply, full of love and amazement. As sensitively as I could I filled Shahirah in on the existence of Verity and my marriage to Bill. I included news of people I hoped she still remembered and volunteered bits and pieces I prayed would jog her memory and make her feel less awkward about our relationship.

One little niggle had to be dealt with.

'Does your father know you have contacted me?' I typed.

In the back of my mind I doubted very much if he did, and instinctively I feared what his reaction might be if he found out.

But for that moment and that day, I allowed myself

unreservedly to feel like the mother of two grown-up children and one little one. I hugged Verity with joy until she squirmed and wriggled away.

What an amazing day! A few minutes had changed my life. After all these years, I had tangible details of the real people my lost children had become.

Chapter 28

A Luddite, a Baby and a Healing

'Mummy!' a woman's voice said to me over a crackly line. 'Hello, Mummy, it's me, your Shah.' She spoke in a musical sing-song tone, slightly tentative and enquiring.

'Shah? Oh my god, Shah! Is that really you? You sound so grown up, sweetie,' was all I managed before a dam burst and all I could do was sob.

'Oh, don't cry, Mummy, it's all right,' Shah soothed me. I was instantly flooded with myriad complex and illogical thoughts: distress that I couldn't recognise my own daughter's voice; relief that one of my heart's desires was coming to fruition; panic as I didn't know what to say to this stranger.

I needn't have worried. After I pulled myself together, we just began to talk – awkwardly, yes, but it was wonderful. I realised that this first phone call needed to be approached with honesty, but also as much nonchalance as I could muster eleven years, six months and fifteen days since I last saw my daughter. No sweat, a little voice inside me urged. Bloody hell!

Shah sounded wonderful, simultaneously intelligent and naive, insightful and giggly and hurt – that was in the undercurrent of her voice. Eleven years of being cut off from me, of having her decisions made for her had taken their toll – there was a fragility to our discussion, as though she and I had still to come to grips with the new reality.

Rationally, I knew that I had lived a whole new life since the kidnapping, and so had Shah. I no longer held a position of authority with her; gone were the days when she was six and I was her all-important mother – and this I had to keep in the forefront of my mind as we talked and cried and talked again.

I tried to keep a level tone and failed abysmally. But I must have done something right, because our tentative relationship somehow blossomed. We both took a leap of faith that day and began to occupy a place, however small, in each other's day-to-day lives. For me, Shahirah's presence was a constant – it had been since the day she was born – but for Shahirah, I had to keep telling myself, I probably would be no more than a secret smidgeon in a private part of her thoughts.

For years, I had privately held the conviction that my children would return to see me when they were adults, but I hadn't expected anything before they each reached the age of about twenty-seven. I'd had to think in those terms: I had calmly calculated the years of education then added the time it would take for them to establish themselves either in a career or in marriage, find their own adult voices and break free of their father's all-pervading presence and control. Yes, I had thought, twenty-seven would be a feasible age to come into one's own in the royal family of Terengganu.

Now I saw I had underestimated the vistas the Internet

could provide, and I had doubly underestimated my daughter's gutsiness. She was apparently very much my daughter after all – a source of headaches to her father and the stepmothers he had provided my children with. I will admit I got a little pinprick of satisfaction from this knowledge.

What an amazing new dimension technology has brought to the world! The children and I had been censored from each other's lives – but a little bit of 'googling' and Shah had been able to track me down herself. She had learned of my aid work and other activities. And now, with the privacy of her own pre-paid personal mobile phone that couldn't be traced or tracked by other parties, a whole spectrum of possibilities opened up for us.

Privacy and secrecy were the biggest worries I had. Such a development of wonderful happiness! Yet I was forced to maintain silence as far as the outside world was concerned. Shah was still a long way off being considered an adult in Malaysia. Twenty-one was the age of majority there, and even then, a member of an Islamic royal house had severely limited options. Iddin, too, was still not legally an adult. Lord only knew what their father would do if he found out about this contact, for during my conversation with Shah, I was able to gather that the proverbial would really hit the fan if he was to find out. My biggest fear was that Shah would be married off without a choice and would be swallowed up in the great royal abyss.

Following my first phone call with Shah, I wrote a list of people I felt I could safely tell our news. It wasn't so much that I couldn't trust a really broad circle of my friends; rather, everyone I told could perhaps let slip in their excitement this wonderful development for my family . . . and in the end it could be leaked to the press out of joy and excitement, not malice.

Sue MacArthur was the top of the list. She is Shahirah's godmother. I was still sad that Rob, Sue's husband, and Shah and Iddin's godfather, had passed away suddenly during the Kosovo war and I hadn't been able to attend his funeral. Sue had known Shah since before she was born and loved both her and Iddin loyally and unwaveringly. She burst into sobs of joy when I told her the good news, and then in the next breath counselled, 'You can't tell anyone, it would be too dangerous for Shah.' My dear friend comprehended the risks involved so clearly that she withheld the news from her two sons, Nick and Ben – young men who had been practically raised alongside my children and who considered themselves their cousins.

Next was Patsy, safely residing in Belgium. I knew that she would understand my emotions, and my conversation with her would be brief – she'd fill in the blanks herself. Then Barry Goodman, my dear friend who had returned to live in London. My beloved Tony Williams had introduced Barry and me over lunch, suspecting that we would get on enormously well. As a result, Barry and I shared our libraries, great conversations and each other's trust. Barry is endowed with wonderful good sense and an uncanny eye for cutting through bullshit. It was he who made sure Verity's first restaurant lunch and art gallery visit was undertaken at the age of eight days with me in tow. Barry makes a wonderful godfather to Verity and would stand as godfather to the new baby as well. Of course, I whispered the news to Deb Gribble, another sister I never had; she had supported me all through the darkest hours and days following the abduction and loved Shah very much – she, too, wept. I contacted Judith Curran in New Zealand to bring her up to date, just as she was about to hop on a flight to film a documentary in some exotic clime, and she promptly sat down, dissolving in a puddle of tears and laughter. Ever practical, her first statement when she pulled herself together was, 'Do you want me to fly over there today and help bring her home? What else can I do?'

My beloved godparents, Auntie Connie and Uncle Kevin, who are more like my surrogate mother and father, took their phone call in the kitchen of the townhouse to which they had retired after they sold their dairy farm. 'My dear, what wonderful news,' said Auntie Connie. 'Be very careful of your own self too, not just the children. We love you all.'

Tall and patrician Heather Brown, burst into tears at her kitchen sink as I let her in on the news. 'Bloody hell,' she sobbed, 'I can't believe it! We can't tell anyone; I've lived in Malaysia, I know the complications for you all. Oh, it's wonderful, I can't stop blubbing.'

I wished that my dear agent, Tony Williams, was still alive for me to confide in, but he had passed away very suddenly from an aggressive type of cancer only three months before. But I could have sworn that I heard his drawling and husky tones as he received the news: 'Play it through, me dear, just play it through. What other choice do you have, me dear?'

Exhausted by the end of a very emotional day, I lay down with Verity's sleeping form cradled in my arms and fell into a deep sleep of warm and unreserved happiness. Towards dawn though, a cold breath of fear stole into my room. I sat bolt upright beside Bill and extricated my arms from around Verity.

I would have to dissemble from now on. I would have to

bend the truth whenever the inevitable question was trotted out: 'Have you spoken to your children?'

How could I get around this innocuous but fraught line of questioning?

And then I came up with my strategy, the manoeuvre that would squeeze me out of the tightest of corners, a stock response that would satisfy the curious. Whenever the question was posed, I would subtly change the subject, just like politicians and diplomats the world over.

'I wish I could hug them, that's all really. It's been so many years now and all I can imagine is how amazing a hug would be. I can't talk about it at the moment because I will burst into tears. I know you understand.' I would finish with an extended hand on the questioner's arm as a thank you – drawing a line under the enquiry and effectively changing the subject.

It wasn't strictly lying, I assured myself shakily; I was telling the truth while avoiding answering the question. Most importantly, and this had to be my paramount concern, I was protecting my children. They had to come first, before any of my prickling sensibilities and the press and public's interest.

But it was enormously hard, I was to find, and so Bill and I began to confine our social activities to either large affairs, like christenings or weddings, or small gatherings with the people who knew what was going on. It was an enormous strain, keeping this huge secret, but it would prove to be worth it for my children's sakes and the tentative steps they were both taking.

My contact with Iddin was initially much more confusing than with his sister. Somehow, with Shah, it had been easy to fall into girltalk.

Luckily, I knew many young men and teenage boys had

difficulty verbalising their emotions. I could only imagine this was compounded in my son's case: though he was at the age when most young men in Western society strive to free themselves of the shackles that tie them to their parents, Iddin was firmly in my former husband's sphere of influence.

Quite shy as a child, Iddin had also been a cautious kid, seldom leaping into any activity without first calculating his ability to undertake the task with some success. He had always been the thoughtful one, ruminating long and hard on issues and solutions, so I could only imagine what a can of worms my presence would bring to his now fairly stable existence. I wanted to know and understand the young man he had become, and I realised that any contact I had with him would have to make my appreciation of his adulthood very clear.

I, of all people, had to give him respect, for I strongly suspected that his father, a consummate ringmaster and puppeteer, would still be trying to control every aspect of our eldest child's existence. Intelligent young men need the security of respect and an acknowledgement of equality from their parents as they mature. Without parental trust in his good character and common sense, a son's self-esteem and confidence cannot grow.

Taking the bull by the horns, I rang Iddin at Shah's urging – she gave me his number. I knew that Iddin had not been that comfortable with the written word when he was a child, having been diagnosed with a mild form of dyslexia. So a very quick phone call might be the best way to start. Besides, he was about to turn twenty, and I couldn't possibly miss one more of his birthdays.

I dialled the mobile number three times and hung up

before it even began to ring but, pulling my nervous stomach into line, I finally allowed the ringtone to begin.

Speed, accuracy and love were my goals. Would I ever get another chance?

The phone answered.

'Hello Iddin, it's Mum. I'm sorry to intrude and I really don't want to make you feel uncomfortable, but I really, really wanted to hear your voice. I love you and I really miss you and I am so sorry that I couldn't get you home and I tried, I really tried, but it was so impossible.'

(Quick gasp for breath.)

'I sent you presents and cards and letters and I don't know if you ever got them. I just wanted you to know that I am really proud that I have you as my son and I will love you no matter what you choose to do in your life.'

(Gasp and sob from me.)

'OK, I'll go now, I'm sorry that I've intruded. I love you so very much—'

'Hey, Mum, don't go! I'm really sorry I didn't email you or ring after Shah got the numbers but, Mum, I just didn't know what to say or how to write it. I'm scared, Mum, and I love you too!'

It was the best ham-fisted, needy and garbled phone call I have ever made. A wave of profound peace swept over me as I heard my son tell me I was loved and remembered. For now, that was enough.

Chapter 29

Lysander the Magnificent

T he importance of finding out who my children were as grown-up individuals was foremost in my mind. Because they had been kidnapped in a pair, it was far too easy to lump them together. I had to make a conscious effort to allow them each true individuality. Their experiences over the intervening years – according to their gender, scholastic achievement, obedience and adaptability – would have varied enormously. Little by little, as we talked and corresponded, I was to discover more about each of these two beloved people.

And all the while I watched Verity grow and thrive, developing into a funny little individual full of unselfconscious smiles and the utter security of being loved by Bill and me. She took to bathing the baby doll we had bought her to ease her into the concept of a little brother, and would press her mouth up against my belly and talk to the baby about painting and food and whatever else came into her head. She had watched a birth video with me and wasn't at all perturbed; rather, she was enthralled with the whole process. She loved the knowledge that she had grown inside my tummy and could still remember being breastfed.

Shah, too, via long distance, had a real fascination with descriptions of the baby's movements inside me and the photographs I sent her via email of my condition and of Verity too. My pregnancy led to lots of talks with Shah about my feelings for her, her birth and what she had been like as a little person. It was obviously important for her to hear the mothering in my voice. Verity and Shah even began to develop a relationship of their own. They would have small chats on the phone and Shah began to call Verity 'V' – her special pet name for her little sister.

The pain came in concentric circles from my lower back. Leaning my forearms over the edge of the bed, I rocked as Bill rubbed my back, and Sue read aloud an article from a newspaper. It was 21 April 2003, a Monday, and I was in labour for the birth of my fourth child.

Verity was safely ensconced with her grandparents, Bill's mum and dad, and would stay with them until her baby brother was born. They would spoil her to death, I knew, as they were utterly devoted to their granddaughter, the first grandchild in the family. Bill would laughingly complain that all the Greek strictness he had been brought up with had completely evaporated when it came to Verity.

The hours went by and I paced and rocked, trying to speed the delivery along. Then I phoned Shah in Malaysia.

'Mum! Have you had the baby yet?' she squealed before I had even said hello. She was completely in the moment and wanted a description of how I was feeling. It was an amazing situation to be in, whispering secretly to my daughter, while she encouraged me to hurry up and give birth to her little brother!

Things don't always go to plan with babies, and so it was with the birth of Lysander. Instinctively, I knew that all was not right – even when the pains increased marginally in strength, they weren't nearly painful enough. Twelve hours of labour had passed, the contractions were 90 seconds apart and I could still talk and joke and walk around. I should have been almost speechless with pain by this stage and approaching the need to push, but the weight in my pelvis felt wrong.

The doctor did another pelvic exam, and the news was not good. The baby had cocked his head backwards and jammed it just above the birth canal. His heartbeat was still strong, but my heart was showing signs of fatigue. To have a successful and safe vaginal birth with a strange head presentation such as this was an impossibility, given my weakened heart muscle. It was going to be an emergency Caesarean section, my biggest dread about childbirth.

Less than twenty minutes later I was flat on my back in an operating theatre, numbed from the waist down and being rocked and pulled as the doctor wrestled our son through the incision in my belly. Bill sat at my left shoulder, perspiration beading his forehead. I knew he was worried he would faint at the sight of so much blood. But then he was swept up in the moment, as Lysander Antonio appeared over the top of the surgical screen spanning my belly. It was 9.21 p.m. on 21 April.

Bill cut the umbilical cord, and I had a moment to plant a

kiss on little Lysander's forehead as he gave a lusty yell.

Groggy joy and relief spilled out of me, and I wept in a slightly befuddled cloud of painkillers. But then, suddenly, things threatened to go pear-shaped – I began to haemorrhage.

Bill was hustled out with Lysander before I had got a good look at him and the surgical team set to work again.

Two hours later, all sewn up and doped to my eyeballs on morphine, I held Lysander in my arms for the first time and inspected our baby son, with Bill hovering at the edge of the bed as I could barely manage Lysander without help. Amazingly gorgeous, and enormous!

Lysander was born the largest of my four children, a whopping 3.9 kilograms (8 pounds, 6 ounces) and 62 centimetres (26 inches) long – we'd better start saving for big shoes, I thought. His head circumference was 37.5 centimetres – suddenly I was rather grateful for the C section.

Lysander had bright blue eyes and blondish hair and extraordinarily long toes and fingers. He took to my breast with gusto, emitting lots of satisfied little grunts before drifting off to sleep.

Handing me the phone, Bill said it was Shah, whom he had called with the news. This was an incredibly emotional chat; the drugs were kicking in and I was so happy I could only weep. Thousand of miles away, my daughter wept with me and I recalled the wonder I felt at the birth of all my amazing children, and hoped I would soon be introducing them to each other.

Chapter 30

Surges and Roller Coasters

N ow my life was filled with lightness of spirit as I threw myself into the wonderful joy of mothering my two youngest children. Verity and Zan loved each other fiercely – when they weren't clashing, as siblings do.

Verity had started kindergarten and was thrilled with it, and Lysander was a happy, relaxed little fellow with blond curls and twinkly blue eyes. Given half the chance, Verity would paint or draw for the entire day and both children would have me read them books and tales for all the waking hours.

Sometimes I couldn't help reflecting that with the wonderful experience of being able to mother children again, my entire world had begun to right itself – my life was loving and peaceful at last.

As the children grew bigger, I began doing some freelance

magazine writing, and started to participate regularly in the Department of Foreign Affairs and Trade's (DFAT's) consular training courses, as a consultant. I was teaching diplomats how to deal empathically with distressed people, like the left-behind parents who might contact them for assistance and guidance. I found it amusing that I had done this sort of work in Washington, for a foreign government, many years earlier. The wheels of change often turn slowly in Australia, although in this instance, through my work with the Department, I came to understand that a new wind was sweeping away all the stuffiness and intractability of old. I was proud of my connection to DFAT and the changes there.

By this time I was working only sporadically at the coalface of parental child abduction – I had just about suffered burnout on this issue – but was immensely satisfied that over the years some of my recommendations were adopted by the European Union, the Australian Attorney General's Department, British Lord Chancellor's Department, Hong Kong Family Law Association, a body of American judges specialising in family law and, most recently, DFAT.

Bill, too, had made a sea change, distancing himself from his former life as senior executive with a multinational telecommunications firm. Already holding a science degree, he returned to university to further his studies, at the same time following his passion for building and construction by starting his own firm. He also kept his hand in the field of technology and continued to consult to large corporations in need of his expertise.

We had decided that we needed more room for our growing family and to cater for the possibility that Shah and

Iddin might want to visit us some day. So Bill set about renovating and extending the house we owned next door – essentially building a house atop a house and cleverly turning a single-storey Victorian terrace into a light-filled four-bedroom modern home. He did the work himself, during 2005, with a crew of employees, and me catering – hot lunch for the workers every day! My amazing father-in-law, Anton, who is in his 70s, insisted on working at the building site every day too. His grandchildren, Verity and Lysander, love their *Papoo*, and revelled in his presence.

Aid work was something I now missed, but taking off to a war or disaster zone at the drop of a hat when you have a family, especially with small children, is out of the question. After the tsunami in South East Asia in late 2004, I did some fundraising for CARE, and was pleased to be able to contribute to the relief effort in this small way. I will probably always twitch when I see places and people I could possibly assist if I were still in the field, and I don't think I will ever get that part of my life out of my blood. I doubt if I really ever would desire to, for it is something I hope my children learn from and are proud that I did.

Contact with Shah and Iddin grew more and more frequent, richer and more intimate. We went to great pains to keep it secret. The weight of keeping this wonderful news to myself in the face of well-wishers enquiring about our family was a daily strain; over and over I reminded myself that the children came first, and held my tongue.

Little by little, I had the honour of knowing that I was becoming Shah's confidante and, little by little, Iddin's friend.

It was a thrill to receive a text message from Iddin, wishing me a happy Mother's Day and telling me I was the best mum in the world. A Christmas wish or just a hello was blissful. The simple and joyous pleasure of a text message, or a call on my birthday after so many years, meant the world. For so long I'd had to pretend that I hadn't experienced twinges of envy when all around me received these markers of normality and love. Now that it was returned to me, I vowed I'd never take my children's love for granted.

Shah had begun to study architecture at university. This course was not something about which she was personally passionate, and it disappointed me that she was not encouraged to follow, or even allowed to discover, her own heart's desire. But some things, like her veil and her studies, were for her father to command, it seemed.

Shah and I had by this time developed pet names for each other. Shah had a deep love of Louisa May Alcott's *Little Women*, and long ago I had cried over the book too. We spoke of the March family often, and eventually I became her 'Marmee', and she my 'Jo Girl'.

Iddin, meanwhile, was a young man trying to find his feet and his own way in the world. I was so proud of him when, late in 2005, he finally found his voice and his passion – photography – and decided to follow his heart instead of his father's dictums. It took a lot of guts to go against those expectations of the royal family.

Chapter 31

The Incy Wincy Spider

'Mum, I'm supposed to go to London and Paris with Abah [her father] and the other kids in a week or so, what will I do? I'm going to be looking after five of them as their mothers aren't going.' Shah was referring to her step-siblings, the children of her father's numerous wives.

Goodness, what was the subtext to this statement, I wondered.

Shah's relationship with her father was quite volatile; she wasn't always the obedient daughter he required. The children had never been allowed any independent travel; certainly the passport issue was a fraught one, yet here Bahrin was offering Shah an international trip, albeit in the dead of winter and to the opposite end of the globe to where her mother lived. Apparently Bahrin staunchly avoided any mention of me to the children, they'd not been allowed a single letter or gift from me in all those long years; he probably felt that his years of indoctrination and unyielding discipline had cleansed their minds of me. He still had no notion that Shah and Iddin were in contact with me; had he known he would surely be apoplectic. After all, this was the man who insisted on choosing his wives' and children's clothes – to match his!

This offer to Shah was a first, and I ran through various scenarios in my head. Did her father mean it as a diversion because he suspected her growing disenchantment with her regimented, restricted life?

Both Shah and Iddin had said they wanted very much to come home to Australia, but the definitive break was proving harder for them emotionally than any of us had expected. To visit me would be a declaration of rebellion against their father and everything that had been drummed into them. In a culture of filial piety and unquestioning obedience, it would be viewed as disrespect of the first order and constitute a grave loss of face for Bahrin among his peers, and before the public at large.

It was also an incredible leap of faith for Shah and Iddin to contemplate leaving Malaysia – all they were familiar with as adults was in that country.

Financially, I wasn't wealthy and simply didn't have the wherewithal to open a cheque book and write Iddin and Shah a new life. I could provide money for tickets, yes; a roof over their heads and food, of course; and bottomless love and unequivocal acceptance – but not the lifestyle and diversions they were used to. Neither of them had ever worked; royals simply don't have after-school jobs at McDonald's. Shah had done a little tutoring for spare change, but that was hardly the reality of student life in Australia. Both were accustomed to a generous allowance from Bahrin, even if there were strings attached. How would they cope back home in Australia?

Two years had passed since Shah's first email, and at times first one and then the other had been ready to make the leap to freedom and Australia, but never, frustratingly, at the same time! We would get a part of the way down the track and then one wouldn't want to leave without the other – the timing was always off.

Now, trying to sound casual, I ventured to Shah that if she wanted it, I could arrange for help to get her home from Paris or London – all she had to do was get to the Australian Embassy and they would assist her. Under Australian law, I reminded her, she was an adult and legally able to do as she pleased. 'Heavens, you can even tell me to take a flying leap and there is nothing I can or would want to do about it,' I assured her.

Tentatively, she began to ask what she would have to do. She worried that she wouldn't be able to find her way around Paris or London alone, so I gave her the telephone numbers of my friends Patsy and Barry. Both of them could be trusted implicitly, and either of them would drop anything at her call and take her under their wing. Barry was living in the middle of London, and Patsy would drive down to Shah's aid in Paris at the drop of a hat.

Shah and I put a plan in place over a couple of days of intense phone calls. If she felt confident enough, she would attempt to leave the hotel in London or Paris on her own, without her father being aware she was missing, having called Patsy or Barry first. Or perhaps she would simply wander into a fitting room at Harrods or Printemps and disappear.

The next thing I did was call the Department of Foreign Affairs. I blessed the fact that I could speak directly to the officer in charge of consular affairs, because of my work with the Department. They swung into action, notifying the various overseas stations and smoothing the way.

Barry and Patsy were primed and ready. I had my fingers crossed and was praying for a miracle. But I pushed my excitement to the background and pretended to myself there was nothing unusual going on.

We moved into the newly renovated house in the middle of Shah's trip to Europe. It was complete except for the kitchen – I had to limit my cooking to barbecues, barbecues and the added flavour of stir-fries cooked on, you guessed it, the barbecue. Thank goodness it was summer.

Setting up the Christmas tree with Zan and Verity, I fastened our bedraggled fairy to the top of the tree and wondered if Shah would see it in place over the New Year.

Christmas drew near. Barry called me two days before the holiday – I held my breath expectantly.

Yes, Shah had been in touch with him on her mobile, a number of times – but then silence had fallen.

I rationed my tears to ten minutes alone in the bathroom. I'd had years of disappointment, I joked to my reflection in the mirror. Time to get on with it again.

Although there was still a chance Shah would activate the plan, I felt instinctively that this was not the time when I would hold one of my older children in my arms. I brought my attention back to the little ones, who had been in a flurry of Christmas wrappings and stickytape when Barry, their godfather, had telephoned.

Shah would later tell me that she simply couldn't leave her

little sisters unchaperoned, marooned and distressed in a large, unfamiliar department store, and that she was too frightened to make the leap. I reassured her that it was OK, it was her decision to make – I wasn't cross, I told her. I loved her whether she was near or far – no ifs or buts and it wasn't dependent on her turning up in my living room. I would see her if and when the time was right for her.

Chapter 32

Down Came the Rain

Tuesday, 14 February 2006, began ordinarily enough. Verity had started primary school a few days earlier, at Bill's old school just around the corner from our house. It was a point of pride to her that she was following in her dad's footsteps, as she delighted in announcing to all and sundry. I was still coming to terms with the rapid passage of time! Verity was now almost five and was suddenly a tiny schoolgirl.

Lysander was less than his exuberant self that day, having had a general anaesthetic and three hours of surgery on his mouth and jaw, for a dental problem, a few days earlier. A Wiggles CD managed to raise a smile and a bit of participation from him, but he was lobbying heavily for a *Thunderbirds* DVD, telling me his mouth was still too 'ouchy' to go and play in the garden in the shady afternoon light. Nice try, I thought, with an inward smile. I was negotiating a play with his train set instead of television when the telephone rang.

'Mummy,' cried the sobbing voice, 'I want to come home now! Now, Mum, I've had enough. I can't do this any more.'

'Shah, what's happened, darling? What's wrong? Are you hurt?' I was in a panic.

'No, Mum, I just can't keep doing architecture – I hate it and I want to come home and see you *now*!'

Gradually I calmed her, and we started to consider how she might come home.

'Shah, have you still got the Malaysian passport you used for the trip to Europe?'

'I've got it, Mum, but what happens if Abah has a security flag on it and I get stopped when I try to leave the country?' Her father could do this, as Shah was still not of legal age in Malaysia.

I tried to think of the right words to say. All I could come out with was, 'Darling, if you want to come home, then we'll make it happen.'

She was still upset, but adamant that was what she wanted; now all I needed was to come up with a plan.

'Give me until tomorrow morning to put all the things in place, but I want you to start getting ready now. If we don't want your father to find out what you're doing . . .'

'I can't tell him,' she wailed. 'He'll stop me for sure and I'll be sent back to Terengganu and I won't be able to see you or even talk to you. He doesn't understand,' she went on. 'I'm not happy here and I can't do architecture just because he wants me to be like him. I need to see you, Mum' – huge gasp for breath and hacking sobs – 'I want to come home. I want to be myself.'

'OK, darling,' I gentled her. 'The first thing is to understand that the best way for you to leave, if you really think that Abah may have an alert attached to you, is to get to the Causeway.'

The Causeway is the bridge that connects the peninsula of Malaysia with the Republic of Singapore. It was a few hours' drive from where Shah was living. Scores of buses and cars crossed the border at this point daily, bringing cheap labour from Malaysia into affluent Singapore. Shahirah would have a better chance of leaving Malaysia at this point than any other. It was normal for Malaysians to drive over to Singapore for a day of shopping; it would appear as if Shah was going on an innocent shopping trip. If she was caught, it would seem less sinister if she was without luggage – it would simply look like she was being a bit naughty and going for a jaunt to buy some trinkets without her father's permission. That she actually needed his permission at the age of twenty greatly angered me. She was an adult; even I shouldn't have control over her.

'You'll have to go across really early one morning,' I told Shah. 'Do you still have a bodyguard following you around?'

'No, not any more, not that I've noticed, not since I've been in uni, but then Abah has arranged for lots of people to keep an eye on me.'

'OK, you're going to have to be very brave and organised and do exactly as I tell you, Jo Girl. You can't tell anyone you're going and you won't be able to take anything with you except a small backpack, like a day bag.'

'My friend thinks I should tell Abah that I'm dropping out of uni. She says she'll come with me, but I'm afraid.'

'Do you think that's a good idea, darling? What do you think might happen if you tell your father?' I cursed this naive friend in whom Shah had already confided, then wondered if the friend perhaps knew which side their bread was buttered on.

'I don't want to speak to Abah, but I do want to tell Iddin what I'm planning and see if he will come as well.'

'OK, that's your decision, but you have to do it quickly, and I'll ring your brother as well.'

Taking a big gulp of air, I outlined more of the plan that was working itself out in my brain.

'You're going to have to find out the bus schedules from Kuala Lumpur to Johore or Singapore and give me the time of the one you think you can catch. Do you have any money?'

'I think I have enough for the bus fare, but that's all, Marmee.' She was starting to sound calmer again, which made me worry less.

'Don't worry about anything else, I'll arrange the ticket out of Singapore to Melbourne,' I assured Shah. 'I'm going to contact the Australian authorities and see what they can do to help us.'

Thinking about the different times zones, I made rapid calculations about whom I would need to call first.

'I'm going to go now. You keep your phone on and I'll call you back later.'

What happened next was an amazing flurry of phone calls, right at the end of the business day, to the Department of Foreign Affairs in Canberra, and some intense conversations. Luckily, I was dealing with Tracey Wunder in Consular Affairs and she simply pulled out all the stops to assist me. Diplomatic cables flew off to the mission in Singapore, though I was careful to make it clear that this could all disappear in a split-second and that Shah was highly emotional.

Within hours I was able to ring Shah back with a solid

plan and a contact number at the Australian consulate in Singapore. Speaking at length to the Consul, Ross Tysoe, I was struck by how level-headed and unflappably sensible he was – and how compassionate.

Fortunately, according to Shah, my former husband was in Dubai on business and so the prospect of him confronting her and physically stopping her departure seemed less likely than I'd feared.

'Mum, my friend wants to drive me to Singapore to say goodbye,' Shah announced, and I bit down my irritation with this friend once more. In any case, it was Shah's choice, and I'd agree to anything to see her safely to the Causeway and her rendezvous in Singapore.

It had been determined that a dawn crossing would be best. The Australian High Commission staff had been put on alert, as had Qantas, that they might have a special passenger in the next few days for one of their flights to Australia. We had made the call that any flight to Australia would do; the imperative was to get my daughter out of the region. If there were no seats available, Shah would travel in the cockpit of a Qantas aircraft, as this was considered Australian territory and not subject to the laws of another country.

'No more mobile calls about the package, Ms Pascarl,' said my final official contact in his best 'M' voice. 'There's always a lot of interest around,' he added cryptically.

'Do you still want to do this, darling?' I asked Shah in our next phone conversation, holding my breath for her answer.

'Yes, Mum,' she answered without hesitation. 'I need to come home. I want to be free.'

'OK, if you are sure. Now I want you to buy a prepaid SIM card for later. When you are safely clear of Kuala Lumpur, you'll have to take your old SIM card out of your phone and toss it away.'

Surely we'd covered all instructions now?

I hardly slept a wink that night: it was only hours until we knew if this plan would work, and erase fourteen years of yearning.

The next day, 15 February, was Iddin's twenty-third birthday. I resolved to call him later in the day when I knew he would probably be alone. I feared putting him in the position of knowing too much if he wasn't coming too. The last thing I wanted was for him to be blamed for Shah's departure. In Bahrin's book, non-disclosure was as bad as outright lying. Grey areas of behaviour were strictly reserved for him.

The following day, Shah and I spoke every three hours from 11 a.m. Melbourne summer time. Malaysia was three hours behind us, and I could barely function that whole long day watching the clock tick over the minutes and the hours. Bill kept Verity and Lysander occupied, leaving me free to fixate. Jumping out of my skin every time the phone rang, I remained in front of the computer taking care of final details with Foreign Affairs.

Whenever Shahirah and I spoke she swung between utter determination and nervous anxiety. I tried to calm her when she started to panic: 'Darling Jo Girl, it will be fine, you just have to be very brave and remember what to do. It will all be fine, sweetie. You're an intelligent grown woman, this is your decision to make as an adult. I love you sweetheart, and so do Verity and Zan – they can't wait to see you. Just hang on, darling, and we'll soon be able to give each other a huge hug. You can do this, darling, just be brave.'

Eventually, I put the little ones to bed and pushed down my gnawing anxiety as I read them story after story. Lying between them both, I listened to their peaceful breathing and occasional snuffles and began to let down my guard and wonder what it would be like if Shahirah arrived in Melbourne the very next night. I wondered what a hug with her would feel like or if she would be too shy to want that. I dreamed of laying the palms of my hands on her face and learning its contours.

Rising from the bed, I walked downstairs to phone Iddin for his birthday, and a very serious chat.

Iddin told me he felt it wasn't time for him to come home just yet. He was also rather worried about Shah's departure.

'Abah is going to be so pissed off, Mum. I don't want to get the blame.'

What could I say to him? All I could ask was that he not obstruct what his sister was about to do.

'I really love you, Mum. Thanks for the birthday call – I'm really sorry I can't come right now, but I will come soon, I promise.'

Hours later, my stomach was churning, as if I was on some unhinged amusement park ride and my nerve endings were uncomfortably electrified. The departure time was scheduled: midnight Malaysian time, 3 a.m. Melbourne time.

Shah's last call had come an hour earlier, at 10.30 p.m., and I was beginning to get worried. The friend who was supposed to drive her to Singapore was trying to persuade Shah to say goodbye to the friend's family, with whom Shah was close. Were we never to have peace from outsiders meddling in our family life?

At 1 a.m., the telephone rang. It was Shah and she was completely distraught. Her friend had persuaded her that it was wrong to run off without telling her father, and she was losing her nerve. The friend had refused to drive her to Singapore and had taken a detour and the opportunity to browbeat her. I was furious! This so-called friend, I felt, was being utterly self-serving and ignoring Shah's wishes. For so many years, people had been telling Shah what to do and here was another example of her powerlessness over her existence and her opinions.

In the middle of a devastatingly emotional discussion, Shah's mobile phone rang.

'It's Abah,' she began to scream hysterically. 'He's coming to see me now! I can't do it – he's back early and I can't do it now – it's too late, Mummy. Oh, Mummy, I'm sorry, so sorry, I love you so, I can't get to you now.'

I heard loud hammering on a door, voices in the background, the sounds of a scuffle.

'Oh, Mummy, I'm sorry I waited too long, I lo—' and the line went dead.

Shredded by fear and worry I began to sob, and dialled and redialled Shah's phone with no answer. Frantic with anxiety at what had happened to my daughter, I tried to recall exactly what I'd heard in the background during the call. Someone had obviously alerted her father to what was going on and he had hotfooted it back from the Persian Gulf. I had my suspicions, but it was too late for me to do anything about it. Shah had been stalled, worn down and manipulated, until time simply ran out.

Gutted beyond belief, I stared into the darkness, waiting for the sun to come up. It was akin to having her kidnapped all over again. That we'd come so close was no consolation.

This waiting game, and always having to pick myself up and keep going, was getting to be too much. I was seriously pissed off at any higher power that was floating around out there pulling the strings of my life.

Chapter 33

On Tenterhooks

It was 2 a.m. in Belgium, and Patsy's voice was toneless. Her amazing and extraordinary Walter, her husband, had suddenly collapsed and died without regaining consciousness.

Walter had been a sturdy bull of a man in his early 40s. Patsy wept, and said he'd just returned from a trekking trip that weekend. He had caught a terrible bug that had attacked most of his organs.

I wanted to jump on the next flight to Belgium, but Patsy insisted I not come yet.

'Come later, when I'm really alone. You're the first person I've told: I knew you and I could understand each other. I've just driven back from the hospital, and soon everyone will be here. After the funeral, when they've gone, then you may come to Ambly.'

Bill and I had both spoken to Walter a few weeks earlier. Now, listening, Bill was ashen; he and Walter had become friends over the Internet. They had very similar personalities and had ribbed each other endlessly.

Melbourne was gripped in a sports-mad fever; the Commonwealth Games had rolled into town, bringing with it elite athletes from around the globe and an arts festival that was a moving feast of activity and colour. The city glowed in the early autumn sunshine and the weather held, bringing the mercury to 35 degrees and the people to the river and the beach and all the places Melbourne offered in between.

So I was pulling myself out of all the doldrums, taking Verity and Lysander to the fun activities put on during the school holidays against the backdrop of the Commonwealth Games.

The city crowd on this glorious day was raucous; roving minstrels added to the cacophony, and the strains of a jazz band competed with the laughter and shouting of children building sandcastles on the artificial beach temporarily lying outside the art gallery. The sky was blue and cloudless, the sun hot and bright.

We had joined Verity's best friend, Lavinia, her big sister, Kiara, and their mother, Andrae Talarico, for this outing. Lysander and the girls were digging delightedly in the sand and Andrae and I sat together watching the fun. The girls had spent two years at kindergarten joined at the hip and were now attending the same school.

I felt a strange vibration in my trouser pocket, and it took me a while to realise it was my mobile phone. Drawing it out at a fumble, I saw Shah's number pop up on the screen.

We'd had very limited contact since the abortive flight to Singapore. It had been several days before I learned that she was unhurt, but very fragile. Weeks had now gone by, and my emotions had evened out and found a safe plateau.

Somehow, Shahirah had managed to keep the full truth

from her father, and he still had no idea that she and Iddin had developed a secret relationship with me. Therefore, the recriminations had been limited. Bahrin viewed Shah's planned 'shopping' trip to Singapore as a caprice, a whim of fancy by a silly and rebellious girl. He hadn't a clue about who our daughter was and what she needed. I wondered if he had ever really looked at her and seen anything other than his own reflection.

'Hi, Mum! When's Verity's birthday party and Lysander's? Oh, and Easter too, when's that?' came Shah's questions out of the blue.

Rising to my feet, I gestured to Andrae that I had to go somewhere quieter to take this call, and moved to a deserted side entrance to the gallery.

Giving the dates, and glancing back at Zan and Verity as I answered, I asked her how she was.

'I'm great, Marmee! I'll be coming to see you next Saturday – Abah's buying me a ticket!'

It was now Wednesday. Fasten your seatbelt, I warned myself, here we go again.

'Mum, are you still there? I'm really coming this time. I've told Abah I want to see you and he's given me permission to come for a short holiday.'

How I wanted to scream now, at that patronising word 'permission' – she was twenty years old. She didn't need permission, particularly to visit the mother from whom she'd been kidnapped. The visit, if indeed it went ahead, would take place just three months short of her twenty-first birthday – and her legal majority under Malaysian law too.

Somehow I mustered a semblance of cautious enthusiasm, not wishing to deflate Shah when she sounded so happy, but feeling very dubious about this storybook chapter unfolding – it was just too good to be true, unless Bahrin planned to bring Shah right up to the wire and then pull the pin on the whole plan.

'Are you pleased? I'm going to be there for Verity's birthday party!' Shah said again.

'Absolutely, darling, but how did all this come about? How much does your father know about us?'

'Not that much. He thinks I've only just spoken to you in the last couple of weeks.'

'Well, this is amazing news, darling, thank your father for me!' And with just a little more bewildering chat, she rang off.

I couldn't help but note that Saturday's date would be 1 April – April Fools' Day – was this Bahrin's idea of a cruel joke?

The next day, I went through the rigmarole of contacting Foreign Affairs again, and putting a game plan together with the sterling assistance Tracey Wunder, who was such a bubbly woman with a great sense of humour and a strong dose of common sense. Worried that this would also prove to be a false alarm, I explained the maze of difficulties and apologised in advance – just in case.

If Shah really did arrive in two days' time, the last thing we wanted was a media feeding-frenzy. Immigration flagged Shah's arrival and ensured it would not be necessary for her to be processed in the public arrivals hall. The manager of Melbourne Airport was brought into the loop; he organised for me to park at the rear of the terminal, out of public view. I could wait for Shah in the government's VIP room, where there was little chance of bumping into anyone who would catch on to what was happening. Customs officers would escort Shahirah off the plane and directly to the room. To avoid my being seen, it was decided I should arrive two hours prior to Shah's flight and bunker down in the VIP room to wait.

I would have to leave home at 4.30 a.m. to get to the airport, and we had decided we wouldn't rouse Verity and Zan. Bill would stay at home with them, and our friend Peter Wallace would go to the airport with me. It was best for Verity and Lysander to remain in ignorance of Shah's possible arrival. Saturday was the day of Verity's fifth birthday party and an early start would be too much for her on such an exciting, busy day. There was also this: if Shah didn't turn up, Verity would be devastated and it would ruin her birthday. So we strove to keep the lead-up to the big day as normal as possible.

Our family friends would be at the party early, sworn to secrecy; and later arrivals would be introduced to Shah as a non-English-speaking exchange student. So with twenty-four hours to go, and a birthday party for twenty-five children to cater for, I rolled up my sleeves and began a baking frenzy. If Shah really did walk off that flight, then I wouldn't have any time for party preparations and it was vital that Verity's big day go ahead as planned. Psychologically, the cancellation of her birthday party should not be linked with a big sister she had never met and who nevertheless promised to change the family dynamic forever. As few waves on the sibling rivalry front, the better.

I finally managed to wrangle an excited Verity and Zan into bed on Friday night. Then I phoned Shah. It was 7.30 p.m. I almost wept when she said she had her ticket in her hand.

At 7.45 p.m. Australian immigration authorities confirmed Shah had an active travel visa in their system.

At 8.30 p.m. I spoke again to Shah: she was still packing and couldn't decide what to bring.

At 8.45 p.m. our friends began to call. Heather rang to check if we were on track; she said she couldn't possibly sleep until she knew Shah was on the plane and made me promise to ring her with an update before I went to bed.

At 8.50 p.m. Sue telephoned to find out if there had been a change of plan.

At 9 p.m. I had Judith on the phone from New Zealand – she was anxious and doing some of the worrying for me.

At 9.10 p.m. Deb wanted to know if Shah was at the airport yet. I said no, still waiting.

With a nervous chuckle I reflected that it felt a bit like being pregnant and all your friends knowing the due date: everyone calls to find out if Mother Nature is running to schedule. In this case we were all hostage to Shah's father, and whether or not at the final hour he would allow her to board the aircraft and let it take off.

By 9.30 p.m. Shah had finished packing and was about to leave for the airport. I told her I wouldn't call again until 11 p.m. my time.

At 9.47 p.m. I talked to Iddin: 'Don't worry, Mum, Shah is going tonight. Love you a lot, Mum, I'm going to come soon too, promise.'

At 10 p.m. the airport duty manager phoned, to go over

security details and arrangements for my vehicle. He was incredibly helpful and also excited for us.

I moved to the computer and began to send out thank-you messages to all those who were helping with delivery of the 'package'. I wanted to ensure that they knew I was grateful for all their thoughtful assistance, regardless of the outcome.

An email I sent to Barry in London that night says it all.

Well, it may just be on for Saturday . . . I won't know until midnight Melbourne time. Proof of the pudding at 8 a.m. on Saturday!!!!!!!!!!!!!! Feel alternately nauseous and paralysed with excitement.

Meanwhile, I'm catering for Verity's fifth birthday party on the same day at 2 p.m. – am up to my armpits tonight in honey joys and chocolate crackles! I also have to bake a mermaid cake!

– Will keep you posted.

Love

Jack xxxx

My feelings and thoughts were a whirl of confusion. I told Bill over and over again: 'She won't come, you know, she's not going to be allowed to get on the plane.' My coping mechanism had flicked onto self-protection mode.

Bill played things very close to his chest, but he spoke of Walter. 'I always thought that when this moment came and the big kids came back, I would talk it through with Walter and ask him what to do – he was the one person I knew who had experienced something like this.'

When I rang her, Patsy had said that Walter was 'up there'

watching over us, orchestrating a positive outcome. But still the manic words continued: 'She's not going to come, she's not going to be on the plane.'

The clock ticked around to 11.30 p.m. and I ventured another call to Shah.

'Hi, Mum, I've just checked in! It's happening!'

'Quick,' I said, 'give me your seat number. I need to notify the people at the airport. You have to stay on board the plane and not get off until a Customs and Immigration officer comes to fetch you. OK darling?'

I scribbled down the seat number, and told her I loved her very much.

'Oh, I love you too,' said her joyous voice. 'I'll be with you soon, Mummy darling, I'll see you in the morning! Verity doesn't know, does she? I really want it to be a surprise for her birthday!'

Assuring Shah it would be and hanging up the phone, I realised that I was trembling. Surprise it would be for Zan and Verity, but would my nervous heart make it through to morning?

I called the special telephone number I had been given by Foreign Affairs. 'The package is in seat 7C and will await collection.' I rang off after an acknowledgement from an unknown voice.

Bill and I sat up to watch a movie, then, bizarrely, unable to relax, I got it into my head to wax my legs. I perched on the kitchen bench slopping burning wax about then ripping it off as Bill winced at my grunts of pain. All the while I muttered under my breath, 'She's not going to be on the plane, she's not really coming, he's going to drag her off at the last minute.'

Just after midnight, I received a text message:

See you in the morning, Love Jo xxx

Bill and I trundled upstairs wearily; tomorrow would either be a very good day, or a very bad one. In any case we would have a birthday party overflowing with five year olds rampaging around the house. It was going to be a very busy day, come what may.

Placing a kiss on Verity, and Zan's brow, I straightened their covers and gently closed the door. If all went well in the morning, their lives would change forever as well. The family dynamic would shift – adjustments would be made by all of us and we'd absorb the changes with love and with each other's help. I said a silent prayer that I would finally have the opportunity to rise to the challenge.

But first, just like a child on Christmas Eve, I had to chase some sleep before I could see what Santa would bring me in the morning.

Chapter 34

The Incy Wincy Spider Climbed up the Spout Again

A sharp rap sounded on the door of the VIP lounge and it swung open. Two uniformed Customs and Immigration inspectors were there, and Bernie Monaghan, the airport duty manager, hovering solicitously and protectively in the background.

'G'day, Jacqueline, my name is Paul and this is Mick,' said the taller of the two officers. 'You won't remember, but you went to primary school with my brother.'

'Of course I remember your brother; what's he up to these days?' I replied with a nervous smile. I could hardly remember my own name at this stage.

'Anyway,' Paul continued, 'I just wanted to say that I've followed your story for years and really felt for you and the kids. We both have' – with a jerk of his head he indicated his partner – 'and we really hope that it turns out all right for you this morning. I just wanted to let you know that the flight has touched down and we'll be heading down to the gate, and then we'll see. Fingers crossed, eh?' He finished with an encouraging smile.

I nodded tremulously, then sincerely thanked them. Until I saw Shah for myself, I wouldn't believe it was true. There was still a possibility it was all another cruel hoax.

The door swung closed and Peter and I sat together in silence. I suddenly thought it was a good thing that Peter was a trauma surgeon – if my heart stopped with grief or joy, he'd know what to do.

'Cheer up,' said Peter, 'we'll know in a little while.' He reached over and gave me a bear hug, then turned to look up at the arrivals monitor. 'It says offloading,' he told me. Peter had been my friend since I was fourteen, had known Bahrin and watched Iddin and Shahirah grow in the years preceding the kidnap.

'By the way, what's with the get-up?' he quizzed, jabbing a finger at my hair and make-up. 'Bit dressed up, aren't you?'

'Well, you don't get many chances to meet your own child all over again and I wanted to make a good impression,' I explained with a tense and embarrassed grin.

Minutes dragged by. I could hear the steady tick of the clock on the opposite wall. I was tortured with anticipation and nerves. 'She's not on the flight, she didn't get on,' I kept telling myself over and over again.

And then a loud knock on the double doors. Peter and I leapt to our feet.

I was halfway across the room when the door opened wide and a whirling blur of brown flung itself towards me as I opened my arms.

A huge wail like a stab of pain echoed round the room. 'Muuummmyyy!' came the anguished cry.

I didn't even see her face, just felt the arms clinging around my waist as we both let out a sob at exactly the same time. Somehow we had staggered across the room and were standing in the doorway, blocking it. Peter gave us a gentle push backwards and firmly closed the door, leaving us alone.

Our embrace did not falter; we couldn't let go as fourteen years of tears began to fall. From a distance I registered the keening sounds of long pent-up grief, and realised Shah and I were the source. We howled like banshees; I had not thought it possible to chorus such a wave of emotion and grief in audible tandem and survive.

No words were spoken, except, over and over again:

'Mummy.' And my reply, 'Shah-shah.'

Sobs and tears caught in our throats and still we clung together not moving a muscle. Shah's head had burrowed itself into the right side of my neck and I grasped her furiously to me, afraid to let go.

We had taken up a kind of rocking sway – a dance of comfort and of grief and comfort again. I was her mother once more, and she my child to be rocked and cradled.

We wept and wept, till surely we could weep no more, but still the tears came.

'Sore neck, change,' I half laughed, half cried, and automatically we switched the sides of our embrace: no talk needed and still no drawing away.

At some point I think the door opened a crack and was rapidly closed again.

'I don't even know what you look like,' I finally murmured when our howls had subsided to occasional gulps of air and big snotty snivels. 'On three, we'll look at each other,' I ventured.

'No, no, not yet,' protested Shah, 'Just a bit longer.'

And so I rocked her some more. Her shoulders shook and her hair was saturated with my tears.

'One–two–three,' I counted then, and drew back to look at my child, the girl I had given birth to all those long years ago.

She was amazing.

She was beautiful.

Dark-brown almond-shaped eyes, red-rimmed from all the crying, looked back into mine. Slim, delicate features and slender wrists. Masses of tousled, brown-black hair and a shy smile.

I cupped her face in both my hands and gently kissed every inch of it in wonder. I ran my fingers through her hair and rubbed them across her ears – they were the same little ears I had played with as she dozed off to sleep as a child.

She had taken off the traditional veil on the plane, she said, running her fingers through her hair. I wanted to ask more, but those sort of questions would wait.

The door opened again. Peter poked his head in and said we'd better leave. He'd already put Shah's suitcase in the car. We hugged each other once more and turned for the door, arms entwined. In the corridor, the two Customs officials, Paul and Mick, beamed at us with tears in their eyes. I hugged them both and Shahirah followed suit. We walked from the terminal to the waiting car within a cordon of protective people. Shah, enveloped in my giant quilted coat, was insulated from the cold. I kept my head down and walked fast. Peter packed us gently into the back seat and we sped away, the tinted windows protecting us. No one saw us; the route we took was deserted.

Shah and I snuggled close and held hands on the drive

home. She immediately pulled a stack of photographs from her bag and began to show me a record of some of the missing years. We grinned at each other continuously and I registered that my face was beginning to ache.

It was still hard to absorb the reality of her presence.

'You're really here,' I kept saying inanely. 'Oh, I've missed you so.'

Then I remembered to tell Shah about the birthday guests who would be coming this afternoon.

Shah laughed at the prospect of impersonating an exchange student who couldn't speak English and turned her attention to the passing scenery.

'This looks so right, the colour of the trees and the sky; Malaysia's always looked weird to me. *This* is what I remember home looked like.'

I knew what she meant. When I lived in Malaysia I found the green lushness both stifling and overwhelming; I suspect lots of travellers feel that way and can't put their finger on what's wrong. That's probably why those who go away to work overseas eventually come home. In Australia, our sky is different and our trees.

When we pulled up outside the house, Shah shot me a nervous and uncertain look. My children were about to meet each other.

She hid behind the front fence pillar as I rang the bell.

'Mummy!' came the excited cry over the intercom. Then Shah and I could hear Bill talking to the kids.

'Mum has a surprise for you. Why don't you go and see?' he suggested.

The gate popped open and Verity and Lysander came running towards me expectantly.

'Where's the surprise?' they demanded as Shah popped into view, crouching down low to say hello.

'Hi, Verity! Hi, Zan! It's me, Shah-shah, I've come for your birthday party.'

'Yay,' squealed Verity, leaping into Shah's arms and almost knocking her over. 'Did you bring me a present too?'

'Tar-tar,' said Zan. He came forward and grabbed her hand.

'Hi, Shah. Welcome,' Bill greeted her. 'This has been a long time coming!' he ended with a quick hug.

We tumbled through the door, a jumble of rowdy children and luggage. There was hardly time to take Shah to her room before the little ones were pulling her away to show her all their favourite things.

Exhausted and elated, I leaned into Bill's arms and let out a sigh of relief. 'I'll give them five minutes and then go and rescue Shah,' I told him.

Eventually, I dragged Shah away from Verity and Lysander and bundled her into her room, after a quick tour of the house. She hadn't slept on the plane, so I hugged her again, showed her the snugly green robe I had bought her and the nightie.

'You just have time for a couple of hours' rest before your godparents arrive.'

Once she had changed, I tucked her up beneath her fluffy white duvet for a nap. Kissing her forehead and stroking her cheek, I savoured the moment, still doubting its reality. Whispering the bedtime blessing from her childhood into her ear for the first time in fourteen years, tears filled my eyes.

'Sweet dreams, god bless. I love you millions, billions, trillions and infinities.'

The rest of the day passed in a blur of joyous happiness: extended hugs; balloons; teary-eyed 'aunts' and friends; Shah's delight at finding the party food included chocolate crackles and honey joys — favourites from her own birthday parties; Lysander earnestly trying to take photographs of the event with his biggest sister, Shah, squatting beside him; Verity's sighs of sheer bliss as she unwrapped the fairy dress and pink accessories Shah had given her; a mermaid-shaped birthday cake.

There was peace and contentment too. Amid a flurry of running and jumping five year olds, a shy Shah beamed at me, at her little brother and sister, at all her friends.

Uncle Eric, Shah's 83-year-old godfather, had wept at the surprise appearance of Shah, and his warm embrace seemed to go on forever. Sue spoke discreet and private words with Shah and her eyes glistened all afternoon afterwards; Heather's matter-of-fact exterior dissolved into a long squeeze punctuated by more tears. Tissues were at a premium in our home that day.

I seemed to hover outside my own body, observing and revelling in the jubilation.

A few friends whom I hadn't had the chance to warn pulled me aside and sceptically quizzed me. That Japanese student of yours looks a lot like you, they said as realisation began to dawn, grins of joy lighting their faces.

We couldn't cope with media, I said over and over, but most importantly, I felt instinctively that for all Shahirah's upbeat bravado, beneath the surface I had a very traumatised girl on my hands. Time and space to get to know each other, and for the family and children to work through the dynamics, was vital. A media circus would impede that and make it much harder to do with natural timing and exploration.

Twenty-eight days was the time limit that had already begun to count down in my head. That was the supposed duration of Shahirah's stay with us – how would I ever let her go.

I decided to push the timeline to the back of my mind and just enjoy the next few days. We would cross that bridge when we came to it.

The guests had all departed, Verity's big day had been a success, the cleaning up had been done and now it was time for bed.

Lysander and Verity climbed into Verity's double bed for their evening story. I lay between them, and Shahirah found room to nestle at my feet across the width of the bed, wrapped in a rug. I read *Possum Magic*, a book as much a part of Shah's early childhood as it was her little brother's and sister's. Afterwards, Shah and I crept out when the small ones were asleep. Going down the stairs, Shah ventured a question.

'Mum, can I have a really deep bath? We don't have hot water over there and I've *really* missed baths.'

'Of course, darling, this is your home too,' I replied.

And then, very shyly, she followed with a rather confronting question.

'Mummy,' she said, her heart-shaped face tilted downwards, 'will you have a bath with me?'

Swallowing my panic at the prospect of revealing my forty-something body to a 'stranger', I answered yes. It wasn't that I had a problem with nudity – the little kids took showers and baths with me all the time, and I'd done the same with Shahirah and Iddin all those years ago. I was just a bit taken aback that Shah was feeling comfortable enough to suggest it, considering her recent religious upbringing. In my mind, there was also an element of worry that I might disappoint or even scare her with my body. Had she grown up with me, she would be used to my body getting older, losing some of its youthful elasticity and ageing as it should. This would have given Shah some perspective on her own physicality and body image. I could already see that we shared an almost identical body type – it was just that my 'gear' was 10 inches wider or lower than it had been. After all, I had breastfed four children. But if Shahirah wanted to have a bath with me, then so be it.

In the bathroom I lit candles and brought out my most delicious perfumed bubbles. Turning on the tap at full bore, I ran us a steaming hot bath, blessing the fact the tub was huge and luxurious.

We sank into the water, settling down amongst the foamy bubbles. After a while in the warm water, Shah began to pour out her heart. She filled in the blanks of the stolen years, the treatment she'd endured at the hands of her first stepmother, Norela. To break down a little girl, over the years Norela had systematically taken every opportunity to tell my beautiful daughter that she was ugly, deformed and useless. My child had been snatched from a foreign country and her real mother; why couldn't Norela have shown Shah compassion and love in an alien land? We touched on the abduction, about which Shahirah was reluctant to speak, so traumatised was she fourteen years later. We talked about her life in Malaysia. Although her father had gone to the trouble of abducting her and Iddin, he'd left it to others to rear the children: Shahirah and Iddin hadn't even lived with him at his house, they'd been put in spare rooms at their grandmother's home next door.

When I heard about her father's brand of discipline for small children I was devastated. Shah gave a chilling account of the punishment for talking back to her stepmother. Bundling Shah into his car in the dark of night, Bahrin would regularly drive her to the cemetery, remove our daughter from the vehicle and leave her to spend the night alone in the deserted graveyard in the pitch black. Iddin had apparently been spared this punishment but was regularly caned.

'Sometimes,' Shah told me in a flat voice, 'I tried to run after his car, and I remember clawing at the tyres as he left.'

It was a small comment at the end of Shah's story that upset me the most. 'I probably deserved it for disagreeing with Norela,' said Shah. My poor daughter didn't realise that no child, especially one who was already traumatised by a kidnapping, deserves to be left in the dark in a cemetery. What was done to her was very wrong, and in most countries a parent would go to jail for treating a child that way.

On the fingers of one hand, Shahirah could count the people who had been truly kind and loving towards her during all her time in Malaysia. Only three had ever said anything positive to her about me, and even they had spoken in whispers out of Bahrin's earshot.

It turned out I had been right: the kidnap was all about possession, not love. The vindication was hollow – I would have infinitely preferred to wave a magic wand and erase all those years of pain my children had suffered.

As the water in the bath chilled, we replenished it again

and again, spending nearly three hours in its warmth, so that by the time we emerged we had begun to resemble wrinkled prunes.

For Shahirah and me, that bath was a rebirth of another kind. We once again became mother and daughter; but we also became women connected by more than genetics and circumstance.

'Stay with me, Mum, I'm too scared to sleep alone,' pleaded Shah. We'd talked for hours more propped up on a mountain of pillows in Shahirah's bed. We talked more, and finally my voice went hoarse and I had to beg to be allowed to sleep.

As I laid my head down next to Shah's sleepy head in the wee hours of the morning, the words of the child's nursery rhyme came back to me.

> *The incy wincy spider climbed up the water spout*
> *Down came the rain and washed poor incy out*
> *Out came the sunshine and dried up all the rain,*
> *And the incy wincy spider climbed up the spout again.*

It just went to show, I reflected, that if you hold on long enough, the sun will come out and the rain will go away.

Chapter 35

The Clamouring Hoards

The next two days were blissfully normal in a strangely abnormal way. Shah's wish list had nothing to do with sightseeing, for she didn't consider herself to be a tourist. She wanted to reconnect with places and things that were familiar. So we drove to our old houses, her school and kindergarten; we stopped whenever she got a prickle of recognition down her spine and she would peer intently at whatever it was that had caught her eye and try to remember why. I had to drag story after story from my memory bank to illuminate the particular incidents and places Shah remembered.

One afternoon we trundled down to the Royal Botanic Gardens to feed the ducks and swans, much to the delight of the younger children. This was an activity chiselled into the stone of Shah's deepest memories, for we had spent many afternoons there when she was little.

Lying on the grass, I felt almost as if I was watching a six year old again, as Shah luxuriated in the mild sunshine and the wide open spaces. Swans and ducks swam to the children and were fearlessly fed titbits by all three of them.

Monday, we had time for a girlie expedition, heading over to my hairdresser, my friend Nicky Reid, whom I had known for more than twelve years and who worked from home. When I introduced Shahirah to Nicky, her floodgates opened and couldn't be closed. But this was more than I had expected: Nicky sobbed and blubbed for an entire hour at the revelation that Shah and I we were reunited.

But our peace was not to remain undisturbed for long. When Shah spoke with her father by phone on Monday, Bahrin let drop that he might have spoken to the media about Shahirah's trip to Melbourne. A couple of hours later, a friend rang to say that speculation of Shah's return was being discussed on the radio.

The phone began to ring, until it was ringing incessantly. It was already too late for most of the media to make print or broadcast deadlines, but I knew what this meant. Taking Bill aside, I told him we'd better pack some bags and leave the house until it all blew over, but he was adamant – we should stay put amidst familiar surroundings.

'You have no idea what it will be like,' I argued, but he remained firm and so I resigned myself to making the best of a very bad situation. I was particularly worried for the younger two children. Shah certainly had some idea about the media, but for the little ones, being trapped inside a house was not a very healthy thing – physically or mentally.

We went to bed with the bell on the phone turned down low.

But by seven next morning, the extent of media interest was clear. Our doorbell was ringing over and over again – as were those of our neighbours, by reporters seeking information and gossip. The house next door was peered into and our telephone quietly rang off the hook – the message machine filled in just an hour. We kept all the curtains drawn and hid inside.

Shah was horrified and burst into tears, then retreated to her room, lying on her bed and staring sightlessly at the ceiling. The distress of all she had suffered during the years of abduction was very deep, and now this media attention traumatised her.

Cars and camera crews choked the street and by, 9.30 a.m., it was almost impossible for passers-by or residents to enter or leave, either on foot or in a vehicle. The police were called and began to issue traffic fines to all and sundry. It proved no deterrent; the reporters and photographers knew their employers would pay and refused to move on.

The only funny thing was that all the camera crews were waiting outside the empty house next door, their long lenses trained in the wrong direction. However, that didn't last long as a police officer wanting to speak to us rang our bell and we were forced to answer the door.

That was when I knew for sure that Bahrin had purposely put out the story. He was the only one who had the incorrect number for our street address. At the last minute before Shah's departure he had asked her for the address and she had inadvertently given him the wrong number.

Over four days, hundreds of calls jammed the phone lines of my new literary agent, Deborah Callaghan, too; her other work must have ground to a halt. And then, in the absence of comments at our end, the media began to chase and broadcast interviews with Bahrin. Shah telephoned him and asked him to desist, describing the rowdy siege outside our house, but he went on fuelling the media fire.

I believe that Bahrin wanted to ruin Shah's trip home to Australia, to make it look as if I was media-hungry and willing to exploit her.

In desperation we asked the police again for assistance and they tried to clear the street. Still, Verity was forced to go to school with a blanket covering her head, and so, too, Lysander.

At night, the paparazzi showed terrible persistence. Donning balaclavas against the cold, they threw stones against our windows in the hope they would tempt us to open the curtains and peer outside, affording them a blurry picture. My two youngest children were terrified by this behaviour and I was hard pressed to get them off to sleep. Friends who visited in the evening had to run the gauntlet of photographers just to drop off food, as we couldn't leave the house to shop.

Shahirah was a mess and I was rapidly turning into an unpleasant manic mother lioness. Lysander was so frightened that I found him sticking Bandaids the length of his bedroom door to 'keep the naughty people out'. Verity was confused and needy; she just wanted her normal life back. Her school had to put guards on the door, as reporters attempted to find an angle to the story there as well.

It had to stop. It was evident that the press would not leave us alone until we gave them part of what they wanted. I understood that they bore us no malice, and that the majority were overwhelmingly pleased for our happiness, but they were ravenous for a picture.

Right smack in the middle of all this insanity, Judith flew in from New Zealand to meet Shah and share in our joy. She was like a bright light being flicked on.

We decided to pull ourselves together and allow the release of video footage and one photograph of Shahirah and me together. We were not interested in exclusives or payments, although we did pause for a while aghast at the huge sums being bandied around. But ultimately we decided that it would be best if the pictures were distributed to every media outlet in Australia and any other interested media around the world. For over fourteen years, people had been so kind and supportive, this was our family's way of saying thank you.

We left the house for the first time in five days.

A couple of paparazzi attempted to snatch a picture. But in general, at last, we were left alone.

One thing that really heartened us was the goodwill shown by people who recognised us. Strangers ran across the street to hug us and burst into tears. When we went shopping, we were hugged and congratulated repeatedly. Many of those parents from our local kindergarten and school whom I had thought aloof in the past expressed their happiness for us, and said that for so many years they had avoided speaking to me as they simply hadn't known what to say or how to deal with our tragedy.

This was behaviour Shah had not experienced before. In general, she explained, Malaysian people had treated her like a royal oddity and, over the years, had been quite rude with their personal and insensitive questions. Kindness was such a revelation to Shahirah it made me want to weep all over again.

We managed a wonderful family holiday over the Easter break, hiding out at the foot of the Victorian snowfields in a log cabin and enjoying a wonderful Easter-egg hunt with our friends, Heather and Graham Brown, at their pub. The children ran around like wild things and we paddled in the river and generally had a great time. If we were recognised, people limited their contact to expressions of congratulations and then left us alone.

My two girls, even though separated by sixteen years, sometimes bristled with sibling rivalry. It was difficult for them to come to terms with each other's existence; on a deeply loving level they did not falter, but when it came to engaging my attention they were competitors. As Verity and Shahirah jostled, I tried to dispel any jealousy, and to give them the tools to sort things out themselves. They were still learning that my love is elastic, adaptable, squishy and big enough to go around all four children. Instant families are very hard for any child to slip into.

Eventually, life found a nice rhythm, and I watched Shah gain confidence and begin to blossom. It was wonderful.

The ordinariness of our daily activities was so elating that I refused to see this precious time through the lens of a camera and only took a minimal number of pictures. For me mundanity was the key and the most extraordinary gift. If I had spent the entire time with a camera in my hand, I would never have experienced the little and intense moments of love, the glue that holds a family together.

One night towards the end of her twenty-eight-day visit, Shah, Bill and I were watching an action movie on television. During a scene in which one of the protagonists fired a pistol, Shah casually remarked, 'That's like the one I use,' gesturing to the gun onscreen.

'What do you mean?' I was amazed.

Shah explained that she and Iddin were taught how to shoot a few days after they were kidnapped. When they arrived in Indonesia on the way to Malaysia, they were given rifles and taught to shoot tin cans. They were told they had to learn to protect themselves from me if I came to get them. After that, Bahrin made sure they trained with pistols, in case I turned up. Iddin and Shah still sometimes went to the firing range to relax.

Great, I muttered in my head, my children not only use weapons, they're taught to shoot their mother!

It was horrifying to learn that Shahirah took guns and shooting so nonchalantly.

'Abah always carries a pistol and all our bodyguards too,' she told us.

I quite literally began to bang my head against the sofa. What else would the years uncover about my children's upbringing in Malaysia?

The day of Shah's departure drew nearer, and finally arrived.

'Mummy, please believe me, I *will* come back soon,' she said as I tried to smile.

Verity and Lysander clung to Shah's legs as she lay on the floor of the VIP lounge with her head cradled in my lap.

Yes, she did have to leave; she had given her word to her

father, and Iddin would suffer the consequences if she failed to return. But the boarding call sounded terribly final, somehow.

'I'll see you all again soon – I love you all so much!' She was sobbing now. And then the airport duty manager, David George, took her away to the departure gate.

I felt a profound emptiness and wept as she disappeared from view. Bill and the little ones did their best to comfort me, and together we went home.

Chapter 36
Row, Row, Row Your Boat

Then, eight days after Shah left, the phone rang.

'Mummy, I don't belong here, I know that now. I want to come home for good. Can you get me out?'

So, twenty-four hours later, Shahirah walked off that plane again – to begin a new life in Australia. She was just in time for Mother's Day.

The decision as to where she lives and what she does was rightly hers: she is an adult and has a right to a life of her own making. She needs to find out what she wants to bring to the world and how she can do that herself. She needs to discover her own tastes and passions, without moral blackmail, without manipulation. She needs to simply live, surrounded by our love and encouragement. Make her own mistakes and learn from them, knowing we will love her no matter what.

We had the great privilege of sharing Shah's twenty-first birthday here in our home – with a cake of her choice baked and iced by me! It was our traditional family birthday cake, double chocolate mocha rum cake. For presents, her list was specifically non-acquisitory and gave some hint of her interests: she requested piano and guitar lessons, reasoning she had a lot of catching up to do on things most Australian children would have experienced by her age. She is exploring exactly who she is and how to nurture and enrich her soul.

I always smile to myself when I hear her singing in her room, for music has been only a partially explored passion until now.

As a mother of an adult woman, I am learning too: learning to fight my protective instincts and not second-guess Shah too often. We are all finding our way in our new family, and that includes the young children as well.

It can be quite amusing when Verity and Shahirah rummage through my wardrobe and openly covet my collection of shoes and evening bags or particular items of clothing – each vying with the other about who will have first dibs on certain pieces now or when, in Verity's case, she is grown up. It's sometimes all sequins and Manolo's at twenty paces between the girls, but I truly relish these 'normal' mother and her daughters episodes. I've also gotten to fulfil at least one motherly milestone with Shah – I taught her how to walk steadily in sky-high heels and not wobble all over the place. A small and trifling moment to most people – definitely a vacuous fashionista moment – but a small maternal triumph after having missed so many.

Sometimes it is frustrating having our own real princess in the house: there is a distinct lack of domestic nous in Shahirah. We had to have a go at domestic boot camp, for Shah had never had to worry about the nuts and bolts of living, or boring chores. But I am incredibly proud that she has dived in head first, having a go at waitressing and reception work in an attempt to find a niche for herself. I have great faith that when she does find her path, she will throw herself into it wholeheartedly, and I will support her in that.

A loud kerfuffle had broken out downstairs. I was nearly dressed but we were perilously close to being late that morning. It was time to leave on the short walk to Verity's school. Tuesday, 22 August 2006, would shape up to be a whirlwind of a day.

The little ones were calling out with great excitement. I dashed out of the bedroom – and saw a burly figure climbing the stairs towards me.

Behind him came Verity dancing, Lysander jumping, and Shah.

'Mum,' the man said to me.

'Iddin!' I shrieked, and he caught me as I teetered on the top step.

I burst into tears, sinking to the floor and being kissed by him and crushed in a strong and wonderful hold.

Flummoxed, shocked, completely at a loss for a sensible thing to say, I couldn't stop touching his face and grasping and regrasping his fingers.

Iddin was trying to halt his own tears, saying over and over, 'It's all right, Mum, I'm here now, I'm home. It's really me, Mum, I'm home. Don't cry, Mum, it's going to be all right. I'm home, Mum, I'm really home.'

I nestled in this fully grown man's arms like a small child, our roles reversed.

Dozens of questions ricocheted around my brain. 'How? When?' was all I could utter.

'Shah helped me, Mum. I wanted to surprise you – did I?' he asked hopefully. The answer must have been clear in my gobsmacked face.

Bill strolled in at that moment, straight from the shower. And he didn't miss a beat – extending his hand and saying, 'Welcome,' then laughing and shaking his head.

Verity presented a freshly created drawing to her big brother, one she had just whipped up in honour of the occasion.

'This is for you, Iddin,' she said shyly and sat down to observe him.

'WELCOME HOME IDDIN', the caption read, and the picture showed her brother and our house and the sun shining down on us all.

Zan just stared in awe at Iddin; I suspect he thought his brother would be the size of a photograph, but here he was sporting a beard. From that moment, my littlest boy imprinted on my biggest boy like a duckling and followed his big brother around with adoration in his eyes.

As I gazed at him, Iddin laughed and volunteered, 'I'm going to shave it off, Mum, but I wanted you to see it.'

I loved it, a young bull showing his manliness to his mum.

After a while Iddin said, 'Mum, if the media comes, let's just give them what they want straightaway; I don't want to waste any of my time with you at all.'

It was sad that Iddin had come to think so pragmatically. I went back for another enormous hug.

How in heaven's name had my small frame produced such a bear of a man? It was utterly befuddling and amazing.

Then I roused everyone. 'Come on, all of you, I want to

walk to school at least once with *all* my children around me.'

And so in the bright spring morning we walked hand in hand to drop Verity at school – Bill, Zan, Verity, Iddin, Shah and me. It was absolutely glorious – it surpassed any daydream I had ever conjured up.

Within hours, the first media outlet had made contact. Fortunately, this time we had an experienced publicist poised to help and a game plan that the media outlets accepted and respected. Iddin's break from university was so short, only ten days – not a second would we waste of family time together.

Bahrin had called a press conference to announce he had magnanimously allowed the children to visit me for a short time. It was a pathetic stab at saving face, but his lack of respect for their independence distressed Shah enormously.

We resolved that the two eldest children and I would appear at our front gates for a photo session and a brief comment the next day. And indeed the media left us alone afterwards, even though we declined all requests for further interviews.

Together we talked an enormous amount, again filling in some of the blanks of the lost years, but for the most part Iddin was more keen on living in the present than the past. He knew without a shadow of a doubt that I had never given up my fight for him and his sister; the lengths to which his father had gone to obliterate me from their minds only confirmed my devotion, he said.

Iddin had a list of wishes for his time in Melbourne. Many

involved me cooking his remembered favourite foods! Catching up with his old school friends was also high on his agenda. He also wanted to find some Quiksilver surf clothing and, like Shah, visit old haunts and familiar places.

The timing was a bit awkward as I was due to have minor surgery that Friday, but we managed to fit in an amazing shopping experience at Quiksilver's flagship store the day before I had to go to hospital. Iddin had a great time courtesy of a lovely woman, Mrs Geraldine Law, of the Quiksilver family, who arranged a special time for us to shop with the manager of the store. After fourteen years to be able to give my eldest child a treat after so many missed birthdays and Christmases was such a thrilling thing to do.

As well, Iddin and I often found quiet times together after everyone else was fast asleep. Cuddling up on the couch, we talked of his love of photography and scuba diving. Watching his face illuminated with enthusiasm made me thank heaven that he had discovered his passions. He was determined to complete his course in photography and wanted to focus on underwater shots – that would marry his two passions.

On the day before his departure, I organised for Iddin to dive with the sharks at the Melbourne Aquarium. Lysander and Verity were mesmerised by the sight of their big brother swimming with stingrays and sharks inside the massive glass tank. I was transfixed by Iddin's body language: he placed himself on the bottom of the tank as colourful fish swam around him and nibbled at the bubbles from his mouthpiece. He looked completely chilled out, like an underwater Buddha.

Being a typical male, Iddin waited until the last moment to express his emotions to me. Four hours before his flight was due to take off, he seemed suddenly aware of all he had left unsaid. Holding my hand, he made sure he had my attention before beginning.

'Mum, I really love you, I want you to know that. I want to finish my course and then come back and live here, but I want to be able to support myself and work. *I am coming back,*' he stressed emphatically. 'Mum, I want you to know that I am really proud of all the work you've done overseas helping people. I'm proud that you're my mum. And I really love you. I know that you never gave up on us, Mum, you never quit. I know you tried everything to get us back.'

'I did, I did,' I said from behind the tears that had started to well up in my eyes.

'Mum, promise me you believe me when I say I'm coming back, that you'll see me next holidays. None of what happened to us was your fault, Mum, I know that, OK? None of it, and I love you, Mum.'

We hugged each other crushingly – I still felt oddly little in my son's arms. How fiercely I loved him and how much I wanted to ask him to stay. But later, as I watched him go through the departure gates, I was proud that I had refrained from doing so.

I was now a parent of adult children, and part of me had to get used to letting go; allowing Iddin and Shah to go their own ways – so they could come back of their own free will.

My greatest wish had been to one day introduce all my children to each other, to reach out my hand and be able to touch their cheeks and not have them disappear in a puff of smoke as they did in my dreams. Blessedly, that day had arrived – and it was truly wonderful.

As to what I want now, not much. I would like to be

allowed the grace to raise Verity and Lysander and watch them grow and help them to flourish. My biggest dream had come true when I stood in my kitchen and watched all four of my amazing, unique, beautiful and individual children sitting together around the dining table, joking and smiling, waiting for me to serve them food I had just prepared. There's not anything else that can surpass what I consider life's greatest and most amazing bonus – my children.

My children Iddin and Shah have always deserved to have both of their parents as a constant presence in their lives. Yes, I suffered over the years, but my main concern was always for my abducted children, and how they were coping. The relationship they have with their father is complex, but I don't begrudge them the validity of the love or allegiance they feel for him. And as hard as it is, as unpalatable as I may find it, my role is to accept and respect their feelings. Bahrin is their father, just as I am and will always be their mother. As adults, the setting of parameters and boundaries is their decision, and we, as their parents, must accept their choices, even if sometimes we may not agree with them. For me, it's always been about love, not power.

In the future, I will tell any mother or father who comes to me after they have lost their child to kidnap, that if they have always seen their child as an individual, not a possession, and loved them with respect for *their* needs and not the parent's own, then love will someday override borders and prejudices and indoctrination and their children will return.

One must always live in hope.

Epilogue

I hope this book and its precursor, *Once I Was a Princess,* serve as a cautionary tale that will encourage parents going through a relationship break-up, or a difficult time with their former partners, to realise that revenge, anger and retaliation are futile and damaging actions. To use children as a weapon against a partner will hurt them terribly, but not their relationship with the left-behind parent. So many years on, my conviction was correct: stolen children always come home when they can. But the relationships they will have with the abducting parent, once they are mature and informed adults, will reflect what was done to them as children.

Anger and revenge are motivations that eat away at one's inner core, and taint any future happiness on the horizon.

Family law is such a complex and emotional minefield; it can mark one's life, and that of one's children, for decades to come. A knee-jerk response to certain situations is not always the most rational or the best long-term plan when dealing with a family or a relationship – even a relationship that has devolved into something alien and bitter. Dignity and commonality are strong principles which will hold a person in good stead when putting down the foundations of a new life after divorce or separation.

Physical control only lasts over one's child while they remain young. How one, as a parent, behaves in the here and now will determine if you are a chore to be 'tended', or a welcome guest and participant at the major milestones of their adult lives.

My story opened countless doors for me around the world. Some I chose to step through, others I did not, and some I was hauled through kicking and screaming. Incongruous as it sounds, I've been equally at home sipping tea in a mud-and-dung hut in Maasailand and sitting in the bar at the House of Lords in London. I've chatted to movie stars in the middle of war zones and shared instant noodles in a Kosovar refugee camp with other aid workers while guided missiles whined overhead; I've travelled round the globe dozens of times and experienced all manner of transport, from luxurious first-class flights to armoured military vehicles, speeding motorbikes and the trailers of filthy garbage trucks in East Timor. I've bathed in a crocodile-infested lagoon and lazed in a Hollywood hot tub, I've dined in embassies and at roadside chipperies in Belgium – each was an adventure and each experience gave me an insight into the human heart.

During the fourteen long years I was without Iddin and Shahirah, I discovered the worst and the best in other people – but most of all, I've found a commonality of humanity around the world which gives me hope that our very

358

ordinariness will be our salvation. For all the turmoil in the world, there is a calm place deep within each of us that –regardless of race, creed or nationality– carries our dreams, hopes and expectations for our children and our children's children. My belief is that at the very core of all humans there is a fundamental desire to nurture and to value the simpler things in life and that through this collective sanity it is possible to celebrate our sameness, and not our differences.

I've learned many important lessons during my fourteen years of stubbornness, reinvention, battling and lobbying, but three, in particular, have special resonance. First, we must never take anyone or anything for granted – especially our children. We simply can't count on tomorrow to say 'I love you'. Secondly, I've learned to never give up, and thirdly I now know always to turn a negative into a positive.

Life is simply a work in progress; the trick is to make sure you apply yourself to the job well.

Acknowledgements

Over the years, I have been fortunate to accrue an amazing host of friends without whom this book would not have been possible. During the years when my children Iddin and Shahirah were withheld from me, my friends are what kept me going. It is to them I proffer my deepest and most sincere gratitude and love.

As well, my love and thanks go to my eldest children Shahirah and Iddin for trusting in my love for them and our memories to make their leap of faith. Verity, you are my sunshine miracle girl and you have been so patient, allowing me to write this new book, thank you with lots of squishy love. Lysander, although you aren't quite four, there is a wise old man behind those eyes and I love you very much. Bill, what a light at the end of the tunnel; you so detest publicity I can't go into more detail HBMMGSLA – thank you!

In no particular order, each of you have been on this rocky journey with me: Sue MacArthur, Deb Gribble, Auntie Connie and Uncle Kevin Coverdale, Gavin McDougall,

Dean White, Heather Brown, Sally Nicholes, Mike Fudge, Barry Goodman, Patsy Heymans, Judith Curran, Chris 'Geeb' Allen, Sarah Beard, Andrew and Caroline Blackman, Charles Tapp, Dawn and Martyn Bradley, Jane Allen (now McLean) and Jason McLean, Valerie Hardy, Maria Balinska and John Udorovic (who always said the sun would come out again).

Special thanks to my extraordinary friend and literary agent, Deborah Callaghan, for chanting, *I think I can, I think I can* during the home-stretch insanity.

Appreciation and thanks to James Fraser, Sonny Mehta, Miss Jackie Collins, Tracey Chapman, John Judge, Shakira Caine, Steven Candries, Uncle Eric Waller, Richard and Joanne Waller, Ingrid Butters, Sonia Patterson, Anthony Blair, Martin Grant, Jocelyn Mitchell, Drewe Balmain, Jane Hill, Sophie Daou and Neil Milne. My thanks to Rove McManus for allowing me to hear Belinda Emmett's music, which motivated me and reminded me to be frank and less than perfect. Our dear Marianne 'Mim' Henneveldt, who helped to wrangle Lysander as I wrote much of this book, and Elizabeth Lew for her sixteen years of 'back-up'. Rob and Janine Goldstein, Lyn and Harold Jossel and all your clan, when the times have called for it, you've been my South African back-up team.

Some of my favourite photographs are reproduced in this book, taken by the talented Tom Stoddart, Luke Hardy and Jeffrey Sales – thank you so much for 'pulling my teeth' painlessly.

Thanks for the wonderful support and the unwavering commitment I have received from Fiona Brownlee and Bill Campbell of Mainstream Publishing, and the sterling work of Deborah Warner, my editor.

Appreciation to the people from CARE International past and present: Antony Blair, Chloe Bayram, Stephen Gwynne-Vaughan, Guy Toussignant and Geoffrey Dennis.

To the people I have had the privilege to meet through aid work, my writing and travels, I owe you a debt that I can't sufficiently repay. You have allowed me to listen to your thoughts and record your stories, reminding my readers that life is so much bigger and broader than our living rooms and the television screens that flicker in the corner.

Sincere thanks must also go to those people who have wished my family well and worried on our behalf about the outcome of this gruelling experience. Your kindness ticking over in the background kept me going.

Thank you, *merci, danku, hvala, tack, grazie, obrigado, danke, assantisana, pakka per fyrir, falemnderit.*

Useful Contacts

Jacqueline Pascarl
www.jacquelinepascarl.com
Email: info@jacquelinepascarl.com
PO Box 282
Hawthorn Vic 3122
Australia

International Parental Child Abduction
Australia
Nicholes Family Lawyers
Specialists in Parental Child Abduction Issues and Hague Convention Law
Level 3, 224 Queen Street
Melbourne Vic 3000, Australia
Tel: +61 (0)3 9670 4122
www.nicholeslaw.com.au
Email: sally@nicholeslaw.com.au

Attorney General's Department
Canberra, Australia
Tel: +61 (0)2 6250 6666
www.ag.gov.au

Department of Foreign Affairs and Trade
Canberra, Australia
1300 555 135 (24 hr hotline)
www.dfat.gov.au

Belgium
Missing Children International Network
Tel: +32 (02) 534 5631 or +32 84 211 461
Fax: +21 84 221 1394

European Union
Child Focus
European Centre for Missing and Sexually Exploited Children
Tel: +32 2 475 44 99 (24 hr hotline)
www.childfocus.org

Canada
Missing Children Society of Canada
Suite 219, 3501–23 NE
Calgary, Alberta T2E 6V8,
Canada
Tel: +1 (403) 291 0705
Fax: +1 (403) 291 9728
www.mcsc.ca
Email: rmorgan@mcsc.ca

France
Collectif de Solidarite aux Meres D'Enfants Enlevees
9 Rue des Chaillots 92190
Meudon, France
Tel: +33 (1) 4534 4910
Fax: +33 (1) 4623 1164
Email: csmee@wanadoo.fr

United Kingdom
Reunite – International Child Abduction Centre
PO Box 7124
Leicester LE1 7 XX,
United Kingdom
Advice Line:
Tel: +44 (0) 116 2556 234
General Enquiries:
Tel: +44 (0) 116 2555 345
Fax: +44 (0) 116 2556 370
www.reunite.org
Email: reunite@dircon.co.uk

PACT
Parents and Abducted Children Together
PO Box 31389
London SW11 4WY
United Kingdom
Tel/fax: +44 (0) 20 7627 3699
www.pact-online.org
Email: support@pact-online.org

United States of America
The National Center for Missing and Exploited Children
(US Central Authority for Incoming Cases)
Charles B Wang International Children's Building
699 Prince Street
Alexandria, VA 22314–3175,
USA
Tel: +1 703 274 3900 (24 hr hotline)
Fax: +1 703 274 2200
www.missingkids.com

Can anyone help locate Audrey Leinoff?
She was abducted in 1988, aged four.
www.audreyleinoff.com

Humanitarian Aid and Development
CARE International
www.careinternational.org
'Click' on the country site most appropriate for you.